International Relations in a Changing Global System

INTERNATIONAL RELATIONS

IN A CHANGING

GLOBAL SYSTEM

Toward a Theory of the World Polity

SECOND EDITION

SEYOM BROWN

Brandeis University

WestviewPress
A Division of HarperCollinsPublishers

Copyright ©1992, 1996 by Westview Press, Inc., A Division of HarperCollins Publishers, Inc.

Published in 1996 in the United States of America by Westview Press, Inc., 5500 Central Avenue, Boulder, Colorado 80301-2877, and in the United Kingdom by Westview Press, 12 Hid's Copse Road, Cumnor Hill, Oxford OX2 9JJ

Library of Congress Cataloging-in-Publication Data
Brown, Seyom.
    International relations in a changing global system : toward a
theory of the world polity / Seyom Brown. — 2nd ed.
        p.   cm.
    Includes bibliographical references and index.
    ISBN 0-8133-2352-5 (hardcover). — ISBN 0-8133-2353-3 (pbk.)
    1. International relations.   2. International organization.
I. Title.
JX1391.B73   1996
327.1'01—dc20   95-23651
                                                                        CIP

The paper used in this publication meets the requirements of the American National Standard for Permanence of Paper for Printed Library Materials Z39.48-1984.

10   9   8   7   6   5   4   3   2   1

To Anne and Carol,
my youngest ties
to the future

Contents

PART TWO: TOWARD NORMATIVE THEORY

Preface and Acknowledgments

The need for new thinking about international relations, which compelled me to write the first edition of this book, has not abated. If anything, it has become more pressing, as a succession of post–cold war crises has increasingly exposed the inadequacies of the institutions and norms of the nation-state system.

This predicament has been reflected in a series of global "summit" conferences—attended by the heads of state or cabinet-level officials of virtually every country: the United Nations Conference on Environment and Development (Rio de Janeiro, 1992); the World Conference on Human Rights (Vienna, 1993); the International Conference on Population and Development (Cairo, 1994); the World Summit for Social Development (Copenhagen, 1995); and the World Conference on Women (Beijing, 1995).

The eruption of international summitry is a symptom of the spreading realization by the peoples of this planet that, like it or not, and despite their differences, they *are* increasingly interdependent. More and more, what happens in one part of the world affects the well-being of people in every continent. The mobility of things, information, and persons and the capabilities of humans (by design or inadvertence) to alter the natural world mean that people who had previously been remote from one another are not only coming into contact but are getting in each other's way—materially and psychologically.

Looked at systemically, the problem is one of growing incongruence, or structural *mis*match, between the emergent world society and the traditional world polity—a polity whose national sovereignty norms and structures are the legacy of a very different social reality. Indeed, without considerable restructuring of the inherited nation-state system, few of the principles and programs endorsed by governments at the global summits can be effectively implemented. Yet such undertakings are being embraced (at least rhetorically) in the absence of the kind of political theory required to assess the feasibility and desirability of the more fundamental structural reforms that are implied.

In other words, much of today's international statecraft is being conducted in a philosophical vacuum. Even the innovative 1995 report of the Commission on Global Governance, despite its attention to "Values for the Global Neighborhood," is largely devoid of the basic theoretical reasoning that its institutional recommendations presuppose.

It would be presumptuous of me to aspire to fill this vacuum. Rather, my more modest purpose is to develop *the case for* a theory of the world polity—a theory responsive to the need of the inhabitants of the planet Earth to learn to live with one another without destroying themselves and the planet in the process.

Unfortunately, the theory I am calling for has neither a rich corpus of recent and contemporary political philosophy nor an appropriate body of twentieth-century thought about international politics to draw on. The political philosophers have concentrated primarily on the requirements of order and justice *within* countries. And the body of thought that focuses on relations *among* countries—"international relations"—has rarely delved beyond the paradigm of sovereign nation-states selfishly pursuing their interests in an anarchic world polity.

Given the extent to which these two realms of theoretical discourse have developed in isolation from one another in recent decades, it is no wonder that a 1979 book written with the explicit purpose of bridging the gulf, *Political Theory and International Relations* by Charles Beitz, was generally regarded as an anomaly by established academics in both fields. Another effort to connect the province of political philosophy to the field of international relations, Terry Nardin's 1983 book, *Law, Morality, and the Relations of States,* suffered a similar fate. One of the few philosophically erudite international relations specialists, Stanley Hoffmann, also tried in his *Duties Beyond Borders,* published in 1981, to sensitize his colleagues to the need and opportunities for ethical statecraft in a world of increasing interdependencies; but Hoffmann's fellow political scientists gave only passing attention to his prescient arguments.

In the 1990s, however—stimulated by the post–cold war controversies over human rights and global poverty—international relations scholars have been rediscovering the importance of normative issues, while political philosophy scholars have been retrieving and reexamining the works of those thinkers whose wisdom extended to the relations among states. Symptoms of the trend are Chris Brown's *International Relations Theory: New Normative Approaches* and the volume of essays edited by Terry Nardin and David Mapel under the title *Traditions of International Ethics.*

Notably, this expanding dialogue has engendered fresh contributions by moral philosophers such as John Rawls and Michael Walzer. Prodded by colleagues to trace out the international implications of his seminal *A Theory of Justice,* Rawls has outlined what he calls "The Law of Peoples" (essentially a reiteration of the ethics of nonintervention) in his 1993 Amnesty International Lecture at Oxford. And Walzer, in his *Thick and Thin: Moral Argument at Home and Abroad,* published in 1994, elaborates on the idea—only touched on in his earlier works—of a "minimalist" international moral code, in addition to the laws of war, to which countries must be held accountable.

The new literature on the normative dimensions of international relations has helped me prepare the second edition of this book. But most of the new work by others—still operating on the assumption that the nation-state system is (and ought to be) the essence of the world polity—fails to move the discourse very far toward the basic explanatory or normative theory that I called for in the first edition.

Meanwhile the gap between how the world actually works and the picture of world politics conveyed by the still-reigning "realist" school of international relations has been widening. And sadly, some of the most sophisticated "realists" have become preoccupied with the need to rescue their paradigm from obsolescence in the face of anomalies that profoundly challenge its key premises rather than help us understand and constructively grapple with the new realities.

My purpose has not been to write a critique of the "realist" paradigm, however. That would only perpetuate its ability to set the agenda of questions about world politics and to define the terms of debate. My agenda of important questions, which is laid out in the Introduction, and which structures the exposition thereafter, is quite different. It is meant not only to provide a framework for reconnecting the theory and practice of international relations with political philosophy but also to provide terms of reference for crucial issues in world politics around which scholars, policymakers, and concerned laypersons can engage in mutually intelligible discourse.

I expect the book may be useful in courses on international relations, foreign policy, and (some, happily, do exist) world politics. But it can best serve its purpose if, in providing an alternative conceptual orientation to the standard texts, it generates a healthy "cognitive dissonance" on the part of students—provoking them to ask fundamental questions not only about the material in these texts but also about the world around them.

Many colleagues and students have contributed to my thinking—too many to fully acknowledge, because the book reflects an interlocutory process extending back through most of my professional career. Special thanks are due, however, to readers of the first edition who offered suggestions for the second edition (namely, Robert C. Johansen of Notre Dame and Marc A. Levy of Princeton) and to the graduate students in my Brandeis seminar on normative issues in international relations (Xianju Du, Christina Kulich, Mariano Parks, William Ruger, Beate Sissenich, Christopher Stephens, and Tatiana Yankelevich) who struggled along with me as I attempted to clarify and reformulate many of the arguments presented here.

I also want to thank Daniel Philpott for the opportunity to participate in the seminar on Ethics and International Relations he conducted at Harvard University's Center for International Affairs from 1993 to 1995. The exchanges in this seminar with Lea Brilmayer, Bryan Hehir, Stanley Hoffmann, Robert Keohane, David Lumsdaine, Terry Nardin, Henry Shue, Michael Joseph Smith, and Alexander Wendt among others have been crucial to the rethinking and rewriting in this new edition.

Once again, I am grateful to Spencer Carr and the editorial staff at Westview Press (especially Linda Carlson, Cindy Rinehart, and Shena Redmond) for helping me to say what I wanted to say more clearly and effectively.

Between the first and second editions, the debt I owe Matthew and Jeremiah has changed its character. No longer merely tolerant victims of their dad's time-consuming preoccupations, the boys have been developing their own theories on what's right and wrong with the world—and have been unsparing in giving me the benefit of their wisdom.

Seyom Brown

International Relations in a Changing Global System

Introduction: The Need for a Theory of the World Polity

A theory of the world polity—as distinct from a theory of international politics or, more broadly, international relations—is needed to help us deal with the central predicament of the human species: the failure to develop systems of governance to keep pace with the expanding power of humans to alter the natural world. This failure increasingly risks even the extinction of the human species, as independent agencies of decision—states, corporations, political movements, individuals—obtain capabilities for destroying the conditions that sustain life on earth.

Significantly, but not surprisingly, the conventional theoretical literature on international relations is not rich in suggestions for how humankind might overcome its predicament of inadequate governance. Rather, its central premise is anarchy, the absence of governance for the international system as a whole. Most orthodox international relations scholars content themselves with explaining how the anarchic international system works.

Prototypically, the anarchic structure of the nation-state system is the starting point for, and also circumscribes, Kenneth Waltz's influential *Theory of International Politics*. Waltz's enterprise in this book is solely to elaborate the essential characteristics of the anarchic structure and to show how this presumably unalterable structure determines behavioral regularities and processes changes in relations among the nation-states. Waltz and his disciples like to call their approach "structural realism." Structural it is; but the extent to which it is realistic can be debated.[1]

Not all "realists" maintain that the anarchic system precludes international cooperation or the establishment of international regimes to institutionalize coordination in particular fields. Indeed, reflecting what statespersons are actually doing, there is a

---

[1]Kenneth N. Waltz, *Theory of International Politics* (Menlo Park: Addison-Wesley, 1979). Waltz's scholarly progenitor, Hans J. Morgenthau, in his seminal work *Politics Among Nations: The Struggle for Power and Peace* (New York: Knopf, 1954), did take up the question of the structural transformation of the anarchic nation-state system into a world state, which he claimed would be necessary to guarantee the avoidance of a nuclear World War III. But Morgenthau concluded that no world state, except one that was imposed by a World War III, would be feasible unless it rested on the foundation of a world community of shared moral and political values; and he did not find the ingredients of such a world community present in the contemporary world or in the foreseeable future (pp. 469–485).

growing scholarly literature on cooperation and regime construction and maintenance under the premise of persisting world anarchy.[2] But even in their work on
cooperation, by disciplining their investigations to relations among sovereign actors
within a basically anarchic system, most of the "realists" avoid more fundamental
historical and normative inquiries into the sources of international anarchy, the reasons for its persistence, and the possibilities for alternative structures of the world
polity supplanting anarchy.[3]

What Needs to Be Explained—and Evaluated

A theory that can contribute significantly to the understanding and possible amelio-
ration of humankind's most pressing issues of governance must pose and attempt to
answer fundamental questions concerning at least these global problems:

1. Anarchy. Why is the world as a whole so anarchic, without a dependable general
system of order and justice, and with each country relying ultimately on its own military forces and military alliances for national security? Rather than starting a priori with
global anarchy as an essentially unalterable political condition of world society, a theory
of the world polity should seek to explain the origins and perpetuation of this condition. It should at the outset be open with respect to whether there are certain unmodifi-
able traits of the human species that necessarily produce and sustain international anarchy, or whether other global political configurations also are consistent with the human
being's essential characteristics. A theory of the world polity ought not to be bound by
the virtually tautological assumption that sufficient explanations for many of the hall-
marks of international politics—especially the weighty role of force and the small influence of moral considerations—can be found in the world's anarchic structure itself.
Rather, the theoretical enterprise should be open to the possibility that these presumed
behavioral constants of international politics, *along with* the anarchic structure, are
products or expressions of other factors that may be more, or less, subject to change.

2. Cooperation. In the context of the world's basic anarchic structure, what
explains the existence of enclaves of international cooperation in particular regions

---

[2]Examples of recent scholarly interest in international cooperation and coordination regimes are
Robert M. Axelrod, *The Evolution of Cooperation* (New York: Basic Books, 1984); Stephen D. Krasner,
ed., *International Regimes* (Ithaca: Cornell University Press, 1983); Robert O. Keohane, *After Hegemony:
Cooperation and Discord in the World Political Economy* (Princeton: Princeton University Press, 1984); and
Kenneth A. Oye, ed., *Cooperation Under Anarchy* (Princeton: Princeton University Press, 1986).

[3]A welcome exception from within the "realist" tradition is provided by Barry Buzan, Charles Jones,
and Richard Little who, in their *The Logic of Anarchy: Neorealism to Structural Realism* (New York:
Columbia University Press, 1993), attempt to show how throughout history, and despite the rise and disintegration of empires, the "deep structure" of interstate anarchy has resisted fundamental transformation.

of the world and, globally, among countries in particular fields of interaction? Why do virtually all countries belong to the United Nations and participate, either directly or indirectly, in the UN's peace and security operations and in its programs in economic development, health, and environmental protection? Is such cooperation "epiphenomenal," being only reflective of (and having little impact on) the main power contests within the nation-state system, or does it represent an alternative way of conducting business that might eventually supplant the anarchic structure and norms of the traditional world polity?

3. War. Is war (and the threat of war) between countries an inherent and normal characteristic of a world polity structured predominantly as a nation-state system? Are there ways to substantially reduce the role of international violence without fundamentally restructuring the polity? To answer these questions we need to be able to stipulate the essential features of a basically peaceful world polity; and we need to be able to outline the conditions—at least hypothetically—under which such a polity could emerge.

4. Wealth and Poverty. What explains the vast disparities in economic condition of the peoples of the world and the fact that most of the poor are non-"white" and concentrated in areas of the globe that were once under the control of European empires? To what extent are the persisting disparities the natural direct result of the global economic market and the economic endowments of particular countries, and to what extent are they the result of political "distortions" of the natural workings of the global economy? Are changes in the structure and functioning of the world polity necessary to reduce the global economic disparities? And would they be sufficient? What is the risk that such politically directed attempts at global economic redistribution would produce significant decreases or increases in gross world product? What is the political feasibility of such restructurings of the global economy?

5. Ecology. Is the existing decentralized structure of the world polity capable of supporting the kinds of mutual forbearance and cooperation from countries (and other powerful actors) required to preserve the planet's essential ecological balances? If not, what modifications of the world polity would be needed, and under what conditions might these modifications be politically feasible? Are modifications of the global political economy necessary preconditions or corollaries of the required ecological policies?

6. Human Rights. How can "human rights" norms be reconciled with the foundational norms of the nation-state system? A cluster of questions is involved, such as: (1) What configurations of the world polity are compatible with the worldwide application of the doctrine that the institutions and policies of government are legitimate only to the degree that they rest on the consent of the governed? (2) If the norms of national sovereignty and noninterference in the internal affairs of countries are essential features of the nation-state system, as is often claimed, what are the prospects of the nation-state system's adaptation to political philosophies and movements premised on universally valid rights of individuals?

Breaking Out of the Confines of "Realist" Theory

To answer these basic questions we will need to avoid the analytical trap of the "realist" school: its assumption that the world polity is essentially (and inevitably) a system of sovereign nation-states.[4] Rather, the essential structure of the world's political system at any point in time—what it has been, what it is today, what it can become—should be continually open to fresh assessment.

Clearly, the contemporary world polity is predominantly a nation-state system. The entire human population is organized into territorially demarcated units of community self-protection and welfare.[5] And it is the interaction among governments of these nation-states—namely, "international relations"—that is the principal, formal, legitimized process for managing conflict and cooperation among the world's peoples.

To recognize the dominance within the world polity of the nation-state system, however, is not the same thing as equating the world polity with the nation-state system. The world polity encompasses more than politics among the so-called nation-states. Transnational and subnational entities of various sorts (corporations, ethnocultural groups, ideological movements, churches and religious movements, labor organizations, professional associations, special interest groups) also perform political roles on the world stage—defining who is on whose side on what issues and helping to determine the global distribution of power and wealth.

Careful "realist" theorists avoid the logical pitfall of simply equating international politics with world politics. Some of them, like Kenneth Waltz, abstract the nation-state system from the larger and more complex field of world politics, thereby allowing for parsimonious explanations of the apparent regularities of international poli-

---

[4]I will continue throughout to put quotation marks around the term "realist" to remind the reader that those adhering to this school are simply making a *claim* of realism, which, according to my lights, has not been adequately demonstrated.

[5]Strictly speaking, most of the world's countries are multinational states rather than simple nation-states, if a "nation" denotes a group of people that considers itself a community with a way of life significantly distinct from other communities. Even following the disintegration of the Soviet Union, most of the nations of the world still do not have states (in the sense of sovereign governments) of their own. But to avoid having to develop a whole new jargon, I continue the tradition of using the term "nation-state" interchangeably with "country" to denote a political unit of world society whose territorial demarcations and legal sovereignty within its boundaries are generally recognized by other such political units. Similarly, my use of the terms "transnational" and "subnational" could be translated to mean "transcountry" and "subcountry."

tics (such as competitive arming between countries with conflicting interests and the formation of alliances to balance the power of countries attempting to establish world empire).[6] But the gain in parsimony is purchased at the price of a loss of relevance to many of the critical predicaments of humankind today and too rigidly isolates an analysis of how countries act toward one another from the human sciences and from social and political philosophy.

The contrasting approach undertaken here treats the nation-state system as a *subsystem* of the world polity, which in turn is seen as a subsystem of world society. This formulation allows for analysis and theorizing about (1) the relationships between what happens in society at large and what happens in the world polity, and (2) the relationships between what happens at various levels of the world polity and what happens in the nation-state system.

Rather than positing international politics as a closed system with an anarchical structure whose essential characteristics are fixed for all time, we can look at the nation-state system (or any other prominent feature of world politics) dynamically and historically—asking how the system in its varying configurations processes "inputs" from parts of world society in varying historical contexts, and seeking to determine the basic historical conditions for the emergence, persistence, and fundamental transformation of the system itself.

Definitions and Distinctions

I define the *world polity* as *the global pattern of structures and processes for conducting and resolving conflicts and making and implementing rules.* The world polity thus comprises interactions of a special kind within the general field of human interaction. This is consistent with the practice in the social sciences of distinguishing between the larger field of human interaction—*society*—and society's distinguishable subfields: the polity, the economy, the ecology, and the variety of ideational or "cultural" connections between people.

It should be noted that neither society nor polity, as defined here, necessarily assumes a membership adhering to common views of right and wrong, nor do they imply any particular degree or kind of organization. Societies or polities may be, but are not always, integrated by ideas or organization. When I want to refer to human aggregations characterized by shared values, rules, and/or institutions, I use the normatively pregnant term *community.*

In this usage, I am somewhat at odds with an important tradition in sociological theory that applies the term "society" to a highly interactive grouping of people, bound to each other by not only material dependency relationships but also com-

---

[6]Waltz, *Theory of International Politics.*

mon institutions and shared values.[7] I also differ with colleagues in the field of international relations who borrow from this sociological tradition. Hedley Bull, for example, writes that a society exists when its members are "conscious of certain common interests and common values," when they "conceive themselves to be bound by a common set of rules in their relations with one another, and share in the workings of common institutions."[8]

I find it useful for analysis and theory-building to treat all such attributes as variables that may be present to some degree in any human aggregate. Accordingly, *world society*, as conceived here, is the multitude of particular societies, some of which overlap in geographic space and in their memberships; but what peoples are included within a particular society is essentially arbitrary or definitional: The criteria for inclusion or exclusion can be set by the members themselves or they can be postulated by observers. There are local societies, national societies, transnational societies, ethnic or religious societies, societies defined by the occupation of their members or other functionally specific traits. World society, so defined, includes them all and has existed in one form or another throughout human history. The extent to which the human species at any point in time does share common values—does indeed manifest features of a community—can remain open to assessment.

By contrast, the province of the *polity* (a special aspect of society) is more specialized—comprising a society's enforceable rules and enforceable authority relationships, and the processes (ranging from voting to violence) by which such rules and relationships are made and implemented.

Thus politics is not simply, in the much-quoted phrase of Harold Lasswell, the determination of "who gets what, when, how," nor is the study of politics only "the study of influence and the influential."[9] In any society the winners and losers may also be determined by a variety of factors, not all of which are "political" as the term is normally used: Natural endowments and skills, the prevailing supply and demand for valued goods, even luck—any of these can affect the distribution of society's amenities. Neither is it sufficient to define the political system as those features of society that "authoritatively allocate values" (a formulation of political theorist David Easton[10]); for in any society the allocation of many "values"—positions, rewards, privileges—are substantially determined by inherited cultural norms (such

---

[7]See the essay on "Society" by Leon H. Mayhew in the *International Encyclopedia of the Social Sciences* (New York: Macmillan and the Free Press, 1968), Vol. 14, pp. 577–586.

[8]Hedley Bull, *The Anarchical Society: A Study of Order in World Politics* (New York: Columbia University Press, 1977), p. 13. Similarly, Evan Luard, *Types of International Society* (New York: Free Press, 1976), contends that the essential characteristics of a society include regular communication and contact among its members and "its own traditions of intercourse, expected norms of behavior, and its own institutions for mutual discussion of common problems" (p. 49).

[9]Harold D. Lasswell, "Politics: Who Gets What, When, How," in *The Political Writings of Harold D. Lasswell* (Glencoe: Free Press, 1951), pp. 284–461.

[10]David Easton, *The Political System: An Inquiry into the State of Political Science,* 2nd edition (New York: Knopf, 1971).

as which kinds of behavior and people are most admired), professionally maintained standards (as in academic institutions), and the market in popular tastes (as, for example, in the entertainment media).

The *polity,* as defined here, comes into play to the extent that enforceable laws or hierarchical power (in the sense of the capacity, if need be, to coerce outcomes) are factors in the determination of who gets what, when, and how. Society's political contests are not over any and all positions of authority, but precisely over those positions of authority that also carry the capacity to compel behavior through the provision or withholding of crucial positive inducements and negative sanctions. Accordingly, the nature of many polities—not all of them, but particularly national polities and the world polity, for reasons to be explained—is closely bound up with the distribution and control of the instruments of violence.[11]

This conceptualization also provides a basis for distinguishing a society's polity from its economy. The *economy* is a society's store of valued resources, goods and services, and other amenities, and its system for managing and exchanging such valued items among its population. The polity intrudes on the economy (and we have a "political economy") to the extent that the performance of these management and exchange functions within a given society is determined not only by the supply-demand situation for various human wants within the society, but also by its institutionalized rules and sanctioning power—its system of governance, its "state."

Delimiting slightly the concept that introduced this section, but retaining its essential meaning, the world polity can be defined as *the worldwide configuration of systems of enforceable societal relationships.* The notion of "enforceability" should be applied flexibly, however, to encompass positive inducements as well as negative sanctions, democratic as well as authoritarian systems for making and implementing rules, and peer relations as well as hierarchies. But the distribution of "power" in this sense (and contests over its distribution) is the very essence of politics.

Toward Appropriate Theory: The Reassertion of Conventional Wisdom

In this work, I do not present a fully worked out and comprehensive theory of the world polity. Rather I offer the outline of such a theory:

- A set of questions that the theory, minimally, should attempt to answer, and some forays of my own toward arriving at answers to these questions.

---

[11]Many contemporary social scientists invoke Max Weber's classic definition of the state as "a human community that (successfully) claims *the monopoly of the legitimate use of physical force* within a given territory." *From Max Weber: Essays in Sociology,* translated and edited by H. H. Gerth and C. Wright Mills (New York: Oxford University Press, 1946), p. 78.

• A set of moral principles for evaluating the world polity (past, present, and future), and some attempts of my own to apply such evaluation to the existing world polity and to suggest reforms of its behavior and structure.

My intention is to generate additional conceptual and empirical work that, in turn, will stimulate those with a theoretical cast of mind—whether intuitive and impressionistic or formalistic—to make their own maps and models of the still relatively uncharted and evolving world polity.

Informed Speculation

One purpose of theory is analytical—to provide understanding of *why* a set of phenomena behaves in specifiable ways.[12] In common speech, "theory" is virtually synonymous with "guess" or "speculation"; and there is an elementary wisdom in this usage which I find entirely appropriate even to the enterprise of academic political theory. Theory, so regarded, typically delves beyond (or below) what is immediately evident or already established as fact.

An injured woman extracted from the driver's seat of an automobile involved in a head-on collision is pronounced dead on arrival at the hospital. If a newspaper reporter covering the event files a story indicating, on the basis of this information, that the driver was killed by the collision, it would be appropriate for the newspaper editor to ask of the reporter: Is this fact or *theory?* The deceased might have had a fatal heart attack prior to the collision; or her husband might have dropped some poison into her orange juice before she left home in her car. As more medical information becomes available, the reporter's original theory may turn into simple fact, but there would still be considerable room for additional theory about why the collision took place: defects in the braking systems of either of the cars? ice in the intersection? running of a red light? some combination of vehicular system failure and the psychological condition of the drivers? What makes these ideas *theory* is that they are indeed speculations purporting to explain why something happened, not that they can be stated in formal mathematical terms or are empirically testable.

Similarly with our attempts to understand world political phenomena. December 7, 1941: The United States naval fleet deployed at Pearl Harbor is attacked by

---

[12]Various premodern and postmodern philosophical approaches may take issue with the fact-value distinction implied here, linking this distinction with the scientism and rationalism associated with the philosophies of the Enlightenment. I plead guilty, if indeed it is an intellectual crime, to making such distinctions for the purpose of analytical and expository clarity, but not to the allegations of scientism and rationalism. Rather, I believe that our values do shape the way we define, select, and categorize the "facts" of the world. I also believe that much of what is happening in the world, especially the suffering humans are inflicting on one another, is subject to factual verification; these occurrences are not simply stories or subjective "texts." Nor do I have to be there to witness the tree (bomb) falling in the forest (on the city) to *know* that it fell and to be profoundly disturbed by the fact.

Japanese aircraft—a momentous event that changed the course of world history. But *why* did it happen? We now know, on the basis of Japanese archival materials, that the Japanese Navy was ordered to launch this attack by a particular faction in control of the Japanese government, and we can identify the influential members of that faction; we also know what was said in the debates leading up to the attack decision in the Japanese cabinet. As research validates this information, even though it is only part of the explanation, it is no longer theory. What remains theory is that part of the explanation for the outbreak of the Japanese-American war that is still conjecture: the role of the U.S. oil embargo in precipitating hostilities, the role of diplomatic miscalculation and incompetence on either or both sides, the effect of intelligence assessments by the Japanese concerning impending improvements in U.S. military capabilities, and the impact of the overall balance of international power in the fall of 1941. Quite likely, all of these factors (and others) were instrumental in bringing on the war, and the assessment of their relative causal weights is the very stuff of debate not only among theorists of the outbreak of World War II, but also among theorists of the causes and prevention of war in general. In debates such as these we are admittedly in the realm of speculation—*informed* speculation, but speculation nonetheless—which, in the conventional wisdom (adopted here), *is* the essence of explanatory theory.

Moral Evaluation and Prescription

Just as concepts of legitimacy and justice are central to many theories about domestic politics and are the subjects of much of the discourse in political philosophy, so such normative concepts are appropriate to a theory of the world polity—both analytically and prescriptively.

Explicit criteria of the *good* polity can provide a basis for a comparative evaluation of historical configurations of world politics and for an assessment of the costs and benefits of contemporary political developments and statecraft. Moreover, scholarly dialogue and debate about the ethical as well as practical validity of alternative structures and norms for the world polity can provide important insights for statespersons, international lawyers, officials of international organizations, and laypersons who are motivated to advance world interests as well as national and more specialized interests.

Although rarely made explicit, normative presuppositions infuse even the scholarly discourse on world politics conducted within the confines of the supposedly amoral "realist" paradigm. The particular political system that is its subject matter—the system of territorially defined sovereign nation-states—was, and remains, supported by normative justifications consciously directed toward the shoring up of the political autonomy of the world's territorially demarcated countries. The normative assumptions sustaining the nation-state system—particularly the principles of nonintervention in domestic affairs and the inviolability of borders—are often taken for granted by "realists" as part of the "structure" of the "anarchic" world polity. But they were not always taken for granted, nor should it be assumed that they will be perpetuated through coming decades as the dominant norms of the world polity.

Embraced by governments as core rules of interstate relations since the middle of the seventeenth century, the principles of state sovereignty and mutual noninterference have been among the essential building blocks of the nation-state system. But it should not be assumed that the nation-state system as we know it could survive the erosion of elite and popular commitment to these principles. Indeed, the statesmen and legal theorists who promulgated them as part of the Peace of Westphalia (1648) ending a century of devastating wars of religion were determined to move out of the simple might-makes-right system under which the peoples of Europe had been slaughtering one another. They pledged henceforth to respect one another's territorial jurisdictions and to refrain from intervening across the borders separating their states, even to aid coreligionists. The principles of mutual respect for the physical integrity and political sovereignty of their respective territorial realms were (and still are) supposed to constrain relations between all states, whatever their ranking in the hierarchies of military and economic power.

Under the inherited Westphalian norms, however, it has been legitimate, in political theory and international law, to violate the sovereignty of another state in defense (or retaliation) against an aggressor state that is itself violating the central noninterventionist norms of the system, particularly if a failure to oppose the aggressor could jeopardize the sovereign independence of one's own state. Here we have the normative underpinnings of both *realpolitik* statecraft and the "realist" model of international relations. The claim that these are normatively neutral approaches to world politics is both philosophically and historically shallow.[13]

One of my purposes in Part One of this book is to uncover and hold up to fresh scrutiny such explicit and implicit normative premises of the currently dominant configuration of the world polity. Along with the analysis of how world politics has been conducted up to now, Part One provides a base for the prescriptive and normatively explicit discussion in Part Two about future directions in the evolution of the world polity.

The False God of Theoretical Parsimony

The questions about the structure and functioning of world polity that beg for answers today are inherently complex. They involve the interactive effects of the polity and the larger society of which the polity is but a part. They involve feedback relationships between the world political system and the world economic system and various subsystems of the world polity and the world economy: countries, intergov-

---

[13]Terry Nardin's *Law, Morality, and the Relations of States* (Princeton: Princeton University Press, 1983), although essentially appreciative of *realpolitik* statecraft, effectively disposes of the mistaken notion that such statecraft (and its "realist" expositors) is devoid of normative presuppositions.

ernmental organizations and regimes, transnational associations, corporations, interest groups, political parties and movements, and influential individuals. There is no presumption that the way the world polity works is determined by material factors more than by ideational factors.

Accordingly, the quest for parsimonious explanation— for that one "powerful" variable or condition, or at least a small set of variables or conditions, to which most of the behaviors we are interested in can be attributed—is not really appropriate to the complexities of contemporary world politics. According to James Rosenau,

> One can only be envious of those analysts who are able to account for the course of events by positing all actors as egoistic power maximizers, or who can reduce modern international history to a clash between security and economic interests, or who can ascribe all causation to the structural requirements of the global capitalist economy, or who use the requirements imposed by the state system to cast a wide explanatory net, or who explain the long cycles of war in terms of one or another master variable. . . . The very parsimony that enables them to explain so much also serves to simplify too much. Virtually by definition, parsimonious theories are compelled to ignore the multiple macro and micro levels at which the sources of turbulence gather momentum.[14]

Like Rosenau, I find no compelling reasons, either in logic or in considerations of usefulness, for restricting a theory of the world polity to a particular unit or level of analysis. The world polity, like any political system, is made up of diverse units (individuals, groups, institutions, rules, norms) that affect one another. What happens at the level of state-to-state interaction affects the relative power, well-being, and behavior of the groups and individuals that make up the involved states, and vice versa. The transnational interactions engaged in by various economic, occupational, ethnic, and religious groups across state boundaries are reflected in governmental policies. The world polity encompasses all of these diverse lines of interaction, which typically intersect one another both horizontally and vertically. Particular units of analysis and levels of interaction (say, the government-to-government relations of countries) can be analyzed as discrete structural and behavioral systems with their own, sometimes unique, characteristics; and we may find it useful to develop theories confined to the special properties of any one of these configurations. Yet in both logic and behavior each of these particular configurations—the nation-state system being one of them—remains a *subsystem* of the world polity, and therefore cannot be adequately understood apart from an understanding of the forces impacting on it from the larger world polity and from other subsystems of that polity.

Nor can the structure of the world polity and the behavior of its influential actors be adequately evaluated (or reformed) on the basis of only one or two normative imperatives—such as the elimination of war, the overthrow of the world capitalist

---

[14]James N. Rosenau, *Turbulence in World Politics: A Theory of Change and Continuity* (Princeton: Princeton University Press, 1990), p. 23.

system, the universal adoption of a market economy, or the spread of democracy. There are too many competing (and quite legitimate) ways of life for it to be anything but fatuous to attempt to impose one value system on the world as *the* essence of the "good" polity. As will be argued in Part Two, a more appropriate normative approach that avoids the pitfalls of both shallow relativism and arrogant universalism would grant the presumptive validity of many of the interests humans value highly and would seek to promote acceptance of a world polity that would require the least sacrifice of such highly valued interests.

An Inclusive Definition of Theory

There has been a good deal of academic ink spilled in debates over what deserves to be called "theory." Most of this turns out to be advocacy of the *kind* of theory the writer employs, or likes to read. Some would categorize as theory only those propositions that can be reduced to mathematical formulae. Others would restrict the label *theory* to statements that can be verified or falsified by quantifiable empirical data. Then there are those who hold *theory* to be a set of interlinked comprehensive explanations of an entire field of interdependent phenomena. I too have my preferences, but it is not my purpose to impose these in the form of a restrictive definition of theory that excludes or denigrates approaches that I find less congenial to my way of thinking.

My agnosticism on what constitutes the true nature of theory having been admitted, I do hope that what I am presenting here will lead to theories of world politics that are stated precisely enough in their key analytical propositions to be confirmable or disconfirmable by historical and contemporary empirical research and argued clearly enough in their normative dimensions to invite reasoned discourse with a wide variety of schools of moral and ethical philosophy. It is not my style, however, to present my work in such formalistic terms as to allow full comprehension only by the mathematically sophisticated. Nor do I like to write in a specialized jargon that requires lay readers to master a new language to adequately understand my arguments.

I will be pleased if those with a more formalistic bent or highly specialized foci of interest wish to translate my discourse into their terms of reference. My exposition here, however, is designed to be accessible to a broad range of scholars from different disciplines as well as to policymakers and concerned laypersons.

Part One

Analytical Framework

1 The Anarchic Structure of the Nation-State System

Throughout the world the most powerful institutions of governance—those vested with supreme rule-making and rule-enforcing capabilities—operate within and on behalf of one of the some 190 territorially demarcated countries, frequently called "states." The entire population of the planet is divided into, and governed by the laws of, one or another of these units. Usually most of the humans living in a particular country consider themselves part of a "nation," a distinct people valuing a particular way of life.

Although there may well be more than one nation within a country, and even though some nations may claim members in more than one country, each of these territorially demarcated complexes of governance is generally regarded as a nation-state; and the pattern of relationships *among* these entities is often referred to as the nation-state system. I will retain this conventional terminology.

What is most striking about the nation-state system, and probably most significant for understanding how it functions in the world at large, is its *essentially anarchic* political structure. A society has an anarchic polity to the extent that it lacks society-wide rule-making and rule-enforcing institutions. International anarchy, it should be noted, does not preclude cooperation among the autonomous nation-states; nor does it necessarily mean the absence of shared international norms or explicit rules of international behavior. Thus, the core norm of the nation-state system—that each country has sovereignty over everything within its territorial jurisdiction—has been the foundation of international law since the middle of the seventeenth century. When the world society's core national-sovereignty norm is threatened by one country's aggressive intervention across another's borders, that norm itself allows each member of the world society the sovereign prerogative of deciding if and how to come to the aid of the victim.

Attempts to overlay this basic structural anarchy with rudimentary global "collective security" institutions (to be analyzed in Chapter 2) have had only limited success, for member governments are determined to limit their freedom of action as little as possible. The United Nations Security Council resolutions in 1990 authorizing members to apply sanctions, up to and including military force, against Iraq for its invasion of Kuwait preserved the right of each member of the United Nations to decide how to implement the resolutions.

Characteristically, in the nation-state system no country is bound by rules to which it does not voluntarily subscribe, and most sanctions on individuals or groups to comply with international rules are administered by the national governments upon individuals or groups within their respective jurisdictions. Yet there are institutions to which most of the nation-states belong (specialized agencies of the United Nations primarily) that are mandated by the UN Charter or special international treaties to make rules for the whole international society and, though lacking substantial powers of enforcement, to oversee their implementation.[1] There are a few selective-membership, international institutions functioning on a global or nearly global basis, such as the International Monetary Fund or the International Maritime Organization, that do have limited sanctioning powers (such as the withholding of funds or technical assistance resources) granted them by their members.[2] Still, efforts to enforce a rule of behavior upon a nation-state against its determined will to resist usually must be undertaken by other nation-states, not directly by the international rule-issuing institution, particularly if the enforcement includes violent sanctions.

There are many detailed rules of interstate interaction subscribed to by large sets of countries and spelled out explicitly in signed treaties that have the force of law within each of the signatory states. But, again, these treaties are negotiated and subscribed to on a voluntary basis. Treaty signatories may charge each other with violation of their subscribed-to obligations and can attempt to enforce obligations on each other through economic or military sanctions. (They can even attempt to mobilize concerted, near-universal sanctions, as the United States did against Iran in the 1979–1980 embassy hostage crisis for Iran's violation of its treaty obligations vis-à-vis foreign embassies.) However, there is no centralized international mechanism for the enforcement of state-to-state treaty obligations.

The view of the nation-state system as anarchic, or essentially anarchic, is widely recurrent in the literature on international relations—albeit with varying terminology and detail in its elaboration. A few theories of international relations, most notably Hans Morgenthau's *Politics Among Nations*[3] and Kenneth Waltz's *Theory of International Politics,*[4] attempt to systematically deduce all of the important behavioral characteristics of international politics, especially the prevalence of war, from this anarchic structure. Basically, they start with international anarchy as a given and

---

[1]Typical rule-making, but not rule-enforcing, international institutions are the Food and Agriculture Organization and the United Nations Environmental Program. The World Trade Organization (WTO) has quasi-enforcement authority; it can find member states to be in violation of its rules, and such findings can be used by other members to justify retaliatory measures against the offending states.

[2]The International Monetary Fund, in its ability to extend or withhold funds for balance of payments relief, for example, has a powerful tool for compelling would-be recipients to adhere to IMF mandates on national macroeconomic policy. The International Maritime Organization can induce relatively poor coastal states to adhere to internationally negotiated standards of harbor maintenance by providing or withholding technical assistance to national port authorities on the basis of their compliance with the international standards.

[3]Hans J. Morgenthau, *Politics Among Nations: The Struggle for Power and Peace,* 5th edition, revised (New York: Knopf, 1978).

[4]Kenneth N. Waltz, *Theory of International Politics* (Menlo Park: Addison-Wesley, 1979).

treat it throughout as a constant. Morgenthau at least makes a gesture in the direction of deriving his characterization of international anarchy from a more basic (albeit questionable) assumption about human nature: namely, his proposition that "The tendency to dominate . . . is an element of all human associations, from the family through fraternal and professional associations and local political organizations, to the state." The nation-state, the largest viable form of human domination, therefore will be engaged in a perpetual struggle for power against other nation-states to avoid falling victim to their domination.[5] Waltz is content to start and stay with a priori assumptions at the observable surface of international behavior: "The parts of international political systems stand in relations of coordination. Formally, each is the equal of the others. None is entitled to command; none is required to obey. . . . Whether those units live, prosper, or die depends on their own efforts."[6]

Neither Morgenthau nor Waltz, nor for that matter any of their prominent disciples, after assuming that the anarchic structure of the nation-state system is the principal determinant of the way things happen in international politics, takes the next step and treats international anarchy as an "independent variable," in the sense of a factor to be manipulated (at least analytically), which would allow them to examine how its diminution or absence might affect other features of world politics.[7] Rather, they treat it as an axiom, from which other features of international relations are to be deduced.

I agree that much of significance in world politics appears to flow from the anarchic structure of the nation-state system; but for that very reason a theory of international politics, and surely a theory of the world polity, would seem to require an *explanation* both of the origins of the anarchic nation-state system and of its persistence. Moreover, to examine systematically just what in world politics is the result of the anarchic nation-state system, we need to think through—hypothetically—how world politics would differ (or remain the same) under a substantially altered structure.

---

[5]Morgenthau, *Politics Among Nations,* quotation from p. 37.

[6]Waltz, *Theory of International Politics,* pp. 88, 91.

[7]Morgenthau, it should be noted, explicitly contemplates the possibility of a post–nation-state system: "Nothing in the realist position militates against the assumption that the present division of the world into nation-states will be replaced by larger units of a quite different character, more in keeping with the technical potentialities and the moral requirements of the contemporary world" (*Politics Among Nations,* p. 10). But while granting the possibility, his writing makes clear that he sees no chance of such a transformation materializing in the foreseeable future, and therefore offers no serious conjectures on the characteristics of a system that would subordinate the struggle for power among sovereign nation-states to the rules of a larger world polity.

For a post-Waltzian attempt, albeit within the "realist" school, to develop an explanation for international anarchy—its origins and its ability to "reproduce" itself—see Barry Buzan, Charles Jones, and Richard Little, *The Logic of Anarchy: Neorealism to Structural Realism* (New York: Columbia University Press, 1993). Buzan, Jones, and Little return to what was at least suggested by Morgenthau, but then pushed aside by Waltz as "reductionist": namely, that the internal structure of states and the strategies pursued by national governments as "agents" of these domestic forces should be important, indeed crucial, elements of a deeper theory of international politics, and that such a theory must attempt to explain the origins, persistence, and changing configurations of international anarchy.

Why Anarchy?

There are material reasons or ideational[8] reasons—usually some combination of both—why any particular human population or society operates without centralized rule-making and rule-enforcement to govern interpersonal or intergroup interaction. Some of these reasons are unique to particular times and places. But there also seem to be some specifiable general determinants of anarchy (while varying in their influence with differences in group size, density, complexity of natural interaction patterns, and the like) that are common across eras of human history and to most societies, ranging from neighborhoods to world society as a whole.

Material Reasons

The material reasons for the presence or absence of anarchy have primarily to do with (1) the natural supply and human accessibility of essential and valued goods, and (2) the capabilities of certain people to control access to what is generally needed and valued. These factors strongly affect both the internal structure of groups and the structure of intergroup relationships.

Where the supply of needed and desired goods is abundant (relative to demand) there is little incentive to control access and distribution, either by commonly accepted rules or by imposition of the selfish and powerful, and an anarchic regime of open access, "first come/first served," tends to evolve. The connection between abundance and relatively benign anarchy has been observed by anthropologists studying simple societies. Small tribes with basically peaceful dispositions tended to develop in regions of abundant natural food and water resources, where a tribe that might encounter another tribe monopolizing the natural resources in one locale could move on to another locale. Characteristically, such peoples fulfilled their subsistence needs more by hunting and gathering than by subsistence agriculture. Prototypical examples from the anthropological literature are the Semai of Malaya, the Arapesh of New Guinea, the Kung Bushmen of Southern Africa, and the Zuni Indians of the American Southwest.[9] Resource abundance also seems to be a good part of the explanation for the basic durability over many centuries of a world ocean regime of open access and free use of the waters and fish of the high seas.[10]

The relationships between conditions of material scarcity and anarchic social structures are more complicated. Where there is not enough of a valued good to sat-

---

[8]I use the term "ideational" rather than "ideological" to avoid the standard (Manheimian) connotation of ideological as an actor's justifications for behavior that is determined basically by material interests. I make no assumption that ideas are less basic or less determinative than material things.

[9]David Fabbro, "Peaceful Societies," in Richard A. Falk and Samuel S. Kim, eds., *The War System: An Interdisciplinary Approach* (Boulder: Westview Press, 1980), pp. 180–203. See also Elizabeth M. Thomas, *The Harmless People* (New York: Knopf, 1959).

[10]Seyom Brown et al., *Regimes for the Ocean, Outer Space and Weather* (Washington, D.C.: Brookings Institution, 1977).

isfy the demands for it on the part of those to whom it is physically accessible, a regime for controlling access and use is likely to develop, either through voluntary agreement or through tests of will and strength among rivals for control. Anthropologists and economic historians locate these changes in the shift from hunting and gathering to agriculture, the latter developing when scarcities generate incentives to establish exclusive communal or family ownership over plants and animals, preferably in a fertile area. Property rights are established and enforced among members of the community, and the frontiers of the area are defended against intruders. Communal rules and organizations become more complex, and common policies are developed to govern any relationships with outsiders. Order *within* territorially demarcated communities concomitant with persisting anarchy—but anarchy of a more competitive, even belligerent kind—*between* such communities are thus the expected political counterparts of economic scarcity.[11]

Some communities, through the development of technologies allowing them to operate agricultural and industrial economies on a large scale and also militarily to subdue (or protect) weaker neighbors, have expanded their frontiers over vast regions, sometimes striving to encompass entire continents. Beginning about 3500 B.C., large parts of the Eurasian landmass and the northern half of Africa were thus divided among huge empires. The earliest of these spanned outward from hierarchically organized communities that had been able to build and sustain large irrigation systems: Mesopotamia, Egypt, Persia, India, and later China. The ancient riverine empires were soon challenged by the great maritime powers bordering the Mediterranean—Greece, Carthage, and Rome. In the Western Hemisphere, regional empires appear to have been centered in what are now Peru and Mexico.

None of the ancient imperial hegemons, however, nor their more recent counterparts (Ottoman Turkey, Ming China, Moscovy, Portugal and Spain in the fifteenth century, France under Louis XIV and then Napoleon, Britain in the nineteenth century, Hitler's Third Reich, Tojo's Japan, and the Soviet Union and the United States after World War II), have come even close to dominating the entire world. Why?

The explanation of the inability of any state to establish world empire, once again, as with the rise of the territorial state in the first place, must give heavy weight to basic material and geographic factors. Imperial expansion beyond a certain size produces negative marginal returns, or what historian Paul Kennedy has termed "imperial overstretch": Distance from the center of power and the vast circumference of the realm make the peripheries increasingly difficult to integrate economically and politically and to defend against hostile outsiders; the need to sustain such increasingly unviable peripheries saps material and human resources away from regenerative and developmental pursuits at the central core of the empire, contributing either to its decline relative to rival empires (sometimes as a result of defeats in wars) or to a

---

[11]Douglass C. North, *Structure and Change in Economic History* (New York: W. W. Norton, 1981), pp. 72–112.

decision by its rulers to cease further imperial expansion, possibly even to retract the realm back to a more viable size.[12]

These material factors preventing global empire, and therefore sustaining some form of anarchic world polity, seemed possibly to have been transcended by the middle of the twentieth century with the development of weapons, transportation systems, and communication systems of truly global range. A superpower with superiority in such capabilities might well be able to establish globally extensive hegemony. Indeed, in the 1950s and 1960s it was commonplace among geopolitical experts in both the United States and the Soviet Union that the rival superpower had such a grand design to establish a world empire and would do so unless stopped by countervailing power. The bipolar organization of most of the world into two rival cold war coalitions was in large part a result, and apparent confirmation, of these assumptions.

As it turned out, neither the Soviet Union nor the United States was able to convert its hegemony into a sustainable empire over even half of the world. Perhaps, were it not for the opposition of its main rival superpower, the new globe-spanning reach and massive destructive power of its strategic nuclear arsenal might have provided the basis for either to hold sway over the rest of the world. But having to face a similarly armed rival not only prevented each from attaining a global imperium; paradoxically, it also undermined the basis of sustainable hegemony over one's own coalition, for two main reasons: (1) It became evident that superpower pledges of strategic protection of its allies were incredible insofar as their implementation would initiate a massive nuclear exchange of blows with the rival superpower. (2) The superpower arms race, and the superpowers' need to assist their respective allies in military buildups, required both the United States and the Soviet Union to divert material resources and human energies to the military sector, meanwhile neglecting to stay sufficiently ahead of other countries in general technological and economic modernization to maintain clear leadership in the global market over other economic powers. Coalition partners came to realize that at moments of truth they might have to fend for themselves—the implication being that they had better develop independent foreign policies and defense capabilities, particularly to service interests that might not fit the cold war priorities of their superpower protector. Meanwhile, particularly in the U.S.-led coalition, revived centers of economic power (Japan, members of the European Community) began to pursue their own interests, including growing commercial intercourse with members of the Soviet-led coalition, more in competition with the United States than under its direction.

---

[12]Paul Kennedy, *The Rise and Fall of the Great Powers: Economic Change and Military Conflict from 1500 to 2000* (New York: Random House, 1987). Kennedy's treatise is one of a long line of studies (including those of Edward Gibbon, Arnold Toynbee, Ludwig Dehio, Quincy Wright, A.F.K. Organski, George Modelski, Charles Kindleberger, and Robert Gilpin) on the rise and fall of imperial or hegemonic powers. For comparative analysis of the theoretical assumptions in these studies, see Joshua S. Goldstein, *Long Cycles: Prosperity and War in the Modern Age* (New Haven: Yale University Press, 1988).

By the late 1980s, just before the collapse of the Soviet Union, there was a growing realization among statespersons that the era of global bipolarity following World War II had been a temporary abnormality. The "natural" configuration of international relations—a decentralized, pluralistic, essentially anarchistic system of competing states—appeared to be returning.

As the Soviet empire started to disintegrate, however, some U.S. policymakers began to think in terms of "*uni*polarity." The belief that the United States had won the cold war against the Soviet Union and was now finally in a position to preside over a global "Pax Americana" was given additional credence by the Bush administration's aggressive leadership of the multinational coalition formed to counter Iraq's 1990 invasion of Kuwait. But these romantic notions were inconsistent with the underlying material and ideational trends in world society that, on the eve of the twenty-first century, were profoundly antithetical to one country lording it over most of the others.[13]

Ideational Reasons

Interacting with, and usually reinforcing, the material factors that create and sustain territorial units of self-government has been the belief on the part of each such community that it is a unique people and should remain so. Archaeological and anthropological studies confirm that an idea-culture was the handmaiden of the agri-culture that generated the first territorially based communities. Stable husbanding of the land required community-wide language and norms for resolving interpersonal conflict, facilitating barter and trade, determining shares of work and output, and maintaining even the simplest organizational hierarchies. Although such social functions were (and are) the requisites of community life everywhere, the ways of performing them evolve differently from place to place; and each society envelops its own practices in a particular set of myths, symbols, and rational justifications that, almost always, are held to be superior to those of other societies. As industrialization produces both a specialization of socioeconomic roles in a community *and* an imperative of integrating the community's diversifying sectors, the ideational features of the community's life also become more elaborate. These cultural elaborations tend to follow a unique evolutionary pattern in each country, further strengthening the justifications for countries to maintain their sovereignty.

The defense of the territorial unit, perhaps originally motivated simply to protect access to and productively exploit scarce resources, becomes inseparable from the defense of the community's way of life. Thus, although varying in their particular

---

[13]This analysis of the disintegration of the cold war superpower-led coalitions is developed more extensively in my *New Forces, Old Forces, and the Future of World Politics* (New York: HarperCollins, 1995), chapters 4–6.

forms, polities the world over seem to have developed according to an underlying elemental logic: (1) the state as simple organizational apparatus to deal with scarce resources becomes (2) the state as a set of institutions for maintaining civic order among those residing in or next to a territorially demarcated jurisdiction, which, in turn, becomes (3) the state as nation, meaning a people with a common culture who loyally subscribe to common norms, rules, and institutions.

Just as the material reasons for self-sufficiency can turn states toward economic imperialism, so the ideational justifications for autonomy can turn nations into presumptuous civilizers of other peoples, even all of humankind. Although, theoretically, the norm of the self-determination of peoples ought to produce a benignly anarchic world polity, in practice people who insist on their own right of autonomous nationhood are often not ready to accord legitimacy to others who claim this right—one of the principal causes of large-scale violence in the world polity.

Imperialistic states with a self-appointed mission to bring civilization and justice to the world inevitably generate resistance to their arrogance. Other rulers who see their own power threatened, peoples proud of their own ways of life or, as a minimum, determined not to be dictated to by foreigners, mobilize (often in alliance with one another) to balance or overmatch the power of the would-be world civilizers. This dynamic has limited in turn the expansionary thrusts of Rome, Islam, Napoleon, the Pax Britannica, Hitler, and the cold war superpowers. The perpetuation of the basic global structure of anarchy has been a result.[14]

The Metamorphosis of State System into Nation-State System

Some of the reasons the nation-state system is anarchic have been shown to lie outside of the nation-state system itself. Anarchy is a generic phenomenon, appearing as a form of polity in societies of very different sizes and constituent units. The world polity of anarchy among countries did not begin with the nation-state system: Its basic anarchic structure (at times expressing itself in rival imperially integrated coalitions) preceded the evolution of actual nation-states. However, as states became nations, both the material and ideational sources of interstate anarchy were reinforced.

If we return to Europe in the middle 1600s, where many diplomatic historians find the roots of the contemporary international system, we find an interstate polity still reflecting some of the socioeconomic and governmental structures of the feudal Middle Ages. The largest territorially defined units of governance were each ruled by a monarch, sovereign within his or her jurisdiction. It was from the monarchical cen-

---

[14]Some of the most insightful writing on the phenomenon of anti-imperialism is by Jean Gottmann, a geographer. See his *The Significance of Territory* (Charlottesville: University Press of Virginia, 1973).

ter of each state that the villages, towns, and cities of the country obtained the necessities of public safety and basic economic security: protection against marauders, the building and upkeep of main roads and waterways, and a common medium of commercial exchange and legal tender within the jurisdiction. Yet most of the monarchical or dynastic states were not yet "nations," in the sense of a population sharing a common culture and considering itself to be one people. Indeed, the monarchs who ran the state system were often culturally alienated from the peoples within their jurisdictions, sometimes not even speaking the same languages as their own subjects.

Although each kingdom was sovereign unto itself, among the monarchs there was a cultural community of sorts: considerable interaction (even intermarriage across dynasties) and shared values—not the least of which was a belief in the virtue of the monarchical form of polity for each of their states, and a derived set of norms for the conduct of interstate relations. They perceived that the perpetuation of their sovereign powers in each of their jurisdictions depended crucially on their mutual adherence to principles of interstate behavior of the kind promulgated in the Peace of Westphalia that ended the wars of religion—in particular, the rule of noninterference by states in the domestic affairs of other states. They did not want to return to the unconstrained brutality of the previous century in which the power competition among rulers involved stirring up violent, subversive religious and ethnic movements in the domains of their rivals.

The monarchical state system codified in 1648 at Westphalia, often referred to as the Classical Balance of Power, thus embodied the paradox (seized upon ever since by "realists") that order *within* states required an anarchical society *among* states, an anarchy constrained by the rule that all states have a right to sovereign independence.[15] This rule was maintained through the power-balancing process: If one state or group of states threatened to become so powerful and expansionary as to negate the sovereign independence of other states, the threatened states would form an alliance to counter the power of the would-be hegemon.

The anarchic system of mutually respectful sovereigns, highly elitist in conception and operation, was profoundly altered by those changes in the material and ideational bases of society that brought on the eighteenth-century French and American revolutions. Though these revolutions were designed to restructure domestic polities, they also contributed to the transformation of the world polity from state system to *nation*-state system.

More and more, a country's security and well-being were a function of the ability of its rulers to gain cooperation from many sectors of the economy to build modern fleets and armies, to construct country-wide transportation and communication systems, and to foster industries that could engage in profitable foreign trade. Ruling groups—whether monarchs, aristocrats, or the new leaders of parliaments—now

---

[15]On the rules of the Westphalian state system, see Edward V. Gulick, *Europe's Balance of Power* (Ithaca: Cornell University Press, 1955).

had to identify with the people of the realm rather than stand aloof from them. They had to speak the people's languages and champion their causes, but fuse them into one overarching concept of the nation-state as an organic whole; and for this it was necessary to enlist the producers of the ideational culture: newspaper editors, writers, and educated persons generally.

This equation of state with nation had both a pacifying and a brutalizing impact on the conduct of interstate—now truly international—relations. As prophesied by Immanuel Kant in his *Perpetual Peace,* states organized on republican/representative lines were less inclined to go to war.[16] But Kant and his disciples failed to anticipate the other side of the coin of democratization: Modern wars, now requiring the efforts of the whole nation to provision them, could not be prosecuted effectively unless supported by a national consensus. Wars had to be fought for *national* causes or not at all. And the determination of necessary and legitimate national interests, even in polities lagging in the development of republican institutions, now was in the hands of the representatives of many sectors of society.

For these very reasons those who wanted to use war as an instrument of national policy would need to whip up widespread popular fear and anger over the issue at hand to assure that a particular conflict with another country was infused with great significance for the entire nation—its honor, its glory, its way of life, its very survival. Once the country was readied in this way for war, negotiated compromises to resolve the precipitating conflict short of war would be more difficult to achieve. And war, once it did start, would be much more difficult to keep limited in its intensity. The enemy, now defined as venal, would need to be severely punished, if not totally destroyed.

Nationalism, in this way, gets turned into a secular religion. Countries inevitably fear interstate intervention, overt and covert, but each is inclined to practice it. The moderating norm of anarchic international society—mutual respect for one another's sovereignty—is honored in the breech. The nation-state system becomes, in effect, a war system (à la Hobbes, a potential war of each state against any other state), which in turn generates the requirement for an even tighter organization of society within the states and a suspicion of cosmopolitan elements of society that appear less than totally patriotic. Statespersons, even if they should want to, are not permitted by parliaments and xenophobic publics to accept the constraints of international law and international institutions.

Ethno-Nationality Conflicts: The System in Crisis

Although equating the state with the nation is an idea that tends to strengthen the state in a country that is, for the most part, ethnically homogeneous, the same idea can be turned against the authority of the state in an ethnically heterogeneous coun-

---

[16]Immanuel Kant, *Perpetual Peace: A Philosophical Essay* [1795] (Indianapolis: Bobbs-Merrill, 1957).

try by those groups who feel that the official national culture of the state does not adequately reflect or respect their way of life. If a legitimate polity is one in which state and nation are congruent with each other, then every nation presumably has a right to a state of its own.

The nation-state system, so conceived, contains the seeds of its own radical (in some cases, violent) disintegration, conceivably into thousands of "sovereign" political entities, as all around the world peoples with distinct cultural identities assert their nationhood and corresponding right to self-governance. There are, of course, many disincentives to an open and active assertion of political independence, including the risk of arrest and imprisonment of members of the secessionist movement and, if independence is in fact attained, the loss of privileged economic access, social services, and other amenities available to citizens of the larger country. Despite such risks and costs, as many as 200 disaffected ethnic communities were attempting to assert their rights against national governments in the early 1990s and, as I write, as many as twenty of these are engaged in overt agitation for political autonomy.[17] And who is to say that any of these communities is not really a distinct nation? A nation is after all essentially a state of mind more than an objectifiable set of attributes.

When we look at the half century that has passed since World War II, it is clear that the systemic impact of the idea that nations are the constituent units of the world polity has been problematical. The reluctant granting by the Europeans of political independence to some 100 of their colonies in the three decades following World War II was arguably their only rational course as the political and economic costs of maintaining their overstretched imperial realms in the face of anticolonial uprisings began to outweigh their benefits; and in this sense, the impact on the world polity was in the main positive and stabilizing, at least temporarily.[18] But the subsequent phases of the national self-determination era—the assertion of the right to independent statehood by ethnic communities within the many Third World countries and throughout the area formerly controlled by the Soviet Union—are threatening to destroy the norms and structural foundations of the state system itself.

The viability of the state system is crucially dependent upon the ability of countries to maintain the loyalty of the populations within their jurisdictions and to secure their borders against unwanted intrusions. But many of the ethnic and religious communities claiming the right to political self-determination comprise populations that span the borders of existing nation-states (such as the Kurds in Iraq, Iran, Syria, and Turkey; and the Hutus and Tutsis in Rwanda and Burundi) or oc-

---

[17]A survey of contemporary ethno-nationality conflicts around the world is provided by Ted Robert Gurr. *Minorities at Risk: A Global View of Ethnopolitical Conflicts* (Washington D.C.: United States Institute of Peace Press, 1993); see also Ted Robert Gurr and Barbara Harff, *Ethnic Conflict in World Politics* (Boulder: Westview Press, 1994).

[18]M. E. Chamberlain, *Decolonization: The Fall of the European Empires* (Oxford, UK: Blackwell, 1985); see also Paul M. Kennedy, *The Rise and Fall of the Great Powers: Economic Change and Military Conflict from 1500 to 2000* (New York: Random House, 1987).

cupy areas of high economic or strategic value to the established jurisdictions (such as Chechnya in Russia). The result has been an epidemic in the post–cold war period of inter-ethnic violence and of harsh repression by threatened governments—much of this challenging the legitimacy and control of established jurisdictions and borders and giving rise to interventions and counter-interventions by outside powers.

The larger implications of these ethno-nationality conflicts for the world polity will be revisited in Chapter 7. Suffice it to say at this point in the analysis that the nation-state system as far it has evolved is not only incapable of keeping such conflicts within tolerable bounds but, paradoxically, is contributing, through its sovereignty norms and anarchic structure, to the spread and intensification of these conflicts.

2 The Phenomenon of International Cooperation

Even though the modern world polity operates largely through the anarchic, presumably self-help, nation-state system, there are many international and transnational associations that exist to facilitate cooperation among their members. Some of these functionally specific and regional associations are highly institutionalized, with formal assemblies, permanent secretariats, and dispute resolution bodies.

In addition, almost every country is a member of the United Nations and thus participates, either directly or indirectly, in the world organization's various peace and security operations and in its programs in economic development, health, and environmental protection.

What explains these enclaves of international cooperation? Are they, as it were, simply "lubricants" of the still basically self-help system of sovereign states to make it work better? Or do they represent a potentially fundamental antithesis—in an embryonic stage of development—to the anarchic structure and norms of the system?

Cooperation Consistent with Anarchy

If we define cooperation as behavior intentionally coordinated by two or more actors,[1] then there is a wide range of international cooperation—cooperation among

---

[1] Robert Keohane defines international cooperation as "a process through which policies actually followed by governments come to be regarded by their partners as facilitating realization of their own objectives, as the result of policy coordination." But Keohane, in attempting to distinguish cooperation from harmony, adds the provision that cooperation between parties "can only arise from conflict or potential conflict" among them. See Robert O. Keohane, *After Hegemony: Cooperation and Discord in the World Political Economy* (Princeton: Princeton University Press, 1984), pp. 51–63 (quotations from p. 63). This restriction, it appears to me, flies in the face of the common occurrence of people and governments deciding to pool their resources and know-how to accomplish some commonly desired task that they could not accomplish by acting on their own. They need not be motivated by a desire to avoid conflict; in some situations the calculation of being better off as a result of cooperation may be sufficient. Surely, the Marshall Plan for aiding European economic recovery after World War II—one of the most dramatic instances of international cooperation—was not entered into by the Europeans and Americans mainly to avoid conflict with one another but primarily to realize the mutual benefits of a revived European economy.

national governments and other actors across national borders—that has been taking place under (perhaps despite) the anarchic structure of the nation-state system.

Puzzling over this phenomenon, a group of American international relations scholars convened a symposium in 1984–1985 to address the question: "What circumstances favor the emergence of cooperation under anarchy?" It was an analytical ground rule of the symposium to "focus on nation-states as the primary actors in world politics, treat national preferences as sovereign, and assume that any ultimate escape from international anarchy is unlikely." Utilizing mainly game-theoretic concepts, the scholars explored the factors in particular types of competitive situations that may induce competitors to coordinate their strategies; but the participants in the symposium were unable to generate general hypotheses about international cooperation apart from the tautological conclusion that cooperation will take place when the relevant actors each calculate that the benefits of coordinated action exceed the benefits of unilateral uncoordinated action.[2]

International relations theorists (who take the sovereign, territorial state system as an unalterable given) do not appear to have been able to add anything fundamental to the ideas about international cooperation developed by the seventeenth-century Dutch legal philosopher Hugo Grotius. An essential characteristic of human nature, argued Grotius, is "sociability," the desire for a peaceful life that leads men and women the world over to establish communities of law and order, or states. The "right reason" that so produces states also leads these states to devise rules for maintaining their respective communities, the most important being the rule of live and let live. Accordingly, the core normative rule for the society of states (propounded by Grotius in *On the Law of War and Peace*) is mutual respect for one another's sovereignty over one's territorial jurisdiction. To this must be added the "customary" rules that countries have worked out among themselves for minimizing conflict and resolving disputes over their boundaries and in commonly used areas such as rivers and seas.[3]

A contemporary version of the Grotian worldview is Hedley Bull's concept of international society as comprising states that are "conscious of certain common interests and common values" and that "conceive themselves to be bound by a common set of rules in their relations with one another, and share in the workings of common institutions."[4] The sense of common interest, Bull explains, may emanate from any number of fears: mutual fears of unrestricted violence, of agreements between them falling apart, of their independence or sovereignty being violated; the

[2]Kenneth A. Oye, ed., *Cooperation Under Anarchy* (Princeton: Princeton University Press, 1986).

[3]H. Lauterpacht, "The Grotian Tradition in International Law," in Richard Falk, Friedrich Kratochwil, and Saul H. Mendlovitz, eds., *International Law: A Contemporary Perspective* (Boulder: Westview Press, 1985), pp. 10–36.

[4]Hedley Bull, *The Anarchical Society: A Study of Order in World Politics* (New York: Columbia University Press, 1977), quotations from p. 13.

sense of common interest may also result from rational calculation by each of the parties that reciprocal restrictions on their freedom of action can produce mutual benefits; and at certain times and places in the world it may also reflect shared values about the good society.

Bull argues that most countries, largely for self-interest reasons, subscribe to a common minimum set of rules of international coexistence—the core rule being the obligation of each country to respect the supreme jurisdiction of every other country's national government over its own citizens and domain in return for reciprocal respect for its own sovereignty.[5] International society also features subsets of countries that have agreed to be bound by more elaborate and complex rules of interaction in the service of a broader scope of objectives than mere coexistence. Such regional or functional enclaves of order, Bull recognizes, are bound to proliferate in an era of growing material interdependence as countries perceive the need for predictability and mutual accountability, particularly in commerce, communications, and ecological matters.

Clearly, cooperation among countries is an option in the anarchic nation-state system and with growing material interdependence may become an increasingly pervasive feature of world society—to the point, even, where it no longer seems appropriate to define the system as essentially anarchic. But so also are coercive domination and war options for countries that get in the way of each other's pursuits. Interdependence, like familiarity, can breed contempt no less than mutual affection. We lack a universally valid theory, however, of under what conditions interdependence will result in hostile interaction and under what conditions interdependence will result in cooperation. We also lack adequate theoretical concepts for explaining when cooperation will spawn institutions superordinate in authority and power to the cooperating actors.

The inability of contemporary international relations theorists to devise a more operational general model of cooperation should not be surprising in light of the fact that international cooperation ranges across a diverse spectrum of relationships: from mere action-reaction sequences at one extreme, say, tacit mutual forbearance by sets of countries from raising barriers against one another's imports, to highly structured organizations at the other extreme, for example, the International Mining Enterprise through which signatories of the Law of the Sea treaty allocate deep sea mineral mining rights to countries and corporations. Military alliances, but also arms control agreements and mutual de-escalations of combat and cease-fires in war; currency convertibility arrangements; multilateral reciprocal trade agreements; the formulation of and adherence to rules on the use of international sea lanes, air corridors, and broadcasting frequencies; intergovernmental arrangements to allocate

---

[5]On the spread of the norms and rules of international society, as defined by Bull, from Europe to the world as a whole, see Hedley Bull and Adam Watson, *The Expansion of International Society* (New York: Oxford University Press, 1984).

ownership shares of joint economic enterprises—all of these cooperative relationships are normal features of an international scene that remains highly anarchic: Each country retains legal sovereignty and there are no global institutions with the standing power to force nation-states to obey international law.[6]

Some forms of bilateral or multilateral cooperation, indeed, can be seen as necessary correlates of global international anarchy. This is particularly the case with military alliances. The constitutive norm of the nation-state system—that all countries should respect one another's sovereignty within each of their territorial jurisdictions—would be unsustainable, given the vast disparities in power among countries, unless the weak could count on the cooperation of friendly countries to assist them in fending off powerful enemies. Military alliances, which involve coordinated commitments (and sacrifice) of human and material resources, are often essential weights in the balances of power that throughout modern history have prevented imperialistic states from attaining world empire.

Similarly, customs unions, common markets, and regional trading blocs have been formed by groups of countries out of fear that their domestic economies, and therefore national autonomy, otherwise would be overwhelmed by more economically powerful states or transnational corporations. Surely, the European Community's commitment to a more fully integrated market was strongly motivated by the shared perception among EC members that the contemplated limitations of national sovereignty are required for effective competition against the United States and Japan. This phenomenon, too, can be viewed as a necessary correlate of international anarchy.

Cooperation "Regimes"

In many circumstances international cooperation proceeds not so much out of a need to organize common defense against political enemies or economic rivals, although such competitive motives may be partly involved, as from mutual calculation of benefits to be gained (as distinct from threats to be avoided) through multilateral collaboration. A flurry of scholarly efforts in the 1970s and 1980s was devoted to understanding the origins and maintenance of such international "regimes"—defined by one prominent group of scholars as "sets of implicit or explicit principles, norms, rules, and decision-making procedures around which actors' expectations converge in a given area of international relations."[7]

---

[6]Oran Young, in his *International Cooperation: Building Regimes for Natural Resources and the Environment* (Ithaca: Cornell University Press, 1989), analyzes the wide range of types of international cooperation. His study cogently conceptualizes the dynamics of different types of regimes, but, like the rest of the contemporary literature on international cooperation, refrains—sensibly—from offering a general covering explanation for the emergence of these different types of cooperation.

[7]Stephen D. Krasner, ed., *International Regimes* (Ithaca: Cornell University Press, 1983), quotation from Krasner's overview essay, p. 2.

International Economic Regimes. According to Robert Keohane, a leading "regime" theorist, whose focus has been mainly on international *economic* cooperation, international regimes come into being and are sustained on the basis of rational calculations of self-interest by national governments:

> international regimes are useful to governments. Far from being threats to governments (in which case it would be hard to understand why they exist at all), they permit governments to attain objectives that would otherwise be unattainable. They do so in part by facilitating intergovernmental agreements. Regimes facilitate agreements by raising the anticipated costs of violating others' property rights, by altering the transaction costs through the clustering of issues, and by providing reliable information to members. Regimes are relatively efficient institutions, compared with the alternative of having a myriad of unrelated agreements, since their principles, rules, and institutions create linkages among issues that give actors incentives to reach mutually beneficial agreements. They thrive in situations where states have common as well as conflicting interests on multiple, overlapping issues.[8]

These conditions are most likely to be centered around clusters of economic issues. In the economic field, more than in the military arena, nation-states (acting out of perceived self-interest) have been willing to subscribe to rules of international behavior, sometimes even to constraints on domestic policies with strong international effects. Post–World War II exemplars of such regimes are the Bretton Woods System for ordering international monetary relations, and the General Agreement on Tariffs and Trade (GATT) for coordinating the reduction of barriers to international commerce.

International Security Regimes. Although harder to come by in the international security field, we do find that groups of countries have sometimes come together not principally to pool their power (as in alliances) against common adversaries but to establish regimes of international accountability, occasionally cooperating in tangible international undertakings in order to stabilize and moderate the rivalrous elements of their relationships that otherwise might drive them to war against one another.

The term "concert" is widely applied by international relations scholars to this kind of cooperative international security regime. Its prototype is the Concert of Europe that prevailed for some seven years (1815–1822) after the defeat of Napoleon Bonaparte, was sustained in diluted form until the Crimean War (1853), and was on occasion activated in the form of ad hoc great-power conferences up until the eve of World War I. The Concert of Europe featured a web of multilateral treaties and agreements among the governments of the great powers (Britain, Russia, Austria, Prussia, and defeated France), committing them to engage in frequent consultations in order to avoid the miscalculations of vital interests that could draw them into war against one another, and, more ambitiously, to facilitate common

---

[8]Keohane, *After Hegemony,* p. 97.

strategies against the destabilizing currents of popular nationalism and radical republicanism loosed upon Europe by the French Revolution. In instituting this system of mutual accountability the statesmen of the time were attempting to prevent the recurrence of two interlinked threats perceived to have brought on the devastating period of the Napoleonic Wars: the spread of political ideas and movements claiming that the sovereign authority of the state belonged to "the people" and not necessarily to the established governments; and the drive by a powerful hegemonic state to establish empire over the other states by exploiting subversive movements within the domain of its rivals.[9]

Generalizing from the case of the nineteenth-century Concert of Europe, some scholars theorize that cooperative security regimes (other than alliances) among the powerful countries in an international system will emerge only in the immediate aftermath of their involvement in large-scale and highly destructive wars and will suffer a demise as the trauma of the war and its disruptive consequences recede.[10]

The post–World War II era, however, exhibits a markedly different sequence, not comprehended by the war-then-cooperation theory:

The hope of the Roosevelt administration to transmute the wartime Grand Alliance between the United States, the USSR, and Britain into a postwar concert of great powers ("Four Policemen," including France, and possibly also including China as a fifth member, all of whom would need to concur for the new United Nations organization to take significant action in the security field), was shattered along the cold war fault-line before the ink was dry on the surrender documents with Germany and Japan. Consultation and mutual accountability between the two most powerful victors, the United States and the Soviet Union, were rapidly supplanted by disassociation, threats and deterrence postures, and the formation of rival globe-spanning alliances. Throughout the first quarter century following World War II, virtually all significant international cooperation took place within each of the two superpower-led coalitions, not between them.

The new worldwide "concert" of powers that, with fits and starts, began to take shape in the early 1970s, and shows promise of being the core of the world order system for the last decade of the twentieth century, was formed less in reaction to the previous world war than in *anticipation* of the mutually suicidal destruction that

---

[9]The essential norms, structure, and operation of the Concert of Europe are richly described by Evan Luard, *Types of International Society* (New York: Free Press, 1976), pp. 95–100, 134–138, 162–166, 193–197, 217–223, 248–252, 275–277, 300–305, and 329–335. See also Richard N. Rosecrance, *Action and Reaction in World Politics* (Boston: Little, Brown, 1963), pp. 149–168.

[10]Robert Jervis states: "Concert systems form after, and only after, a large war against a potential hegemon. . . . After such an experience, the winners will be highly sensitive to the costs of war and will therefore be hesitant to resort to armed force unless their most vital interests are at stake. That is particularly true because in most cases the war against the hegemon will have been accompanied by, or will have led to, large-scale social unrest. . . . Concert systems decay . . . [as] the passage of time alters the unusual postwar situation and reestablishes the balance-of-power assumptions." Robert Jervis, "From Balance to Concert: A Study of International Security Cooperation," in Oye, *Cooperation Under Anarchy,* pp. 60–61.

another world war would unleash. (The bipolarized cold war system had been in large measure a reaction against the excessive "concerting" among the great powers in the pre–World War II period—particularly the appeasement of Hitler at Munich—and marked a return to reliance primarily on countervailing military power to restrain aggressors.)

Ironically, it was Henry Kissinger, one of the theorists of the futility of attempting to integrate the post–World War II "revolutionary" power, the Soviet Union, into a new global concert,[11] who was the central catalyst of the U.S. demarche in the early 1970s to do just that with both the USSR and the People's Republic of China. It was clearly a concert *weltanschauung* that permeated the "Basic Principles of Relations" (largely drafted by Kissinger) signed in 1972 by President Richard Nixon and General Secretary Leonid Brezhnev. Issued at the time of the successful conclusion of the Strategic Arms Limitations Talks (SALT I) and a series of accords on trade, technological cooperation, and cultural exchanges, the Basic Principles document, in addition to renouncing the use or threat of force, committed the superpowers

> to negotiate and settle their differences by peaceful means. Discussions and negotiations on outstanding issues will be conducted in a spirit of reciprocity, mutual accommodation and mutual benefit.
>
> Both sides recognize that efforts to obtain unilateral advantage at the expense of the other, directly or indirectly, are inconsistent with these objectives.[12]

Similar pledges were exchanged by Nixon and Kissinger with Mao Zedong and Zhou Enlai during the U.S. president's historic 1972 visit to China.[13]

Although the promised era of "cooperation not confrontation" in U.S.-Soviet relations suffered important setbacks from the mid-1970s through the mid-1980s (continued military and covert aid to Middle Eastern and Third World clients, the refusal of the U.S. Congress to extend normal trading privileges to the USSR, the Soviet invasion of Afghanistan and power-play against Poland, reactive economic sanctions by the United States, non-ratification of the SALT II agreements, competitive medium-range missile deployments in Europe, altercations over the Reagan administration's Strategic Defense Initiative), the two superpowers continued to

---

[11]Henry Kissinger introduced his study of the Concert of Europe period, *A World Restored: Metternich, Castlereagh, and the Problems of Peace* (Boston: Houghton Mifflin, 1973), with the argument that the "revolutionary power" (Napoleonic France) had not been a fit partner for cooperation since its search for total security did not allow it to be satisfied until it inflicted total insecurity on the status quo powers. In his policy-oriented writings before taking an appointment in the Nixon administration, Kissinger explicitly invoked similar reasoning to caution against attempting to negotiate any kind of modus vivendi with the Soviets.

[12]"Basic Principles of Relations Between the United States of America and the Union of Soviet Socialist Republics," *Department of State Bulletin*, Vol. 66, No. 1722 (June 29, 1972), pp. 898–899.

[13]Text of Joint Communique, issued at Shanghai, February 27, 1972, *Department of State Bulletin*, Vol. 66, No. 1708 (March 20, 1972), pp. 435–438.

adhere to the basic restraints on their strategic arsenals negotiated during the SALT process and to convene the Standing Consultative Commission to deal with alleged violations of the strategic arms accords. The concert principle of mutual account-ability—and consultations—was weakened but holding, at least in those realms that could decisively shift the global balance of military power. Then, beginning again in 1985, promoted by a series of conciliatory moves by Mikhail Gorbachev, the super-powers appeared to be returning to the elaboration of the many-leveled concert rela-tionship initiated in the détente of 1972. (After the breakup of the USSR in 1991, Russia aspired to take on the role of concert counterpart of the United States, but for a time, at least, would be too preoccupied with its internal reconstruction to engage in an active foreign policy.)

My explanation of these developments runs contrary to the prevailing "realist" wisdom that sees cooperative security regimes of the nineteenth-century European Concert and U.S.-Soviet (1972–1979, 1985–1990) détente as anomalies. It is, rather, that *cooperative security regimes are fully consistent with and the most rational responses to the security dilemmas facing modern great powers under the anarchic nation-state system.*

The classic "security dilemma" of countries in the anarchic nation-state system—that efforts undertaken to enhance one's security often will threaten the security of one's opponents—is increasingly seen by national leaders as a problem requiring their cooperative attention, given the prospect that such miscalculations could trig-ger a holocaust that literally would destroy all sides. Given the assumption of the persistence of the anarchic structure of the world polity, the only means of sur-mounting the security dilemma is through international accountability regimes that allow participants to confirm for each other their nonhostile intent. Such confirma-tions can be as tangible as mutual or international agency on-site inspections of mil-itary deployments and facilities to verify adherence to arms control accords. They can also take the form of institutionalized exchanges of information, on budgets, inventories, and the like, particularly through standing commissions in which experts from the member countries can interrogate one another. Periodic "summit"-level meetings among mutually suspicious rivals can be a very important means of mutual education about the range and priorities of geopolitical interests on each side; for developing sensitivity to what each considers most provocative; and for dis-covering common or interdependent interests outside of the security field per se, whose enhancement would provide additional incentives against the exacerbation of conflict. Treaties to codify and publicly legitimate such technical arrangements and political understandings are often crucial elements of cooperative security regimes, for they tend to solemnly commit at-large national constituencies to the undertak-ings and thereby make it more politically costly for governments to renege on their international obligations.

Another security dilemma—that alliances designed to protect national security may undermine it—has also become more severe as war involves all facets of society.

This dilemma, too, has created new imperatives, increasingly recognized by statespersons, for non-alliance or trans-alliance security regimes.

An alliance, insofar as it contains advance commitments by the parties to go to war against a common enemy if that enemy attacks either of them, allows crucial war/peace decisions to be importantly determined by foreign governments. Because of this, the governments subscribing to an alliance will always retain the prerogative of making their own final decisions to enter a war on the side of an attacked ally, even though they have committed their nations in advance to do so; but the alliance commitment establishes a strong presumption that any such deliberation before deciding would be only to determine whether a situation encompassed by the alliance had in fact occurred, not to reopen the question of whether the alliance obligation was in the national interest.

Such precommitments to go to war pose a more profound dilemma to the contemporary nation-state than they did in previous historical eras. This exacerbated security dilemma is a function of three interacting factors: (1) the deepening and widening economic interdependence among countries, virtually assuring that some influential domestic groups will oppose total disruption of commerce with the common "enemy" short of any clear and present threat to one's own country; (2) the destructiveness of modern war, which severely inhibits countries from joining the fray on behalf of alliance partners, particularly if participating means subjecting one's own country to retaliation by weapons of mass destruction; and (3) the domestic support required for sustained military operations (modern arsenals and armies must be fueled and replenished by many sectors of the domestic economy), which further inhibits forthright, let alone automatic, fulfillment of alliance commitments at moments of truth. In sum, only when the consequences of nonfulfillment of a standing alliance commitment are perceived by broad elements of domestic society to be more tangible, immediate, and disruptive to their particular interests than would be the effects of going to war are countries likely to actually honor their alliance commitments; and in the contemporary period, modernized nation-states will realize this condition only in very rare and extreme circumstances.

As smaller and weaker countries find they can no longer rely on "big brother" protectors to redress their imbalances of power vis-à-vis local aggressors, incentives are enlarged to rely on or create neutral international agencies to provide conflict resolution services and/or buffering peacekeeping presences in zones of confrontation. The post–cold war preoccupation with the international security services that are supposed to be available through the United Nations is a reflection of the maturing of this alliance security dilemma.

An alternative to reliance on universal collective security agencies to compensate for the declining credibility of alliances is the attempt by weaker countries to obtain their own "great equalizers"—weapons of mass destruction. Indeed, the fear that many countries might succumb to this temptation has brought about and sustained the seemingly anomalous (in light of traditional "realist" theories) international security regime of the Nuclear Non-Proliferation Treaty (NPT) of 1968. Jointly drafted in concert by the United States, the Soviet Union, and the United Kingdom, the NPT commits the nuclear-armed states (France and China initially refused to sign) not to transfer nuclear weapons or any equipment for producing nuclear weapons to countries without nuclear weapons; and it commits its some 169 signatories without nuclear weapons to refrain from obtaining such weapons in any way. As a part of the bargain, the five nuclear-armed powers pledge to assist the other signatories in building peaceful nuclear power plants. The International Atomic Energy Agency (IAEA) is empowered by the treaty to monitor the peaceful nuclear facilities of the nonnuclear weapons signatories to assure that they are not also engaged in the production of materials or devices for nuclear weapons.[14]

The fact that some of the large importers of nuclear materials and technologies, such as Iran, North Korea, Pakistan, India, and Israel, have been suspected of attempting to develop their own nuclear weapons has induced the major nuclear-exporting countries to form a special concert, the London Suppliers Group, to coordinate and be accountable to one another in their nuclear-exporting policies in order to avoid any contributions to the nuclear-arms potential of their foreign customers. The embarrassing revelations after the 1990–1991 Gulf War, that components for Saddam Hussein's fledgling nuclear arsenal had been finding their way from Suppliers Group countries to Iraq, has led to renewed efforts to tighten the mutual accountability obligations among members of the nuclear weapons club.

Even though the NPT was extended "permanently" by the May 1995 conference of its signatories, there are grounds for considerable uncertainty as to the durability of the nuclear nonproliferation regime. How long will the "have not" countries put up with their second-class status? The significance of the NPT regime for a theory of the world polity, however, lies in its reason for existence in the first place, namely: the recognition even during the cold war on the part of the two military superpowers that, despite their rivalry, they needed to cooperate in a regime of mutual restraint and accountability in the transference of military capability to other countries and to jointly impose their regime on other countries, lest they lose their superpower status and their ability to assure that international conflicts, including their own, did not get dangerously out of hand. Like the Concert of Europe, the nuclear nonproliferation regime demonstrates that great powers can, and will at times, subordinate their power competition vis-à-vis one another to their common interest in at least a minimally predictable and controllable world public order.

Contrary to one of the academically popular theories of cooperation under anarchy, the superpowers in dealing with the nuclear proliferation problem did not need

---

[14] *Treaty on the Non-Proliferation of Nuclear Weapons*; text in U.S. Arms Control and Disarmament Agency, *Arms Control and Disarmament Agreements* (Washington, D.C.: U.S. Government Printing Office, 1984), pp. 91–95.

to go through a repetitive "tit-for-tat" mutual sanctioning process in order to realize that each had more to gain from faithfully cooperating in a regime of mutual forbearance from transferring nuclear weapons to allies than from defecting from such a regime.[15] Each superpower could independently calculate, without having to be threatened by its rival, that if either defected and provided its allies with nuclear weapons, the other would be hard-pressed by its allies to follow suit in order to avoid drastically disadvantageous inter-alliance balances of military power, and that the security of both superpowers would be diminished thereby. Nor did either superpower need perfect information on the other's intentions and capabilities in order to adhere to the regime of mutual forbearance. All each needed was to attribute to the other an ability to perceive and act upon the inherent logic of the situation.

Even so, classic "Prisoner's Dilemma" temptations could prompt rival nuclear have-not countries to defect from a mutual forbearance regime. If one of a pair of countries faithfully abstained from any nuclear weapons program, under the assumption that its rival was also abstaining, but in fact the rival was clandestinely developing a capability for use in a future conflict between them, the trusting country would be severely jeopardizing its security; both sides (for example, India and Pakistan, Israel and its Arab neighbors, Argentina and Brazil) might well suspect the worst of each other, and consequently might pursue clandestine programs that are more costly and dangerous to each than would be their mutual adherence to the nonproliferation regime. Where such mutually paranoid rivals do truly abstain from developing their own nuclear weapons, the reason most likely is their fear of economic and other sanctions from the United States and other members of the London Suppliers Group.

The Role of Hegemonic Powers in Inducing Cooperation

The regime against the spread of nuclear weapons (including the IAEA), the international monetary regime (including the IMF), and the regime for limiting barriers to international trade (the WTO) all might seem to confirm another notion—popular among "realist" international relations scholars—that international cooperation owes most to the presence of a hegemonic power capable of imposing its preferred pattern of relations among other countries. The hegemonic power during the post–World War II period, at least in the non-Communist world, was the United States.

---

[15]The fascination among contemporary conflict theorists with "tit-for-tat" strategies as a means of transcending "prisoner's dilemma" situations (wherein the trusting co-conspirator would lose badly to the untrusting defector, so both defect and lose more than they would if they cooperated with each other) owes much to the imaginative experimental gaming conducted by Robert Axelrod. Axelrod's simulations demonstrate that after repeated rounds of such self-defeating play the participants may well learn to cooperate. Axelrod's *The Evolution of Cooperation* (New York: Basic Books, 1984).

Following the demise of the Soviet Union's power in the late 1980s and early 1990s, devotees of this school of thought looked toward a new era of globally extensive cooperation under U.S. hegemony. A series of dramatic Soviet concessions on arms control, German unification, and regional conflicts, along with the U.S.-led military expulsion of Iraq from Kuwait and then, finally, the breakup of the Soviet Union, gave the Bush administration to believe that it could press its ideas for "a new world order" on the rest of the international community.

According to Robert Gilpin (a leading academic proponent of the "hegemonic stability" theory), throughout history where we find countries peacefully interacting with one another over time, we almost invariably find a dominant power with the will and resources to induce adherence to the kind of cooperative regime it desires. This arrogated "right to rule" on the part of the global or regional hegemon is attributable to three factors:

> First, it is based on its victory in the last hegemonic war and its demonstrated ability to enforce its will on other states. . . . Second, the rule of the dominant power is frequently accepted because it provides certain public goods, such as a beneficial economic order or international security. Third, the position of the dominant power may be supported by ideological, religious, or other values common to a set of states.[16]

The first of these factors—demonstrated power to impose one's will coercively—is widely held to be the crucial determinant of the hegemon's ability to induce cooperation. A common value system is not given much weight in the academic literature (but this could be changing in light of the Eastern European defections from the Soviet orbit in the 1989–1991 period).

Some hegemonic stability theorists (notably, Charles Kindleberger) give the dominant country's economic power primary weight in explaining cooperation. Others (Gilpin, in particular) regard the international distribution of economic capabilities as highly significant for the hegemon—both as object and means of the hegemonically sustained regime—but ultimately derivative of the prevailing distribution of international political/military power.[17]

The presence of a hegemon with overwhelming power (whether military or economic) and the will to use its power to get its way, coercively if need be, may be sufficient to induce less powerful states into cooperative relationships with the hege-

---

[16]Robert Gilpin, *War and Change in World Politics* (Cambridge: Cambridge University Press, 1981), pp. 34–36.

[17]See Charles P. Kindleberger, "Dominance and Leadership in the International Economy: Exploitation, Public Goods, and Free Rides," *International Studies Quarterly*, Vol. 25 (1981), pp. 242–254. Robert Keohane, in his *After Hegemony: Cooperation and Discord in the World Political Economy*, hews closely to Kindleberger's emphasis on the economic determinants of hegemony. Alternatively, Robert Gilpin's book, *The Political Economy of International Relations* (Princeton: Princeton University Press, 1987), can be read as a political scientist's attempt to reestablish the primacy of the geopolitical over the economic determinants of a stable hegemonic order.

mon; indeed, such induced cooperation is presumed by the concept of hegemony. The relatively benign Pax Britannica of the nineteenth century, in which Britain presided over a globally extensive regime of international free trade, is the favorite model of the hegemonic stability theorists. The U.S.-led grouping of advanced industrial countries and the Soviet-led "socialist commonwealth" in the post–World War II cold war period are also examples.

More significant than the question of whether a hegemonic power *can* induce cooperation (the positive answer is included in the definition of hegemony) is the question of whether the presence of such a hegemon is *necessary* for the emergence and maintenance of cooperative regimes.

Robert Keohane properly challenges the hegemony-is-necessary proposition on theoretical grounds: The motivations of states he and other regime theorists stipulate as conditions for cooperation—in particular, the desire to reduce the costs and risks of highly unpredictable rivalries—are just as likely, perhaps even more likely, to be found in situations of rough but uncertain equality of military and economic capability among a set of countries as during a period when one of them is clearly the preponderant power.[18] To be sure, a period of declining hegemonic power *could* result, as Gilpin and others postulate, in a "hegemonic war" to give the declining hegemon a new lease on her predominance or to determine who will be the new hegemon.[19] But it could just as well result in an enlarged set of internationally agreed-upon constraints to preserve order in what otherwise, in the absence of the hegemon's heavy hand, might be a destructively volatile period of sorting out new power relationships.

The historical record, surely, disconfirms the "hegemony is necessary for cooperation" thesis.

It was the exhaustion of the powers of Europe in the wars of religion and the decline of Hapsburgian hegemony, not the emergence of a new hegemon able to impose its will on the others, that resulted in the Peace of Westphalia in 1648—essentially a codification of Grotian rules of mutual respect for state sovereignty. And it was the defeat of the would-be hegemon, France under Napoleon Bonaparte, that brought together the states of Europe in 1814 to establish consultative and mutual adjustment mechanisms to prevent any of them from making a bid for hegemony in the future.

Similarly, the elaboration of webs of East-West cooperation in the 1970s and early 1980s (even before the Gorbachev era) was mainly an adaptation to the recognition on *both* sides that neither could achieve global hegemony and that the attempt by either to do so could provoke a planet-destroying war. The fears on each side that such a mutually suicidal war could nevertheless break out during international crises

---

[18]Keohane's challenges to the hegemonic stability theory are most fully developed in *After Hegemony.*

[19]See Gilpin, *War and Change*, passim.

as a result of misperception of the other's intentions led to the negotiation of "confidence building measures" between the rival Soviet-led and U.S.-led alliances, requiring detailed exchanges of information on movements of troops and military deployments and even the on-site observation by the other side's military officers to verify the nonhostile orientation of such deployments.

Also, the most impressive attempt in modern history to develop a new supranational community among a group of states previously very determined to maintain their sovereign prerogatives—the evolution of the European Union in the last decades of the twentieth century—would not be taking place if any one of the involved states were perceived by the others to be capable of becoming the community hegemon.[20]

ϾϿ

The efforts at international cooperation thus far discussed, whether motivated by balance-of-power considerations or the need to adapt to increasing international interdependence, are not fundamentally at odds with the anarchic structure of the nation-state system—at least not by the intention of their champions, even though, as I will argue later, some of the cumulative effects may be system transforming. Even the more ambitious hopes for the evolution of the European Union into a supranational polity, like the evolution of the separate American states into the United States of America in the eighteenth century, are premised on the persistence of a decentralized world society, with the new multinational Europe becoming one of the sovereign units of the world polity. (To be sure, some of the more visionary champions of a United Europe have regarded it as the embryo of a world process of merging separate sovereignties, leading eventually to a supranational world federation of regional states;[21] but at the level of active statecraft, this grander distant possibility does not appear to have had any current operational significance.)

By contrast, the two great experiments of the twentieth century in global institution building—the League of Nations following World War I and the United Nations following World War II—have been regarded by some influential political leaders and theorists primarily as efforts to transform the anarchic structure of the world polity. A parallel set of expectations has also been attached by some theorists to various functionally specific global institutions operating in technical fields (such as communications and transportation) where reliable worldwide cooperation is a practical imperative.

---

[20]See Ernst B. Haas, *The Uniting of Europe: Political, Social, and Economic Forces, 1950–1957* (Stanford: Stanford University Press, 1958).

[21]Amitai Etzioni, *Political Unification* (New York: Holt, Rinehart & Winston, 1965).

Efforts to Overcome Global Anarchy

The perception that the amount of cooperation the world needs is unattainable as long as the world polity operates largely as an anarchic nation-state system has stimulated two different types of transformative projects: (1) efforts to establish directly a centralized authoritative system of governance for world society as a whole, and (2) efforts to overcome global anarchy in bits and pieces, sector by sector, wherever trans-country "functional" interdependencies are sufficiently matured to allow for the institutionalization of international, possibly even supranational, cooperation.

Centralized Global Governance

For the reasons adduced in Chapter 1, efforts by particular states to establish global governance through imperialistic subordination of the others have not worked. But what about a voluntarily negotiated merger of sovereignties to establish on a world scale a system of law and order analogous to those prevailing in domestic polities? Throughout history this possibility has been explored by philosophers and occasionally advocated by prominent political leaders. Some of the architects of the League of Nations and the United Nations believed that they were erecting the scaffolding of such a world government, even while preserving, at least for the time being, the sovereignty of the member states.

Early Proposals for a World State.   In the seventeenth century, the French monk Emeric Cruce proposed, in his *The New Cyneas,* that representatives of the various European states, Turkey, Persia, India, China, the kingdoms of Africa, the Pope, and the Jews meet in a permanent Council of Ambassadors to make world laws by majority vote binding on all members. These world laws would be enforced, if need be, by the pooled military strength of the majority. A similar plan was developed and publicized in the 1690s by the American colonizer William Penn. The most elaborate of these early proposals was the Abbé de Saint-Pierre's *Le projet de paix perpétuelle (Project of perpetual peace)*, which the prominent cleric submitted to the the French monarchy in 1713. The Abbé's plan envisioned a permanent Senate of Peace composed of two members from each member state, presided over by a "prince of peace" chosen weekly by rotation among the members. No states could enter into treaties or decide on their own on territorial adjustments unless approved by a three-fourths vote of the Senate, and states refusing to abide by decisions of the Senate would be compelled to submit by the combined military power of the Union.[22]

---

[22]For these early world government proposals see F. H. Hinsley, *Power and the Pursuit of Peace* (London: Cambridge University Press, 1963); and Edith Wynner and Georgia Lloyd, *Searchlight on Peace Plans* (New York: Dutton, 1949).

Such proposals for a world state were given short shrift by the monarchs of the time, anxious to retain the fullest possible sovereignty over their respective territorial realms. They were delivered an intellectual *coup de grâce* by Jean-Jacques Rousseau's 1762 publication *Judgment sur la paix perpétuelle* (criticizing Saint-Pierre's project) and his subsequent treatise *L'Etat de guerre*. Rousseau argued that the voluntary establishment of an effective world government was "an absurd dream," because it required sovereigns to perceive, and then act upon the perception, that the common interest in peace outweighed all of their particular interests. This could never come about, Rousseau pointed out, because the rulers of states do not regard peace as an end in itself but, like war, only a condition or means for the realization of other interests. Echoing Thomas Hobbes, Rousseau reasoned that the only way such a subordination of national sovereignties to a universal government could be accomplished would be through imperial subjugation—the imposition of a Leviathan, the re-creation, as it were, of a New Rome. But, Rousseau insisted (in prophetic anticipation of Napoleon's attempt to do just that), this would involve violence on such a scale as would stagger humanity. In sum, the acceptance of international anarchy, the correlate of national sovereignty, was paradoxically the necessary condition for a tolerable world public order.[23] Some recent scholarship on Rousseau, however, shows him to be dissatisfied with having to conclude the Abbé's project could never be realized and argues that his pessimism must be read in the context of his larger critique of society's institutions and juxtaposed against the normative political education he prescribed in his later writings. According to this revisionist reading, Rousseau was definitely not *endorsing* international anarchy. Rather, his deeper message on war and peace was that if human society could be restructured from the ground up in a more enlightened way, then the smaller communities that made up the larger community of humankind might well be able peaceably to put together a global polity to deal in a just way with issues arising between the constituent communities. This, indeed, was the philosopher Kant's reading of Rousseau's political theory.[24]

The Kantian Solution. Much less ambitious in structure than the Abbé's plan, but more demanding in its required transformation of the ethical norms of statecraft, was the proposal by Immanuel Kant for a permanent parliament of still-sovereign nation-states through which they would bargain to adjust their differences nonviolently. As outlined in his pamphlet *Perpetual Peace,* published in 1795, the design of the central world parliament was only of secondary importance to the imperative

---

[23]See Stanley Hoffmann's essay, "Rousseau on War and Peace," in his *The State of War: Essays on the Theory and Practice of International Politics* (New York: Praeger, 1965), pp. 54–87. For the relationship of Rousseau's ideas on international relations to his overall political philosophy, see Roger D. Masters, *The Political Philosophy of Rousseau* (Princeton: Princeton University Press, 1968).

[24]This revisionist view of Rousseau's attitude toward the Saint Pierre *Project* is strongly developed in Grace G. Roosevelt, *Reading Rousseau in the Nuclear Age* (Philadelphia: Temple University Press, 1990).

that the member governments commit themselves to policies of mutual restraint, based on respect for each other's domains, national values, and citizenry. Kant held that such an interstate regime of nonviolent bargaining, accountability, and mutual respect was really sustainable only among countries with republican-style representative domestic polities. In Kant's view, republican countries, in contrast with monarchical or despotic ones, could be depended upon to reflect the natural inclination of the ordinary citizenry to engage in domestic pursuits without the disruptions caused by war, and therefore the self-interest of republican governments would be compatible with the moral imperative of nonviolent deliberation among countries to adjust their differences.[25]

The League of Nations and the United Nations. Kantian confederal premises, more than world federalist designs, are reflected in the Covenant of the League of Nations and the Charter of the United Nations. In a *con*federation, each of the member states retains full legal sovereignty in the sense that the interstate organization cannot legally compel any member to act in accord with a decision of the organization that it opposes; the constitutional device for assuring this is the rule that substantive decisions must be made by unanimous vote. In a federation, each member is legally bound to adhere to all decisions of the interstate organization, even those it opposes; and various important substantive decisions may be rendered by nonunanimous majority vote.

The national sovereignty norm of the nation-state system was reaffirmed by Article 10 of the League, where it was stipulated that the organization was designed to "respect and preserve against external aggression the territorial integrity and existing political independence of all Members." Similarly, Article 2 of the UN Charter states that "The Organization is based on the principle of the sovereign equality of all its Members," and guarantees that "Nothing contained in the present Charter shall authorize the United Nations to intervene in matters which are essentially within the domestic jurisdiction of any state or shall require Members to submit such matters to settlement under the present Charter." The inability of the world organization to override a member's will was assured in the League by the rule (in Article 5) requiring almost all substantive decisions to be based on unanimous vote of all members present, except the parties to a dispute (a party to a dispute almost invariably would have at least one friend capable of voting). In the United Nations, various agencies, including the General Assembly, can act on the basis of majority vote; but the Security Council, the essential institution for peace and security matters, can act only on the basis of the affirmative vote of all of its five permanent members: the United States, Russia, the United Kingdom, France, and China (Article 27).

---

[25]Immanuel Kant, *Perpetual Peace: A Philosophical Essay* [1795] (Indianapolis: Bobbs-Merrill, 1957). The relevant features of Kant's approach are succinctly presented in Sissela Bok, *A Strategy for Peace: Human Values and the Threat of War* (New York: Pantheon Books, 1989).

Nevertheless, the League covenant and the UN Charter, in contrast to Kant's primary reliance on the self-restraint of republican states, anticipate that uncooperative or aggressive states will continue to be a part of the international scene and will need to be collectively sanctioned by concerted economic and military actions of the world organization's members. A world organization with capabilities for coercively enforcing its decisions, despite the deferences to national sovereignty in the Covenant and the Charter, is central to the new system of international relations contemplated by both of these twentieth-century experiments. Both the League and the UN thus embodied the potentially fatal contradiction of assigning a characteristically federal mission to an organization built on confederal foundations.[26]

The League's Article 16 was explicit in defining any member's resort to war in violation of the organization's rules as "*ipso facto* . . . an act of war against all other Members of the League." Members were then supposed to sever all diplomatic and commercial relations with the aggressor and to "contribute to the armed forces to be used to protect the covenants of the League"; but at crucial moments of truth, the League membership could not, or would not, deliver on these core obligations: When Japan conquered Manchuria in 1931, the League resolved that the new Japanese-controlled government was illegitimate, to which Japan responded by resigning from the League; but the Japanese stayed in control in Manchuria as the League failed to apply the economic or military sanctions provided for in Article 16. The closest the League came to acting up to its potential in a major international conflict was in response to Italy's 1935 invasion of Ethiopia. Branding Italy an aggressor, the Council voted to apply Article 16 economic sanctions, and fifty-two countries cooperated in embargoing the sale of "strategic materials" (except oil!) to Italy. Hardly hobbled by the sanctions, Italy could only have been compelled to desist from its blatant power-play by a threat of military counteraction by either of the two most powerful League members, France and Britain (the United States never joined the League). But both of the Western European democracies were preoccupied with domestic problems, and neither felt a direct threat to its own national interests by Italy's aggression in Africa. The major aggressors of the period were emboldened by the League's impotence. Japan launched a full-scale invasion of China in 1937–1938 and, again, suffered no Article 16 sanctions. Hitler knew the League's collective security system had collapsed when in 1938 he began his series of aggressions (the Anschluss with Austria, the occupation of the Sudetenland and then all of Czechoslovakia, and his 1939 invasion of Poland) that brought on World War II.

The UN Charter, to the disappointment of many who had hoped to create a substantially strengthened collective security institution to keep the peace after World War II, is a variation on the League system. Once again, the countries of

---

[26]On the inherent contradictions in the League and UN systems, see Inis L. Claude, Jr., *Swords into Plowshares: The Problems and Progress of International Organization* (New York: Random House, 1984).

the world are provided the legal wherewithal to collectively make rules binding on all members of the world organization, particularly in matters of international peace and security, and to collectively enforce these rules. Any substantive action in the peace and security field is the province of the fifteen-member Security Council, on which the five permanent members of the council each have a veto. In addition to any nonmilitary sanctions the Security Council may ask members to employ against aggressor states, Chapter VII—designed to be the enforcement teeth of the Charter—gives the Security Council authority to "take such action by air, sea, or land forces as may be necessary to maintain or restore international peace and security. Such actions may include demonstrations, blockade, and other operations by the air, sea, or land forces of Members of the United Nations" (Article 42). All members are to earmark certain contingents of their military and hold them ready for contribution to such UN operations (Articles 44 and 45). Strategic direction of any armed forces placed at the disposal of the Security Council is to be provided by a Military Staff Committee consisting of the chiefs of staff (or their representatives) of the permanent members of the Security Council plus other national military authorities whose participation may be required for particular operations (Article 47).

These collective security potentialities in the UN Charter remained a paper shell throughout the cold war as the global rivalry between the United States and the Soviet Union made it virtually impossible to forge a UN consensus in any important case on who was aggressor and who was victim, let alone to form a multilateral UN military force with a command structure and missions acceptable to both superpowers. (The United Nations Peace Action in response to the invasion of South Korea by North Korea in 1950, including the establishment of a UN military combat force, was in reality a U.S. response draped in the UN flag. Without the temporary absence of the USSR from its seat on the Security Council, the authorizing resolutions would never have obtained the required unanimous vote.[27])

The deeper structural cause of the inoperability of the UN collective security system against acts of aggression launched by, or encouraged by, a great power was also the source of the League's basic failure: As long as the primary units of the world polity are nation-states, determined above all to protect their independence, and run by leaders accountable to domestic interests ahead of world interests, no member of

---

[27]With the return of the Soviet Union to the Security Council, the United States was able to preserve the formal fiction that the U.S. military action in Korea was a UN collective security operation by garnering majority support in the General Assembly for the "Uniting for Peace" resolution, which asserted the General Assembly's authority to act instead of the Security Council "if the Security Council, because of a lack of unanimity of the permanent members, fails to exercise its primary responsibility for the maintenance of international peace and security" (United Nations Document A/1481 [1950]). All subsequent UN authorizations for the U.S. actions in Korea were in the form of General Assembly resolutions passed by majority vote, over the protest of the Soviet Union that they were illegal under the Charter.

an international collective security association (whether regional or global) can be relied on to participate in actions likely to put its independence and domestic interests seriously at risk—unless the collective action is clearly required to protect the country's own independence and domestic interests. As I have argued above, even with regard to military alliances, the increasing costs of war preparations and the holocaust dimensions of contemporary warfare make it doubtful that, short of the need to defend themselves against direct attack, most countries will involve themselves (except perhaps by inadvertence or miscalculation) in large-scale war on behalf of the security and well-being of other countries, let alone on behalf of the principle of nonaggression or other world-order values.

In the lead-up to the Gulf War of 1991, simultaneous with the apparent end of the U.S.-Soviet rivalry, these inhibitions on the implementation of the collective security provisions of the United Nations seemed to have been overcome. In response to Iraq's August 1990 invasion and announced annexation of Kuwait, the Security Council, acting under Chapter VII of the Charter, passed a series of resolutions over the next few months mandating members of the United Nations to stop all normal commerce with Iraq in an effort to coerce Saddam Hussein's regime to withdraw totally and unconditionally from Kuwait.[28] Meanwhile, under Article 51 (the "individual and collective self-defense" provision of the Charter) the United States deployed military forces into Saudi Arabia to prevent a further southward move by Iraq against the Saudi oil fields. As Iraq showed no inclination to withdraw despite these pressures, the United States was able to gain backing for the historic Security Council Resolution 678 (November 29, 1990) authorizing member states, if Iraq did not comply with the foregoing resolutions by January 15, 1991, "to use all necessary means to uphold and implement . . . all [the] relevant resolutions and to restore international peace and security in the area."[29] Resolution 678 was universally understood to mean that it would be legitimate to use military force against Iraq to compel its withdrawal from Kuwait. But what Resolution 678 did *not* do was equally significant: Unlike the resolutions on economic sanctions, it did not mandate members to use force. Moreover, it did not prescribe any *collective application* of force, leaving it entirely up to each country to decide between unilateral or multilateral military moves. This was precisely the freedom of action the Bush administration wanted—rather than being hamstrung by having to obtain Security Council or other UN agency consensus for how military force was to be applied—particularly in the face of indications that most of the other Security Council members who voted

---

[28]United Nations Security Council Resolutions: 660, August 2, 1990; 661, August 6, 1990; 662, August 9, 1990; 664, August 18, 1990; 665, August 25, 1990; 666, September 13, 1990; 667, September 16, 1990; 669, September 24, 1990; 670, September 25, 1990; 674, October 29, 1990; and 677, November 28, 1990. Texts in *United Nations Security Council Resolutions Relating to the Crisis in the Gulf* (United Nations: Department of Public Information, November 1990), DPI/1104–41090.

[29]*Ibid.,* Addendum of December 1, 1990.

for the relevant resolutions had no intention of joining in a collective military action. Under the authority of Resolution 678, therefore, the United States acted henceforth in the traditional mode of coalition leader, mobilizing other states to join it in its initiation of military action against Iraq after the expiration of the January 15 deadline; but the operation was run out of the Pentagon essentially as a U.S. unilateral military campaign, with no obligation to clear its actions with other countries, let alone with the United Nations. As it turned out, the Gulf War of 1991 constituted no more of a United Nations "*collective* security" action than did the Korean War four decades earlier.

It would be wrong to conclude, however, that the twentieth-century experiment in international governance has failed. The factors working against genuine collective security have not prevented the United Nations, nor did they prevent the League, from providing important conflict resolution and peacekeeping services for the society of nation-states, particularly in situations not immediately and directly implicating the vital interests of the great powers. These services could well become even more important now that the world-spanning military alliances organized by the superpowers after World War II are no longer available as stabilizers of regional and global balances of power.

More modest in mission than the international forces contemplated in the Covenant and the Charter for repulsing or defeating aggressors, a succession of so-called peacekeeping forces have been created under UN auspices and deployed into troubled locales.

Most of the UN peacekeeping contingents have had the limited function of observing and monitoring compliance with border arrangements, truces, and armistice agreements that have already been accepted by the belligerents. Characteristically, in such cases the United Nations is officially neutral with regard to the substance of issues over which the belligerents are fighting, as are the governments that contribute military personnel to command and staff the UN units. Peace observation forces of this type, typically involving a few hundred troops, have been deployed at various points along the borders of Israel and its Arab neighbors, in Kashmir, in West Irian, and along the Yemen-Saudi Arabia border.

More substantial UN forces, sometimes numbering in the thousands, have been used when their function, in addition to monitoring compliance with a cease-fire, has included the occupation of a strip of territory from which the belligerents have disengaged. The objective is to compel any party that would violate the cease-fire or zone of disengagement to deliberately and visibly rupture the UN line. Such UN forces have been deployed on the Israel-Egypt border on the Gulf of Aqaba, in demilitarized zones in the Sinai, between the Greek and Turkish communities on Cyprus, and—ineffectively—in the Yugoslav civil wars raging since 1991.

The conflict-intervention capabilities of the United Nations were strained to the utmost in the 1961 Congo crisis, when a UN force of 20,000 troops from twenty-five countries was injected into the Congo under a loosely worded Security Council mandate to keep the peace and stabilize control in the chaotic political situation left by the departing colonial power, Belgium. Stretching its mandate to the limit, over the protests of the Soviet Union, UN Secretary General Dag Hammarskjöld authorized the international force to engage in limited offensive military action against troops of the secessionist province of Katanga. Although the UN Congo operation failed in its ostensible mission of bringing order to a chaotic situation, it nevertheless served a vital international community function in substituting for competitive military interventions in the strategic heart of Africa by the United States and the Soviet Union at the height of the cold war.

An even more ambitious peacekeeping mission was taken on by the United Nations in the October 1991 peace settlement for Cambodia signed by the Cambodian government, three guerrilla factions, and eighteen other nations. The United Nations was given the responsibility for administering the country for two years and then organizing election of a constitutional assembly that would draft a new charter for a self-governing Cambodia. The UN's two-year governing role put the world organization's personnel in charge of the key ministries of defense, foreign affairs, finance, and communications.[30]

Such UN peacekeeping activities, based on the voluntary acceptance by countries of agencies and personnel of the world organization within their jurisdictions, are still consistent with the norms and structure of the nation-state system. They do, however, symbolize—and give flesh-and-blood body to—the putative world interest in preventing massively destructive regional or global escalations of local conflicts. By embodying this world interest, the UN peacekeeping efforts have begun to lay the groundwork, despite the recent false starts in Somalia and Bosnia, for the eventual permanent supranational institutionalization of that world interest.

New Proposals for World Order Reform. Many have felt a profound dissatisfaction with the extent to which both the League of Nations and the United Nations have been creatures of the anarchically structured nation-state system and not really efforts to fundamentally transform that system. This has motivated the work of the World Order Models Project of the Institute for World Order in New York City. The most widely discussed model to emerge from this project is the "preferred world polity" formulated by international lawyer Richard Falk.

Falk proposes a "central guidance system" that has the attributes of a world supranational state. It would have armed forces of its own to enforce worldwide disarmament agreements and, if necessary, to assure that the decisions of its legislative and judicial bodies are carried out. But he envisions enforcement of the new world law largely by nonviolent techniques that would have become ingrained during the process of institution building and then installed in globally representative structures and processes of decision-making. Falk's fully matured world polity would feature a

---

[30]"4 Parties in Cambodian War Sign U.N. Peace Pact," articles by Philip Shenon and Alan Riding, *New York Times*, October 24, 1991.

three-chambered, central deliberative body with different bases of representation in each chamber and checks-and-balances voting arrangements among the chambers to assure that world laws are based as much as possible on the consent of the governed.[31]

The influential Norwegian social scientist Johan Galtung, by contrast, envisions a more peaceful and just world community growing out of a radical *de*centralization of the world polity. Galtung believes that the only way to have a polity truly based on the consent of the governed is to root it in "self-reliant" communities smaller than the average contemporary nation-state. These small polities would be territorially demarcated and have substantial local autonomy, but would be crisscrossed and tied together by a web of nonterritorial organizations, "putting everybody in community with local neighbors as well as with distant neighbors." There would also have to be "some central authority that can make and enact plans for such matters as world food distribution, world employment, world ecological balance, world water and oxygen budgets and that can administer the riches that belong to all, such as the seabed and the oceans, the bio-atmosphere, the cosmos, [and] subterranean deposits."[32]

Although largely sympathetic with the world-order proposals of Falk and Galtung, the Indian social scientist Rajni Kothari cautions against the Western, Eurocentrist orientation of even these post-nationalist thinkers. Kothari, along with other Third World theorists, worries that the new models of globalism and world order can unwittingly "perpetuate international hegemonies, class exploitation within and between nations, and structures of government that are repressive and inhumane." The challenge we face, argues Kothari, is that of "moving towards a new states system, at once more diffuse and participant and more cooperation based and integrated. . . . But it is not possible to move towards such a world without first going through . . . the counter-assertion of national and regional identities and solidarities . . . comprising hitherto submerged political and economic entities, both in the Third World and elsewhere."[33]

Falk, Galtung, Kothari, and those with similar radical outlooks are realists in the sense that they are formulating world-order designs for the distant future. And in their pessimistic moments they grant that it might take a catastrophe—say, an immediately looming threat of severe global climate change or the proliferation of weapons of mass destruction to globally active terrorist organizations—to shake loose the attachments of elites and publics to the existing nation-state system. Yet they continue writing and speaking to persuade as many people as they can that such radical reforms are necessary if humankind is to survive its own genius for altering the natural world.

---

[31]Richard A. Falk, *A Study of Future Worlds* (New York: Free Press, 1975).

[32]Johan Galtung, *The True Worlds: A Transnational Perspective* (New York: Free Press, 1980), pp. 92–94, 344–352.

[33]Rajni Kothari, *Toward a Just World* (New York: Institute for World Order, 1980), pp. 23–24.

"Functionalism": Old and New

Meanwhile, unwilling to wait for a fundamental shift in human values, some limited supranational institution building has been under way in several of the specialized agencies in the larger UN system, particularly those that deal with the global economy and the planet's ecology, such as the International Monetary Fund, the World Bank, the United Nations Environmental Program, the World Health Organization, the Food and Agriculture Organization, the World Meteorological Organization, the International Maritime Organization, and so forth. This development is something of a historical surprise, for the thrust of reformist scholarly analysis and political rhetoric in the immediate post–World War II period had focused on the supranationalist opportunities (or threats) contained in the "high politics" peace and security provisions of the Charter. Increasingly since the early 1970s, most hopes (or fears) for transforming the sovereignty-based nation-state system are focused on the "low politics" arenas of economics, the environment, and technical cooperation.[34]

Some insights into the implications of these developments for the world polity may be retrieved from the "functionalist" theorizing of the 1940s. Most prominently represented in the works of David Mitrany,[35] the early functionalism emphasized functionally specific and/or regionally concentrated enclaves of international cooperation, usually of a technical nature on matters initially not involving important political stakes for any of the participating countries. Existing models were the international "public unions" created in the late nineteenth and early twentieth centuries to coordinate international communications and commerce (the International Postal Union, the International Telegraphic Union, various international river and maritime commissions, and the International Labor Organization established under the League of Nations). As put by Mitrany:

> Functional schemes are at best complementary, each helping the others, and at worst independent of each other. Any one can be started at any time whether or not the others are accepted or not, and any one may live and prosper even if the others fail or are abandoned. A scheme started by a few countries for transport, or for oil, and so on, could later be broadened to include belated members, or reduced to let the reluctant drop out. . . . Functional "neutrality" is possible, where political "neutrality" is not. In addition, functional arrangements have the virtue of technical self-determination, one of the main reasons which makes them more readily acceptable. The nature of each function tells of itself the scope and powers needed for effective performance. . . .

---

[34]The movement of theory and research on international institutions away from the peace and security arena and into the arena of international political economics, the environment, etc., is reflected in the changing balance of articles since the 1970s in the premier scholarly journal, *International Organization*. However, I detect a resurgence of theoretical writing during the last few years on the international institutional aspects of security issues, perhaps reflecting some of the trends identified in this chapter.

[35]See especially, David Mitrany, *A Working Peace System* [1943] (Chicago: Quadrangle Books, 1966).

These characteristics of the functional approach therefore help to mitigate the problem of equal sovereignty. In this approach it is not a matter of surrendering sovereignty, but merely of pooling so much of it as may be needed for the joint performance of the particular task.[36]

In Mitrany's vision, the gradual buildup of such functional cooperative associations may eventually create a global community capable of accepting supranational governance:

If one were to visualize a map of the world showing economic and social activities, it would appear as an intricate web of interests and relations crossing and recrossing political divisions—not a fighting map of States and frontiers, but a map pulsating with the realities of everyday life. They are the natural basis for international organizations: and the task is to bring that map, which is a functioning reality, under joint international government, at least in its essential lines. The political lines will then in time be overlaid and blurred by this web of joint relations and administrations.[37]

The central problem with the early functionalist *theory* (though not necessarily with the actual practice of functional cooperation) was its failure to explain how the presumably apolitical interstate agencies operating in the technical fields would at some point assume substantial political functions—making authoritative allocations of goods, services, privileges, and other amenities among the constituent countries. The optimistic predictions of the early functionalists, looking toward a virtually automatic "spill-over" from highly technical coordination to value-significant authorization, had no more theoretical justification than the pessimism of "realists" who predicted an inevitable bottling-up of functionally specific cooperation to prevent it from eroding the sovereign prerogatives of the national governments.[38]

In fact, what has been transpiring in the various arenas of functional cooperation among countries (inside and outside of the UN system) has, more often than not, involved allocations of significant economic and political value to important national, subnational, and transnational interests.[39] Most of the deliberations in international special agencies—in the International Monetary Fund when it provides balance-of-payments support, in the World Bank when it extends development loans, in the

---

[36]*Ibid.*, pp. 162–163.

[37]*Ibid.*, p. 164.

[38]Later functionalist/integrationist theorists saw the process as indeed highly politicized, and therefore considerably more complicated than Mitrany had envisioned; but they did not as a result conclude that it was doomed to failure. Quite the contrary. See especially Ernst B. Haas, *Beyond the Nation-State: Functionalism and International Organization* (Stanford: Stanford University Press, 1964). See also Karl W. Deutsch et al., *Political Community and the North Atlantic Area: International Organization in the Light of Historical Experience* (Princeton: Princeton University Press, 1957).

[39]These developments are richly described in Harold K. Jacobson, *Networks of Interdependence: International Organizations and the Global Political System* (New York: Knopf, 1984).

International Telecommunication Union when it allocates broadcasting frequencies and orbital slots for space satellites, in the International Maritime Organization when it specifies navigation rules—are politically charged from the start.

Countries are coordinating their actions and sometimes entering into deeply penetrating cooperative relationships in these fields not because they are isolated from the primary concerns of publics, parliaments, and powerful interest groups. Rather, politically influential groups are increasingly insisting that their governments enter into international cooperative relationships precisely because they perceive that, with growing intersectorial and international interdependence, their interests will be substantially affected by the actions of foreign actors whether or not there is international cooperation, and that on balance they have more to gain than to lose by the stability and predictability that institutionalized cooperation can bring.

Far from being devoid of politics, contemporary efforts to forge mutual political and legal accountability obligations among those who are materially interdependent are political from top to bottom. The international obligations (whether in the form of treaties or membership in international organizations) are translated into domestic law and can determine who are the winners and losers in the domestic economic and political arena as much as does legislation with a purely domestic focus.

As the substance of international cooperative undertakings increasingly determines who gets what and how, the international institutions in which these undertakings are negotiated become crucial arenas for coalition building among states and transnational agencies rivaling the national governmental arenas. Through this process the new—and very real—functionalism, provided it is given a substantial push by the normatively oriented statecraft called for in Part Two of this book, could well begin to transform the nation-state system into a less anarchic world polity.

3   The Prominence of War

Conservatives and reformers, "realists" and "idealists" alike affirm the sad truth of Hans Morgenthau's observation that throughout history "nations active in international politics are continuously preparing for, actively involved in, or recovering from organized violence in the form of war."[1] A few analysts see a modern countertrend leading toward the obsolescence of major war in relations among the advanced industrial states, while still granting the essential validity of the Morgenthau proposition as a historical generalization.[2]

There is wide disagreement, however, over the causes of the prominence of war in human society, with different explanations carrying profound implications for efforts to reduce its role.

In this chapter I review and evaluate alternative explanations for the prominence of war, including those that find the roots of war in human nature, those that emphasize the structure of society, and those that locate the problem mainly in prevailing cultural norms.

War as "Normal" Human Behavior

Various political philosophers, social scientists, and biologists hold that war between countries is but one expression of the natural propensity of humans to act violently toward those with whom they come into conflict. Peaceful means of dealing with conflict, presumably, need to be imposed by social institutions or, failing this, by

---

Many of the ideas in this chapter are discussed in greater detail in my book *The Causes and Prevention of War* (New York: St. Martin's Press, 1994). The present treatment, however, is not an abbreviated recapitulation of that book; rather, it is part and parcel of my argument for a comprehensive theory of the world polity.

[1]Hans J. Morgenthau, *Politics Among Nations: The Struggle for Power and Peace,* 5th edition revised (New York: Knopf, 1978), p. 42.

[2]For the thesis that major war among the advanced industrial states is becoming an anachronism, see John E. Mueller, *Retreat from Doomsday: The Obsolescence of Major War* (New York: Basic Books, 1989). A more circumscribed conjecture, focusing on countries highly involved in international commerce, is suggested by Richard Rosecrance, *The Rise of the Trading State: Commerce and Conquest in the Modern World* (New York: Basic Books, 1986).

parties to particular conflicts threatening one another with such harsh consequences that they choose to avoid violent battle for the time being.

From St. Augustine to Thomas Hobbes to Sigmund Freud to Konrad Lorenz we encounter the view of the human animal as innately disposed to behave violently, not only in response to direct threats to life and possessions but also in anticipation of raids on one's food, territory, material possessions, or sexual partners. From this premise it is often deduced that a society in which humans have a reasonable prospect of safety and security for themselves and their families requires a superordinate state—Hobbes's all-powerful Leviathan,[3] or at least a government that, as in Max Weber's concept,[4] monopolizes the capabilities for legitimate violence.

There is no expectation on the part of such theorists, however, that a world made up of internally peaceful domestic societies will be a peaceful world. Rather, those who believe that humans are strongly disposed to act violently expect that when the violent propensities are subordinated or repressed in domestic society they may well seek increased outlets in the still-anarchic interstate arena. This, indeed, was the conclusion of both Sigmund Freud and Albert Einstein in their celebrated exchange of letters on the problem of war, in which the psychoanalyst and the physicist concluded that the only way to end war was to establish a worldwide system of "central control which shall have the last word in every conflict of interest."[5] Accordingly, Einstein actively championed the ideal of world peace through world government. But Freud, echoing Rousseau, strongly doubted the feasibility of a world state, although granted its logic in the abstract. "It is all too clear," said the theorist of human passions, "that nationalistic ideas, paramount today in every country, operate in quite a contrary direction."[6] Moreover, Freud's basic thinking on the subject of violence, along with that of biological instinctivists such as Konrad Lorenz,[7] implied that whatever the imposed law-and-order structure, violence will find its own level rather than disappear; and that therefore even if a world government could be established, there still would be plenty of war, although it would be called "civil" war.

Most theorists of international relations who label themselves "realists" accept the instinctivists' conclusion (if not their biological assumptions) that the propensity to resort to violence in conflictual situations is a natural human characteristic. By

---

[3]Thomas Hobbes, *Leviathan* [1651] (London: Penguin Classics, 1985), edited by C. B. Macpherson, Chs. 14 and 15.

[4]Max Weber, "Politics as a Vocation," in H. H. Gerth and C. Wright Mills, *From Max Weber: Essays in Sociology* (New York: Oxford University Press, 1946), pp. 77–78.

[5]Sigmund Freud, Letter to Albert Einstein, September 1932 (Geneva: League of Nations, International Institute of Intellectual Cooperation, 1933), reprinted in William Ebenstein, *Great Political Thinkers: Plato to the Present* (New York: Rinehart, 1951), pp. 804–810.

[6]*Ibid.*

[7]Konrad Lorenz, *On Aggression* (New York: Harcourt Brace & World, 1966); Irenaus Eibl-Eibesfeldt, *The Biology of Peace and War: Men, Animals, and Aggression* (New York: Viking Press, 1979).

extension, war is regarded as one of the normal instruments of interstate conflict—"a continuation of political commerce . . . by other means," as Karl von Clausewitz put it.[8]

Although the proposition that war is a normal occurrence in human society may be sustainable as a historical generalization, the theory that war is an expression of an innate human tendency to violence is highly debatable.

As indicated in Chapter 1, anthropologists have found some tribal societies to be basically peaceful in both their internal and external relationships. Intratribal and intertribal violence appear to correlate with scarcities in life-sustaining resources, and peaceful relationships are found particularly among hunter-gatherers in regions of abundance (such as the Zuni Indians of the American Southwest, the Kung Bushmen of southern Africa, and the Semai of Malaya).[9] The existence of even a few simple and politically underdeveloped societies in which the resort to coercive physical force (actual or threatened) is rare would appear to negate the theory of a strong human instinctual predisposition toward violence. It should be noted, however, that even in these societies cultural myths and rituals are relied upon to dissuade members from violent behavior.

The bulk of modern psychological studies on aggression and violence also tend to disconfirm the instinctivist explanations. Rather, most of the relevant psychological studies support or refine the frustration-aggression hypothesis formulated in the 1930s by John Dollard and Leonard Doob: Violently aggressive human behavior usually is induced by "frustration"—that is, substantial interference with or blocking of goal-directed activity. The violence frequently will take the form of attempts to hurt or destroy the person or group perceived to be the source of one's frustration. But not all cases of frustration, even severe frustration, lead to violent aggression. Frustration-aggression theorists recognize this, and are among the first to point out that humans exhibit a wide variety of adaptations to frustration, some of them creative and constructive. And empirical studies confirm that similar types of frustration will produce different responses—some violent, some nonviolent—in different individuals and in different social contexts.[10] When strongly frustrated, most humans experience a natural buildup of blocked energy that seeks release, but why this natural store of energy will produce fighting in one case, running away in another, negotiating activity in another, and gas pains in still another cannot be adequately explained by biology.

---

[8]Karl von Clausewitz, *On War,* translation by Michael Howard and Peter Paret (Princeton: Princeton University Press, 1976), p. 147.

[9]See David Fabbro, "Peaceful Societies," in Richard A. Falk and Samuel S. Kim, *The War System: An Interdisciplinary Approach* (Boulder: Westview Press, 1980), pp. 180–203.

[10]See Leonard Berkowitz, *Aggression: A Social Psychological Analysis* (New York: McGraw-Hill, 1962). The original version of the frustration-aggression hypothesis was presented by John Dollard et al., *Frustration and Aggression* (New Haven: Yale University Press, 1939).

The frustration-aggression hypothesis holds that where violent and destructive behavior is present the aggressively behaving persons *usually* are reacting to an intensely experienced interference with activity that was directed toward the satisfaction of a strongly desired objective. The hypothesis has no convincing explanation, however, for violence as a means of interpersonal or intergroup competition in the absence of frustration, as personal or mass recreation, or as malicious and sadistic fun. The understanding of such violence, which is often present in the wartime behavior of nations, requires more than the behaviorist stimulus-response explanations. Some probing of the unconscious sources of violent behavior (perhaps on the basis of Freudian individual-centered or Jungian collectivity-centered psychological theories; perhaps on the basis of biological theories of species evolution) and their cultural reinforcements in different sociopolitical settings would seem to be a necessary part of our understanding.[11]

If we cannot demonstrate that the human animal has an innate strong propensity for violence, neither can we demonstrate that most humans are naturally peaceable.[12] Violent and nonviolent methods of dealing with conflict are equally "normal"—in the sense of being integral with the flow of events in all historical periods, occurring within virtually every ethnic and religious group, type of political system, and type of economic system. War, defined as large-scale organized violence between countries, can be seen as merely one expression of the fact that the humans have a range of normal behavioral responses to conflict, violence being one of them.

To say that something is normal, however, is not to say that it is acceptable or not worth trying to eliminate. All manner of diseases are normal in human society, but we devote a great deal of effort to their prevention and control. And such an attitude toward war—as an all-*too* normal, all-*too* prominent phenomenon that needs to be eradicated—seems to be growing, at least in some segments of world society. (See the discussion of "the normative culture" below.)

Structural Explanations of the Prominence of War

How society is structured—whether its polity is autocratic or pluralistic, whether its economy is socialist or capitalist, whether its economic classes are rigidly stratified or fluid and changeable in their memberships, whether certain linguistic, ethnic, or

---

[11] A probing and insightful exploration of cultural/psychological sources of violent behavior is provided by Andrew Bard Schmookler, *Out of Weakness: Healing the Wounds That Drive Us to War* (New York: Bantam Books, 1988).

[12] For a brief survey of the important behavioral studies bearing on tendencies toward either violent or peaceful responses to conflictual situations, see the entry "Aggression" in Robert M. Goldenson, ed., *The Encyclopedia of Human Behavior: Psychology, Psychiatry, and Mental Health* (Garden City: Doubleday, 1970).

religious groups are highly privileged vis-à-vis the rest—provides at least part of the explanation for the prominence of violence or lack of it in domestic society, even for those theorists who assume that humans are innately combative. Analogous features of world society also provide part of the explanation for when and how countries resort to war, even for those theorists who regard war as a "normal" means of statecraft. Such frequently invoked structural factors range all the way from the most general (the anarchic structure of the world polity as a whole) to highly specific features of particular military balances (for example, the counterforce exchange-ratios of the opposed strategic nuclear missile forces of the United States and the USSR).

The Nation-State System as a War System

"Because no authoritative agency can be called upon to resolve disputes among states," write Robert Art and Kenneth Waltz, reiterating the "realist" explanation, "statesmen often find it convenient, and sometimes necessary, to threaten the use of force or actually to use force. Military force is important, if not central, in international politics. It brings some order out of chaos, and it helps to make and enforce the rules of the game."[13] Violent self-defense, or at least a credible and visible readiness to violently defend one's interests—rather than being an extreme fall-back position in cases where community law-and-order agencies have not been able to get to the scene of conflict—is a standard ingredient of international statecraft. National governments that fail to provide their countries with military arsenals (and military help from allies when needed) sufficient to protect the country's vital interests against internal or external enemies are widely viewed as unfit, if not treasonably negligent.[14]

The "realists"—like some of the "idealists" they criticize—either strongly imply (Hans Morgenthau) or explicitly state (Kenneth Waltz) that the principal cause of international war is the absence of a world state. This basic structural diagnosis has antecedents in a long line of prominent thinkers—not only the ancestors of modern "realism," such as Niccolo Machiavelli and Thomas Hobbes, but also the proponents of world government such as Emeric Cruce, William Penn, John Bellers, the Abbé de Saint-Pierre, Bertrand Russell, Albert Einstein, Robert Maynard Hutchins, and Richard Falk.[15] Indeed, it is virtually a self-evident premise of members of the United World Federalist movement that to achieve world peace "nothing less will suffice than a comprehensive plan whereby there would be established on a world scale institutions corresponding to those which have been found essential for the

---

[13]Robert J. Art and Kenneth N. Waltz, eds., *The Use of Force: Military Power and International Politics* (Lanham: University Press of America, 1988), p. 1.

[14]Costa Rica, which does not maintain military forces for external use, is a notable exception.

[15]See Brown, *The Causes and Prevention of War*, pp. 140–147.

maintenance of law and order in local communities and nations."[16] Agreeing with the diagnosis but not the prescription, the "realists" see no politically feasible way of transforming the anarchic nation-state system into a durable world state. If there is too much war in the system at any particular time, strategies to reduce its prominence must be sought *within* the basic structure of anarchy: by a more rational use of the principal mechanism for prosecuting and regulating conflict, the balance of power.

However, theories that blame war on the anarchic structure of the nation-state system, whether advanced by "realists" or world-order reformers, cannot adequately explain the fact of durable nonviolent relationships among groups (including some sets of nation-states) coexisting without a state above them, and such theories cannot adequately explain the explosion of violent revolution or civil war in hierarchically organized states. Just as centralized government is neither a necessary nor sufficient condition for peace, anarchy is neither a necessary nor sufficient explanation for war.

I am not saying that the essentially anarchic structure of the world polity is only a marginal factor in the prominence of international violence. Undoubtedly, where parties to a conflict are tempted to resort to violence, the absence of a government superordinate to them may well be a crucial determinant of escalation to lethal combat. But this is hardly always the case. Other factors usually are also required to explain not only the temptation to prosecute a conflict through violence but also the decisions to actually give vent to the temptation.

The International Distribution of Power

Much of the theoretical writing in political science that attempts to explain the prominence of war in various times and places gives primary weight to the pattern of power relationships among the relevant countries—in particular, the distribution of military and economic power. To be sure, there are many differing definitions of "power" proffered by political scientists, and there is the additional problem of being able to measure the phenomenon even after defining it; but it is sufficient for purposes of the present discussion to conceive of the international power of a country in the general sense of its ability to control the behavior of other countries. Despite the obvious fact that a country's international power, so defined, is the aggregate resultant of numerous factors (internal and external), a good deal of international relations theory attempts to trace out the consequences for war and peace of different distributions of power. The international distribution of power is treated as an

---

[16]The call for a "comprehensive plan" is by Grenville Clark and Louis B. Sohn, *World Peace Through World Law* (Cambridge, Mass.: Harvard University Press, 1960). In this volume Clark and Sohn proposed a detailed constitution for the world, which includes a world police force more powerful than the armies of the member countries.

"independent variable" (although this terminology often is not used) and the likelihood of war is treated as a "dependent variable."

The basic power-distribution model generates a wide range of sometimes contradictory hypotheses about the causes of war. For example:

- States considering themselves to be disadvantaged by the existing distribution of power are prone to the temptation to revise the distribution by force, sometimes by concerting with one another to attack those advantaged by the status quo.[17]
- A country currently at the top of the heap, fearing an impending change in the distribution of power that would negate its hegemony may initiate (or provoke) war while still in possession of superior capabilities in order to hobble its potential rivals.[18]
- Countries configured in a rather even distribution of power may individually or in combination strike at one of their number to prevent a would-be hegemon from realizing its pretentions.[19]

If such a wide range of alternative distributions of power among countries can be invoked as explanations of decisions for war, what happens to the neat causal models of the "realists"? Are not other factors in addition to the international distribution of power also essential to the explanation of both particular wars and for the prominence of war in particular periods and regions of the international system?

A crucial determinant, surely, is the *subjective importance* to the key decision makers of the prevailing or impending international power distribution. No less crucial is the assessment of such decision makers of the prospects that war will significantly and positively (from their point of view) change the prevailing distribution. Finally, how decision makers of the potential belligerents estimate the costs of a prospective war in terms of resources to be sacrificed and other values foregone (or enhanced—such as national "honor" or discipline) can be decisive in their determination of whether to take their chances on the battlefield or around the negotiating table.

When a major country or group of countries has, over time, been intensely dissatisfied with existing international territorial jurisdictions, spheres of influence, privileges of commercial and navigational access, and the like (dispositions often imposed

---

[17]Morgenthau, *Politics Among Nations,* pp. 42–76.

[18]Robert Gilpin, *War and Change in World Politics* (Cambridge: Cambridge University Press, 1981), especially Ch. 5.

[19]This standard "realist" explanation of war (or threats of war) being a characteristic response to a prospective attainment of dominance by one country over the entire international system (or a response by countries within a region to a prospective regional hegemon) works best for the period of 130 years or so preceding the French Revolution, referred to by diplomatic historians as the Classical Balance of Power. See Edward V. Gulick, *Europe's Balance of Power* (Ithaca: Cornell University Press, 1955); and Morton A. Kaplan, *System and Process in International Politics* (New York: Wiley, 1962), pp. 49–50.

by the victors in a previous war), then a rough equality in military power and wealth, such that both sides believe they can acquit themselves well in combat, tends to be conducive to war.[20] Frequently referred to as "hegemonic war," the hostilities may be initiated by either the dissatisfied countries who, having finally caught up in power, feel in a position to rectify the "illegitimate" situation heretofore imposed on them, or by the status quo countries (often led by a hegemonic great power) in order to avert in time the attainment of superior power by the dissatisfied group.[21]

Even with such high incentives to preserve or change the existing distribution of power, however, war sometimes breaks out, sometimes not. Why? For many analysts, the single most important variable for determining whether any particular power-distribution conflict turns violent is the *military* balance of power between the rival countries.

Military Balances as Crucial Determinants

For most "realists," with their basic assumption of an anarchic world polity, war is omnipresent as a trump card—the *ultima ratio*—in virtually all interstate bargaining over conflicting interests; but it is a trump that need not always be played. The reason war does or does not result where there are major interstate conflicts (whether over hegemony or more particular interests) is sought primarily in the existing balances of military power, real or perceived.

Presumably, rational decision makers will not take their countries into wars they are convinced they will lose. The exceptions, and there are some, are (by definition) "irrational." It is when the antagonists on *both* sides believe they have a reasonable prospect of winning that wars are most likely to occur (and persist). Conflicts are war-prone (and ongoing wars are difficult to stop) when at least one side is confident it can win militarily, and the other as a minimum is confident that it can creditably defend itself.[22]

The "realist" paradigm, in its focus on the military balance of power, surely isolates what is an essential variable in the explanation of why and how wars are fought. (My objection is to its claim of explanatory sufficiency.) And it directs our attention to a crucial problem for statecraft concerned with the prevention of war: namely, the difficulties countries have in calculating correctly the balance of military power between themselves and their rivals prior to the full test of actual combat.

The military balance-of-power assessment problem inheres not only in the changing technologies of the instruments of warfare, but also in the uncertainties rivals

---

[20]For supportive arguments in favor of the proposition that rough equality rather than one-sided preponderance is conducive to war, see Geoffrey Blainey, *The Causes of War* (New York: Free Press, 1973).

[21] Robert Gilpin, "The Theory of Hegemonic War," in Robert I. Rotberg and Theodore K. Rabb, eds., *The Origin and Prevention of Major Wars* (Cambridge: Cambridge University Press, 1989), pp. 15–37.

[22]Blainey, *The Causes of War*, Ch. 8.

have over their enemies' real valuation of the territorial or other interests in dispute; for the latter will affect the *will* on each side to expend blood and treasure in combat—an essential determinant of the actual balance of military power that will be brought to bear on any particular conflict.

The characteristic uncertainties of alliance commitments further compound the difficulties in calculating the actual balance of military power relevant to any particular conflict. If the Kaiser knew in advance that he would, in fact, need to pit his armies simultaneously against the main forces of Russia, France, and Britain—not to speak of the United States—it is unlikely that he would have backed Austria's invasion of Serbia in the summer of 1914. In the contemporary period, if India attacks Pakistan, will Pakistan's ally China enter the fray by heating things up on the Sino-Indian border in order to pin down a large portion of India's troops? What if Pakistan is the aggressor? What countries' military forces need to be weighed in the Arab-Israeli balance?

Such uncertainties can sometimes work to deter war, denying potential attackers confidence that they can control their risks. It is widely assumed, for example, that the uncertain risks of escalation to strategic nuclear war are what deterred the Warsaw Pact, with its nonnuclear military advantage in Europe, from aggression against the NATO countries for over forty years.[23]

At other times, however, uncertainties about the real military balance can engender overly optimistic miscalculations of the strength of one's coalition or the weakness of the rival coalition. The Soviet Union evidently encouraged North Korea to invade South Korea in July 1950 on the basis of the obvious military superiority of the North over the South, totally discounting the possibility that the United States would enter the war on the side of the South. The United States, similarly, disastrously miscalculated China's propensity to enter the war on the side of North Korea four months later as General Douglas MacArthur's forces drove up toward the Yalu River.

The raw elements of the military balance between parties to a conflict thus are not a particularly reliable predictor of whether there will be war or, if war starts, which side will do better. The decision to resort to arms on the part of the principal prospective belligerents and their coalition partners will be at least as much determined by their respective valuation of the stakes, which in turn will be a function of each of their nonmilitary domestic, international, and transnational situations. How else can we explain the twenty-year war between the United States and North Vietnam and the fact that the military superpower was in the end defeated!

In sum, anticipation of a grossly unfavorable military outcome may well be sufficient to dissuade a country from going to war; but within the realm of situations wherein the military outcome is not so readily calculable (which usually is the case),

---

[23]See Charles Kegley, ed., *The Long Postwar Peace: Contending Explanations and Projections* (New York: HarperCollins, 1991), for scholarly arguments for and against the proposition that the fear of nuclear war is what prevented the cold war from becoming a hot war.

the crucial war/peace decisions are likely to be determined more heavily by the overall geopolitical situation as perceived by the key actors. The crucial geopolitical calculations of which military capabilities of what countries to count in the balance of power relevant to an impending war will in turn be influenced by the prevailing pattern of international alignments and antagonisms—including the number of coalitions into which the world system is polarized and the extent to which such coalitions are tightly or loosely organized.

The Pattern of International Polarization

There does appear to be a relationship between the basic pattern of polarization (the number of major coalitions in the international system at any particular time and the internal cohesion of such coalitions) and the incidence and intensity of wars.[24] Two general tendencies can be hypothesized:

1. The fewer the coalitions into which the entire system of international relations is divided (assuming that most of the countries *do* belong to a coalition), the less likely it will be that intense conflict between countries will result in war.
2. The more tightly members of coalitions are bound to their coalition partners, in the sense of being irrevocably committed to come to one another's defense, the more likely it will be that war anywhere in the system will escalate to continental or even global dimensions.

The strategic logic behind these propositions is simple: If it is virtually certain that in attacking another country, an aggressor will have to take on all members of the victim-country's large coalition, the expected costs of war to the potential aggressor are likely to appear greater than the potential gains (in other words, the victim's coalition acts as a deterrent); but if war breaks out nonetheless, the probability that the war will in fact draw in many countries rises to the extent that the initial belligerents are members of wide and tightly integrated coalitions.

Thus, if the entire world were divided only into two opposed coalitions and each of these was tightly organized, unilateral war-provoking actions by individual members of either coalition against each other would be rare; and there would be little room for miscalculation of the dimensions of the war that would ensue. War anywhere in the system would become world war. This configuration corresponds to the pattern of cold war bipolarity that many statespersons and analysts during the 1950s and 1960s saw as the evolving and durable structure of the post–World War II world polity.

---

[24]For elaboration of the effects of the pattern of international polarization on war, see Brown, *The Causes and Prevention of War*, pp. 71–77; see also Richard N. Rosecrance, *International Relations: Peace and War* (New York: McGraw-Hill, 1973); and Michael Haas, *International Conflict* (Indianapolis: Bobbs-Merrill, 1974).

At the other extreme, if the world were a polyarchy of multiple and loosely organized coalitions and nonaligned countries, countries would find more opportunities to attack one another, gambling that by adroit diplomacy they could dissuade friends of the opponent to abstain from participating in the hostilities. Wars therefore might break out more easily, but would be more likely to be localized and to dissipate before engulfing the whole system.

By these indexes of war-proneness, the most dangerous international configuration would be a loosely organized but still basically polarized international system. The ambiguity of mutual security commitments would lead to opportunities for miscalculation and bluffing among members of the rival coalitions. Countries might start "limited" local wars under the assumption that the risks of escalation could be controlled. But still there would be temptations for great-power interventions in local conflicts, and smaller powers would feel the need to invoke coalition ties, however loose, to deter their adversaries from ganging up. Indeed, once war started, considerations of prestige, credibility, the avoidance of "domino" effects, and the like might well stimulate a re-tightening of the rival coalitions, turning locally originating and presumably controllable conflicts into wider, even global war.

Despite the dangers, a considerable looseness in the world's coalition structure seems to be the most likely pattern for the foreseeable future. However conceivable in certain realist, balance-of-power theories,[25] the world in actuality has rarely, if ever, approximated the "ideal type" stability of either the tight bipolar or tight multipolar system any more than the enforced peace of world empire. The natural propensity of states, nations, and cultural groupings being to preserve as much autonomy as is consistent with their survival and well-being, the existence of tight globe-spanning coalitions will occur only as temporary expedients to rectify extreme worldwide power imbalances (such as occurred in the aftermath of World War II with the destruction of virtually all preexisting centers of great international power other than the United States and the USSR).

If the world when viewed along its polarization dimension is likely to be rarely and only temporarily in a configuration that, in theory, should make the resort to war unlikely, then surely the degree to which the international system is polarized, even when combined with variations in the international distribution of military power, cannot provide an adequate explanation for the fluctuating prominence of war that characterizes the long course of international history.

My judgment that such structural theories are weak and insufficient in their explanatory power is supported by the historical record, showing that periods of relative peace, no less than periods of war, often coincide with periods of flexible and shifting international alignments.

---

[25]See Kenneth N. Waltz, *Theory of International Politics* (Menlo Park: Addison-Wesley, 1979), pp. 161–193.

Domestic Structure and Interstate War

There is considerable disagreement among scholars over the weight to be accorded domestic factors in explaining patterns of war and peace. Generally, historians have tended to emphasize developments *within* particular countries and political scientists specializing in international relations have tended to emphasize changing balances of power *among* countries.[26] But this apparent disciplinary dichotomy is too neat, being cross-cut by prominent schools of thought and philosophy: Marxists, whether they happen to be political scientists, economists, or historians, see war in the modern era as an external expression of the "contradictions of capitalism" within nonsocialist states; neoclassical economists are wont to find the sources of war in the imperialist/mercantilist conflicts produced by statist distortions of the free market; various political sociologists, following Joseph Schumpeter's analysis of Germany's aggressiveness prior to World War I, attribute the international pugnacity of various governments to the domestic political insecurity of particular elements of the ruling classes who turn to war as a means of enhancing their influence in the high councils of power and generating militant support for themselves from the masses; and many liberal democrats operate from the Kantian premise (sometimes unaware of their intellectual progenitor) that states structured according to republican principles of representation and democratic accountability are basically pacific whereas autocracies are usually the instigators of war.[27]

Does the historical record support any of the theories that locate the sources of war mainly or substantially in the domestic structure of the hostile states?

Statistical studies seeking to determine the correlation of the frequency and/or intensity of wars with particular interstate and intrastate conditions have not been able to demonstrate a significant correlation between the form of government and the onset or dimension of war.[28]

Some manipulations of the data reveal a correspondence between the objectives (other than direct self-defense) for which a country participates in war beyond its borders and the country's political structure: Military actions to enlarge a country's

---

[26]For a balanced review of the debate between historians and political scientists on the importance of internal factors in explaining war, see Jack S. Levy, "Domestic Politics and War," in Rotberg and Rabb, *The Origin and Prevention of Major Wars*, pp. 79–99.

[27]Kant's prescription for world peace—a universal confederation of states that would nonviolently resolve their differences—assumed that the leading countries would have republican/representative forms of government. Governments accountable to the people would reflect the attachments of the ordinary citizenry to the domestic pursuits of family, business, and profession. Such governments would be inhibited from engaging in imperialistic power-plays that could plunge the country into war with all its accompanying societal disruptions. Immanuel Kant, *Perpetual Peace: A Philosophical Essay* [1795] (Indianapolis: Bobbs-Merrill, 1957).

[28]J. David Singer, "Accounting for International War: The State of the Discipline," *Journal of Peace Research,* Vol. 18, No. 1 (1981), pp. 1–18.

territory of dominion over other peoples are seemingly more likely to be undertaken by governments with unlimited executive authority and domestic systems allowing for very little political competition. By contrast, military interventions in support of national self-determination and democratization (like the U.S. actions in the Spanish-American War or Vietnam) are more likely to be undertaken by governments of open, competitive, and pluralistically organized polities.[29] Yet this distinction fails to account for quite a number of major historical events. Britain, for example, forcibly acquired many of its colonial possessions when it was the most democratic of the European countries. And ostensible "wars of national liberation" have been launched by autocrats like Napoleon Bonaparte, Adolf Hitler, and the rulers of the Kremlin.

The statistical studies on international military conflict do, however, appear to strongly support the theory that pluralistic democracies do not go to war against each other (provided that this category excludes the War of 1812 between quasi-monarchical Britain and the United States and "domestic" conflicts such as the U.S. Civil War and colonial wars for independence).[30]

Perhaps the general lack of wars between industrialized democracies has more to do with the geopolitical configurations of rivalry during the nineteenth and twentieth centuries than with the underlying dynamics of domestic structure. Yet there does seem to be something of the dynamics at work that were postulated by Kant. If war goes largely against the grain of republics, then we would expect such polities to be unable to generate the domestic consensus required to overcome their pacific predispositions unless required to by reasons of self-defense or in fulfillment of alliance obligations to a friendly country—conditions that would rarely, if ever, pit the industrialized democracies on opposite sides of a war.

Some theorists find the apparent peaceableness of industrialized democracies to be a function more of their economies than of their polities. Among states with market systems open to the world economy, and particularly those states whose domestic prosperity depends on a flourishing export trade, militarized foreign policies may be regarded as unduly burdensome. For such states, international conflicts of interest, especially those with major trading partners, are better prosecuted and resolved on the basis of nonviolent bargaining than through threats of military action. Bargaining through military threat, even short of hot war, can

---

[29]William K. Domke, *War and the Changing Global System* (New Haven: Yale University Press, 1988), pp. 72–106.

[30]Levy, "Domestic Politics and War," pp. 87–88. See also Michael W. Doyle, "Kant, Liberal Legacies, and Foreign Affairs," *Philosophy and Public Affairs,* Vol. 12 (1983), pp. 205–235; Bruce Russet, *Grasping the Democratic Peace* (Princeton: Princeton University Press, 1993); and William J. Dixon, "Democracy and the Peaceful Settlement of International Conflict," *American Political Science Review,* Vol. 88, No. 1 (March 1994), pp. 14–32.

engender total nation-to-nation hostility and a cessation of commerce between the antagonists; militarized diplomacy is likely to divert material and human resources away from sectors essential to maintaining international commercial competitiveness.

Moreover, in a country whose society, economy, and polity are organized primarily on the premise of a nonmilitarized foreign policy there will be influential interest groups disposed to lobby against militarily hawkish policies. This is the argument of Richard Rosecrance, who in *The Rise of the Trading State* sees more and more countries, as a condition of their effective participation in an increasingly interdependent global economy, faced with the choice of whether to adopt a substantially demilitarized foreign policy on the model of contemporary Japan. Rosecrance differs from the traditional "realists" in his thesis that, even under the premise of an anarchic interstate system, governments of major powers could well choose, on the basis of a rational (and valid) cost-benefit analysis, to pursue an essentially demilitarized grand strategy.[31]

The Normative Culture

Are inclinations of countries to resort to war significantly affected by prevailing ideas about the legitimacy of the use of force in world politics? Clearly, the role and substance of such norms in relations between nations differ importantly from their role and characteristic substance in relations among members of a national community, where they have comparatively much greater influence. But ideas about permissible and impermissible military action are not without weight in international relations.

Recurrent intergroup or antigovernmental violence *within* a country, a government's violent repression of dissidence, civil war—all of these actions are generally regarded as indications that something is drastically wrong either with those who are behaving violently or with the structure and processes of the domestic polity itself. Domestically, if an individual or group is unable to secure possessions against predators or prevent presumed rights from being violated, the usual expectation is that the official agencies of the whole community—the state—will be available to restrain the aggressive parties, to adjudicate the conflict, and to enforce the results of such adjudication. Murder and mayhem, however pervasive, are universally held to be inconsistent with the norms of domestic civil society, not simply a continuation of politics by other means.

---

[31]Rosecrance, *The Rise of the Trading State.* See also Domke, *War and the Changing Global System,* for statistical evidence showing a negative relationship between exports as a share of national output and decisions for war (pp. 107–139).

By contrast, there is no consensus that interstate war is pathological or presump-tively illegitimate. Indeed, in many quarters war—at least a credible threat and capa-bility to initiate war on behalf of one's important national interests—continues to be regarded as fully consistent with the accepted anarchic structure of the world polity and one of the necessary instruments of foreign policy.

There are variations, however, in this normative culture, which can affect the propensity of countries to rely on military power. It makes a difference whether those responsible for a country's foreign policy (be they elites or wider constituencies) regard war as a last resort or simply one of the standard instruments of statecraft. Periods of history, relations among nations in particular regions of the globe, and the characteristic international behavior of certain countries can be distinguished on the basis of prevailing beliefs about the permissibility of war: Is war permissible only after all nonviolent alternatives have been exhausted, and then only in defense of unam-biguously vital national interests? Is constant war-readiness and periodic exercise of one's forces in actual combat a necessary aspect of diplomatic bargaining in an anar-chic world? Or are military adventures part of the very spirit and fiber of the nation?

There is a widespread consensus among international lawyers from virtually all countries, a consensus that cuts across various ideological schools, that the use of mili-tary force to defend against, or retaliate for, violent attacks upon the nation's territory or citizenry is justifiable. Threats of war and actual military operations for the purpose of protecting the "territorial integrity" of the country presumably are legitimate. But the consensus breaks down, with differences between cultures and nations (and between "hawkish" and "dovish" factions within countries), over the question of how imminent an attack must be before it is legitimate to use force against the potential aggressor. Moreover, there are disagreements over the appropriate targets and the mag-nitude and timing of reprisals: Some strategists urge proportional "let the punishment fit the crime" responses; others favor awesome "massive" retaliation. And there is no consensus over whether the purpose of military retaliation should be solely to deter future attacks or, additionally, to avenge and provide national catharsis for past wrongs.

Medieval Christian Norms

In Europe during the first fifteen centuries of the Christian Era, the Church (over the objections of its pacifist wing) developed a "just war" doctrine that was highly elastic in its criteria for when it was legitimate to enter into war. The Catholic "just war" concepts had firmer constraints on the *means* of warfare (certain weapons were held to be unfair; levels of violence were to be proportionate in relation to the stakes at issue; noncombatants were to be spared).[32] In this the Church was in tune with

---

[32]National Conference of Catholic Bishops on War and Peace, *The Challenge of Peace: God's Promise and Our Response* (Washington, D.C.: United States Catholic Conference, 1983).

the dominant practices of the secular feudal rulers of the time. War, like interpersonal duelling, was the normal way of settling quarrels among rival dynasts—whether they were contesting over territorial boundaries, rights of navigation, marriage partners, or slights to their knightly honor. By the late feudal period,

> War was a way of life. . . . The landed aristocracy, who were almost everywhere the ruling class, had no other serious occupation, and indeed no other valid excuse for existence. Kings existed to lead them from one war to another and thus to keep them from one another's throats.[33]

Regarded as an honorable undertaking among Christian princes, war was supposed to be fought chivalrously and according to the "just war" rules set by the Church. The rule book could be thrown away, however, if the war was against Muslims (as during the Crusades) or other non-Christians.

The Wars of Religion

Not surprisingly, therefore, with the sixteenth-century breakup of Christendom into its Protestant and Catholic camps—each side regarding the other as doing the work of the devil—war among Christian states became as self-righteous and vicious as wars against the infidel. Whereas in medieval Europe war was fought between princes as a matter of honor, war now was fought out among the legions of the faithful as a duty to God. Defenders of the faith in one state felt justified in intervening with force in another state on behalf of their co-religionists; and religious minorities sought such help from great powers on their side of the Protestant-Catholic conflict. Cycles of intervention and counter-intervention were the order of the day. Such intervention was often undertaken (and justified by legal theorists of the time) preventively, in anticipation of religious repression; and wars to block such intervention were initiated preemptively against states thought to be preparing to intervene.[34]

Chivalrous restraints on fighting were also discarded. Towns were laid siege, populations of the rival faith were starved. The century-long era of European religious wars pitting Catholics against Protestants culminated in the horrible Thirty Years War—one of the most brutal periods in world history. Within three decades the population of the German and Austrian region was nearly halved from intercommunal killing and attendant diseases. Some 29,000 of Bohemia's 35,000 villages were turned into ghost towns. In many localities the countryside was so devastated that

---

[33]G. Mattingly, "International Diplomacy and International Law," in *The New Cambridge Modern History* III (Cambridge: Cambridge University Press, 1958), p. 150, quoted by Evan Luard, *War in International Society: A Study in International Sociology* (New Haven: Yale University Press, 1987), pp. 331–332.

[34]Luard, *War in International Society,* pp. 337–345.

the peasants were reduced to eating the remnants of dogs, cats, and rats. In some places they resorted to cannibalism.[35]

Westphalia and the Classical Balance of Power

By the mid-1640s, the princes and priests of Europe had experienced enough of such carnage. It took them four years of bargaining to work out a modus vivendi, promulgated in 1648 as the Peace of Westphalia, to allow the predominantly Protestant states to remain Protestant and the predominantly Catholic states to remain Catholic—with each tolerating the practice of the minority religion within its jurisdiction. However, of greater lasting importance were the principles of relations *among* the states of Europe embodied in the documents and undertakings signed by the delegates to the marathon negotiation in Westphalia. Even to this day two principles of interstate relations codified in 1648 constitute the normative core of international law: (1) the government of each country is unequivocally sovereign within its territorial jurisdiction and (2) countries shall not interfere in each other's domestic affairs. As argued by classical authorities on international law (most notably the seventeenth-century theorist Hugo Grotius), if most states, particularly the great powers, would indeed adhere to these principles, substantially fewer wars would occur; and the conduct of war could again be restrained within civilized bounds.[36]

Remarkably, for nearly a century and a half, even though wars were plentiful, the behavior of the great powers toward each other did approximate the Westphalian norms. Reinforced by the diplomatic and military norms of the Classical Balance of Power system, the monarchs of the day by and large respected one another's sovereign authority, refrained from sponsoring subversive movements within one another's territorial jurisdictions, and when they went to war did so for limited ends and with constrained fighting strategies.

But ideational norms are likely to govern a system of relationships over time only if they are sustained by the distribution of material sanctioning power within the system. How then could the norm of sovereign equality be sustained in an anarchic system of states unequal in military and economic power? By posing the question we uncover the elemental connection between the anarchic society of states and a flexible power-balancing process, which in turn leads to an appreciation of why the Classical Balance of Power remains for many theorists the ideal configuration for the anarchic world polity. Simply put: A relatively weak state unable to fend off a more

---

[35]Will and Ariel Durant, *The Age of Reason Begins,* in Vol. 7 of *The Story of Civilization* (New York: Simon and Schuster, 1961), p. 567.

[36]G.I.A.D. Draper, "Grotius' Place in the Development of Legal Ideas About War," in Hedley Bull, Benedict Kingsbury, and Adam Roberts, eds., *Hugo Grotius and International Relations* (Oxford: Clarendon Press, 1990), pp. 178–207.

powerful state that threatens to violate its sovereign integrity can form an alliance with other states to balance the power of the imperialistic state. Groups of states, similarly, facing a would-be hegemon or world imperial power can (and are likely to) combine against it to preclude its dominating the system. But because a lesser member of any alliance (even an anti-imperialist alliance) could easily be converted into a dependent satrap of its great-power protector in the Classical Balance of Power system, all states had to retain great flexibility for realignment with yesterday's enemy against today's friend.

Happily for the durability of the system, the traditions of diplomacy, military capabilities and strategy, and socioeconomic structure of the major states of Europe during the latter half of the seventeenth century and most of the eighteenth century combined to reinforce the flexibility of alignment that was the Classical Balance of Power system's equilibrating mechanism. States were not yet true nations, so their rulers and diplomats could make balance-of-power deals without the need of public accountability. The weapons and military organizations of the time (often based on hired mercenaries) were conducive to limited military engagements—easily initiated, but also easily terminated by negotiation before the belligerent countries had decisively damaged one another.

The Nation in Arms

In contrast with the Classical Balance of Power, the successor era of nationalism was not that compatible with the culture of moderate international relations. The American and French revolutionary doctrines claiming that governments derive their just powers from the consent of the governed (reflecting the practical need of monarchical and aristocratic elites to obtain the support of the rising middle classes in order to govern effectively) had a paradoxical impact on war. On the one hand, confirming the prophecies of Immanuel Kant, the new republican nationalism gave power to sectors of society that preferred the stability and predictability of peace to the disruptions of war. On the other hand, precisely because war now had to be fought for the vital interests of the nation or not at all, and if undertaken would require enthusiastic contributions from the entire nation, wars once started were very difficult to terminate before one side or the other had won decisively.

Moreover, the new military capabilities and strategies, increasingly based on the ability of countries to mobilize the basic industrial sinews of the country for war, put a premium on continual preparedness. Leaders with their eyes trained on the military balance vis-à-vis potential international adversaries felt compelled to keep alive a martial nationalism, lest their country be handicapped for tests of strength that were bound to come sooner or later. Yet the popular nationalism required to sustain sufficient military preparedness might also give rise to intense international affinities and antagonisms that could propel the leaders of a country into wars that their more rationally calculating strategic advisers would regard as unwarranted by balance-of-power considerations. Typically, such pressures operated on Louis Napoleon in the late 1860s and had much to do with France's disastrous involvement in the Franco-Prussian War of 1870. It was also unbridled nationalist sentiment, fueled by Germany's disgruntled Junker class, that led to Kaiser Wilhelm's 1890 dismissal of the arch *realpolitik* statesman, Otto von Bismarck, and the Kaiser's adoption of the foolhardy expansionist policies that helped provoke World War I.

The first great war of the twentieth century, it is sometimes forgotten, was at the outset a popular war. A standard history of the period reminds us that the first week of August 1914 featured

> cheering, singing, marching masses. It was the same before the Winter Palace in St. Petersburg, on the Unter den Linden in Berlin, on the Champs Elysees in Paris, in Trafalgar Square or the Mall in London.
>
> It was as if . . . the unconscious boredom of peace over so many unbroken years had stored up in the nations a terrific potential, which only waited for an accident to touch it off. Far from being innocents led to the slaughter, the peoples of Europe led their leaders. Ministers of Tsar, Kaiser, King, and President watched the press and the streets during these demented days and fell victim to the hysteria as helplessly as any of the nameless multitudes about them. It was as if some historic fatality, expressing itself in a sort of elemental mass passion, for a moment had suspended all the normal processes of humanity.[37]

The terrible human consequences of World War I (more than 10 million killed and 20 million wounded) did generate a popular antiwar culture that after the armistice of 1917 constrained the leaders of the great powers for a dozen years or so. The creation of the League of Nations, which in Woodrow Wilson's vision and the popular imagination would do away with the military alliance/balance-of-power system that caused the war; the seven-nation Locarno Pact of nonaggression and the Rhineland demilitarization treaty of 1925; the Kellogg-Briand Pact of 1928 by which over sixty countries renounced war as an instrument of statecraft—these interstate undertakings reflected the widespread revulsion at the seemingly senseless levels of destruction that now seemed inevitable in modern warfare. Still, the revulsion was hardly universal, even within the policy establishments or publics of the countries whose governments championed the antiwar instruments. Particularly within the dissatisfied major powers of the post–World War I period—Germany, Italy, and Japan—the ascendancy of peace parties proved to be only temporary, as these countries polarized internally into, on the one hand, groups urging constructive participation in the emergent community of nations and, on the other hand, groups hoping to rectify perceived international maldistributions of territorial control and wealth, much of which they attributed to the punitive peace settlement imposed by the Western Allies against Germany and its allies.

---

[37]Frank P. Chambers, Christina Phelps Harris, and Charles C. Bayley, *This Age of Conflict: Contemporary World History, 1914 to the Present* (New York: Harcourt, Brace, 1950), p. 16.

During the 1930s, virulently nationalistic and aggressively expansionist parties achieved ascendancy in Germany, Italy, and Japan; and the governments of each of these countries, with popular support, used brute force unsqueamishly against their domestic and international opponents. As against the rise in the dissatisfied powers of a political culture glorifying violence, the war-weary attitudes that were the legacy of World War I tended to persist in the victor democracies (Britain, France, and the United States) to constrain them from organizing a military counterpoise to the aggressors. Clearly, this asymmetry in normative culture between the satisfied and dissatisfied countries was a crucial determinant of the imbalance of power that tempted the aggressions of Mussolini, Tojo, and Hitler, which finally brought on World War II.

The destructive dimensions of the 1939–1945 war (at least 50 million fatalities, nearly 35 million of them civilians) dwarfed any previous episodes of violence in human history, made a mockery of the "just war" rules of proportionality and non-combatant immunity, and—in its final atomic incineration of Hiroshima and Nagasaki—produced a vast cultural aftershock: worldwide recognition that another world war might spell the extinction of the human species. The new antiwar culture was more widespread than ever, pervading even the military establishments of the superpowers where strategies for deterring war through keeping its awesome horrors omnipresent gained ascendancy over strategies for fighting war.

Winston Churchill, one of the toughest of the cold war leaders, articulated the emergent awareness of the dangers *and* opportunities:

> It may well be that we shall, by a process of sublime irony have reached a stage in the story where safety will be the sturdy child of terror and survival the twin brother of annihilation.[38]

The term "cold war" itself expressed the conviction in both the United States and the USSR, even among factions most hostile to the rival superpower, that the enmity should not, could not, become a hot war. In the face of complaints by the Communist Chinese that the Russians yielded too much in the 1962 Cuban missile crisis, the Communist Party of the Soviet Union, revising the Leninist forecast of the inevitability of war, recognized that the workers of the world now had more to lose than their chains and that in another world war millions would die for every capitalist that died.

Some analysts attribute the emergent antiwar culture (relating to wars among the great powers, not necessarily to wars by the great against lesser powers or among the lesser powers themselves) almost entirely to the fear of nuclear holocaust.[39] Others,

---

[38]Winston Churchill, speech in House of Commons, *Hansard,* March 1, 1955, Vol. 537, 5th ser., cols. 1894–1895.

[39]Art and Waltz, *The Use of Force,* p. 28; Bernard Brodie, *Escalation and the Nuclear Option* (Princeton: Princeton University Press, 1966); and Gilpin, *War and Change in World Politics,* p. 218.

while reluctant to see the threat of nuclear war as a sufficient explanation for the nonoccurrence of World War III, consider the possession of nuclear weapons by the superpowers as a necessary part of the explanation of the Soviet-U.S. "long peace."[40]

The historian John Mueller advances the counterfactual hypothesis that even if nuclear weapons had never been invented, the superpowers would have been deterred by the prospect of another war on the scale of World War II.[41] Indeed, Mueller sees the ascendancy of an antiwar culture in the industrially developed world not as a post–World War II discontinuity with the past, but rather as the product of an evolutionary process, albeit proceeding with fits and starts, traceable back to reactions to the Napoleonic Wars and the U.S. Civil War and operating on both rational and subrational levels: On the level of rational calculation of national interests, there is substantial agreement "that prosperity and economic growth should be central national goals and that war is a particularly counterproductive device for achieving them"; and on the deeper psychological level, Mueller finds war to have become "a thoroughly bad and repulsive idea . . . like dueling and slavery, subrationally unthinkable and therefore obsolescent."[42]

Yet it is difficult to credit the notion that use of military force has become repulsive to the great powers in the wake of World War II—considering the U.S. involvement in the Korean War (1950–1953) and the Vietnam War (1963–1973); the Soviet interventions in Hungary (1956), Czechoslovakia (1968), and Afghanistan (1979–1989); the British war against Argentina over the Falkland Islands (1982); and the U.S.-led high-tech war in the Persian Gulf in 1991 to drive Iraq out of Kuwait. The great powers may be repelled by the prospect of terrible damage to themselves, a substantial risk should they initiate military hostilities against the rival superpower or one of its principal allies; but against those they think they can easily overpower war has hardly become "unthinkable."

෫෨

This chapter must conclude by reiterating the sad truth with which it started: War remains very much a part of the structure and culture of the world polity. It is doubtful that its prominence in human affairs can be substantially reduced without a major shift in the habits of heart and mind of its statespersons and publics concerning the legitimacy of using violence for national ends and without a corollary enhancement of international conflict-management processes and institutions. The normative imperatives and political implications will be explored in Part Two.

---

[40]For a careful yet strong elucidation of the essential role of nuclear weapons in keeping the cold war from becoming a hot war, see John Lewis Gaddis, *The Long Peace: Inquiries into the History of the Cold War* (New York: Oxford University Press, 1987).

[41]Mueller, *Retreat from Doomsday,* pp. 110–116.

[42]*Ibid.,* p. 219.

4   Vast Economic Disparities
Among Countries

The immense differences in the economic condition of countries is another striking fact about world society—both a cause and a result of important features of the contemporary world polity.

The rich industrialized countries contain less than a quarter of the world's population but consume over three quarters of the world's goods. The standard forecasts looking toward the twenty-first century project an even more drastically skewed distribution. For if the world's population growth continues to be concentrated in the poor areas of the globe, as it has been since World War II, and if it continues to outstrip the economic development of these areas, as it did during the 1970s and 1980s, it is highly probable that by the year 2000 the economically underdeveloped countries will contain as much as four-fifths of the world's population but will have to support them on as little as one-sixth of the world's product.

Another way of comprehending the maldistribution of amenities among countries is to compare the share of the world's goods and services theoretically available to each of the world's nearly 6 billion people (if everyone received an equal portion) with the actual per capita gross national product (GNP) of each country. On the assumption of an annual world product of over $20 trillion (a reasonable approximation of the goods and services produced annually in the mid-1990s), each person could have goods and services worth over $3,300 a year. But the real world doesn't work that way: The annual per capita GNP of more than half of the world's countries is below $2,400, and for the poorest 25 percent of the countries it is below $700.[1] Meanwhile, sixteen countries are enjoying a $15,000 per capita GNP or better.[2]

---

[1] Per capita GNP estimates are from the International Bank for Reconstruction and Development/The World Bank, *World Development Report 1993* (New York: Oxford University Press for the World Bank, 1993).

[2] In the mid-1990s, the countries with greater than $15,000 per capita GNP included the United States, Canada, Japan, Germany, France, Switzerland, Sweden, Norway, Denmark, Finland, France, Austria, Belgium, the Netherlands, and two Arab oil-producing countries (the United Arab Emirates and Kuwait).

When we get behind the country aggregates, and focus on the numbers of people involved, the situation looks even worse: Over one billion of the people in the poorer countries must try to survive on less than $370 a year each, not enough to provide even minimally necessary food, clothing, shelter, and medical care—a situation that the World Bank calls "staggering" and "shameful."[3] In sub-Saharan Africa and South Asia, the poorest regions of the globe, roughly half of the people fall below this minimum subsistence threshold; and of these, about 420 million (whom the World Bank classifies as "extremely poor") are suffering on less than 75¢ worth of food, shelter, and medical care a day!

The poverty translates into disease and premature death: Twenty percent of the children in sub-Saharan Africa die before they reach the age of five, most of them from diarrhea or hunger-related diseases. Adults as well as children in the poorest parts of the world are disproportionately infected with tuberculosis (estimates range to about 10 million cases annually, of which 3 million die). Cholera, typhoid fever, dysentery, and other water and sanitation diseases are endemic to vast regions. The World Health Organization reports that over 1 billion people in the developing countries are without safe water. AIDS, the new sexually transmitted scourge of humankind, might seem on the basis of reported cases to be a threat in the affluent more than the poor countries. International health agencies, however, estimate that in per capita terms many poor countries have more serious AIDS epidemics than does the United States—in part because of overcrowding and the lack of protective birth control and medical information. Some UN-sponsored studies forecast that nearly half of the 6 million AIDS cases expected in the 1990s are likely to appear in Africa.[4]

What explains such terrible poverty in so much of the world and the inability, or unwillingness, of the rich minority to do much about it?

Historical Sources of the Global Poverty Gap

Undoubtedly, part of the explanation for the poverty of most of the Third World countries in comparison with the countries of Western Europe, the United States, Canada, and Japan lies in the colonial system and its legacies. About eighty of the approximately ninety countries with per capita GNPs below $3,000 received their

[3]International Bank for Reconstruction and Development/The World Bank, *World Development Report 1990: World Development Indicators* (New York: Oxford University Press for the World Bank, 1990), p. 1.

[4]World Resources Institute, *World Resources 1988–89* (New York: Basic Books for the World Resources Institute, 1988), p. 27; and John W. Sewell, "The Metamorphosis of the Third World: U.S. Interests in the 1990s," in William E. Brock and Robert D. Hormats, eds., *The Global Economy: America's Role in the Decade Ahead* (New York: W. W. Norton for the American Assembly, 1990), pp. 120–146.

independence from their European colonial overlords after World War II. Most of the rest are located in Latin America and attained independent statehood in the nineteenth century. The only wealthier countries that were once European colonies are the United States and Canada, Australia and New Zealand, Israel, the city-state of Singapore, and a half-dozen oil-producing countries of the Arab world. A few countries in the under $3,000 category—notably China, Turkey, and Thailand—were not formally colonies of any of the European powers, but for most of the century and a half before World War II they nevertheless were de facto economic, if not political, dependencies or arenas of competition of the rival European imperiums.

The high correlation of poverty with ex-colonial status is clear. We are in the realm of historical conjecture, however, when we try to ascertain a causal dynamic behind this correlation. Nevertheless, the basic facts of both the colonial and post-colonial systems have been sufficiently established by historical research to generate a set of explanatory conjectures that appear presumptively valid.

First, during the period of overseas colonial empires (which can be dated roughly from 1500 to 1950), the European metropolitan powers often weakened the indigenous economies of the peoples they took over. Particularly during the period of the industrial revolution (1750 to 1900), the share of world industrial output by areas we now call the "Third World" declined from over 70 percent of the total to close to 10 percent.[5] This was in many places more than a relative decline compared to the dynamic, technology-driven growth in manufacturing output centered in Europe and the United States. It was also an absolute decline in the ability of indigenous peoples themselves to provide for their own basic material needs, a consequence of the colonial conquerors taking over the role of manufacturing finished products (clothes, shelter, household furnishings) from local weavers and craftsmen. The new manufacturing facilities were frequently located in the metropolitan country, thereby relegating the colonized peoples to the function of provisioners of raw materials and personal services, and, not incidentally, also consumers of the everyday products now being produced in the industrialized world. Even for the provision of raw materials, however, mass native populations were often conscripted as laborers for the large plantations and mining operations of their overlords, and for the construction of transportation networks and seaports—all of this overwhelming and ultimately destroying indigenous landholding and agricultural patterns, and distorting, if not obliterating centuries-old cultures.[6]

---

[5]See especially P. Bairoch, "International Industrialization Levels from 1750 to 1980," *Journal of European Economic History,* Vol. 11 (1982), cited by Paul M. Kennedy, *The Rise and Fall of the Great Powers: Economic Change and Military Conflict from 1500 to 2000* (New York: Random House, 1987), pp. 148–149.

[6]The process of *de*-industrialization of the colonized world is described by Kennedy, *ibid.* A similar characterization of the process is offered by Barbara Ward, *The Lopsided World* (New York: W. W. Norton, 1968), pp. 49–66.

Later, in the wake of World War II, when the Europeans were compelled to relinquish their colonies they left behind indigenous economies specialized primarily in the production of agricultural commodities and minerals, and substantially lacking in ability to produce their own industrial goods. This put most of the newly independent states in a quadruple bind:

1. The now-Westernized cities' transportation and communications systems, indeed even the basic agricultural and mining sectors of the new states, could not continue functioning without the modern machinery, technology, and chemicals obtainable only from the industrialized countries.

2. The only way these Third World countries could earn enough foreign exchange to import the necessary industrial goods was to continue to specialize primarily in raw-material exports and to sell these cheaply enough so as not to be edged out of the world market by producers in the industrial countries.

3. Alternatively, if the ex-colonial states tried to develop manufacturing sectors to diversify their economies and reduce their dependence on foreign imports, they would have to keep out foreign competition through tariffs and other trade barriers; but the more expensive locally manufactured industrial goods meanwhile would increase the costs of producing the basic commodities and thus reduce their international competitiveness.

4. Finally, if the new states attempted to overcome these deficiencies by either borrowing heavily from the lending institutions of the affluent world or accepting large direct investments by multinational enterprises, they might have to subject themselves to new forms of dependency on, and intrusion by, the United States and/or some of the very countries that had exploited them in the past—some call it *neo*colonialism; Latin Americans use the term *dependencia*.

Some economic historians argue that even without exploitative colonialism and its legacies in the contemporary Third World, the great economic disparities between the "Western" and "non-Western" countries would have materialized. Colonialism was one of the symptoms of the economic development gap that emerged between Western and non-Western worlds after 1500, reinforcing it, to be sure, but not its principal cause. From this perspective, the global economic development gap is traceable to a confluence of factors present in Western Europe that were lacking in other vigorous civilizations such as Ottoman Turkey and China.[7]

---

[7]A proponent of this view of Western Europe's ascendancy is E. L. Jones, *The European Miracle: Environments, Economies and Geopolitics in the History of Europe and Asia* (Cambridge: Cambridge University Press, 1981).

One variant of this thesis emphasizes the pluralistic and conflictual nature of Western society: Europe's lack of political centralization made for perpetual inter-state economic and military rivalry. Geographic factors determined that much of the economic and military rivalry among the major West European states would be oceanic—for control of preferred fisheries, for new sources of spices, fibers, and precious metals, and for command of crucial navigation routes. Science and technology were stimulated by these intra-European mercantile and military rivalries at a time when the Near East and Far East were relatively quiescent under the domination of their respective Ottoman and Chinese hegemons, both of which were preoccupied more with imperial consolidation than with imperial expansion. The rest of the world, heretofore largely beyond the reach of the imperially aggressive and technologically advanced cultures of Europe, became a highly tempting and accessible arena for competitive exploitation and colonization. The Western Europeans easily overpowered whatever resistance they encountered from the indigenous peoples of southern Asia, Africa, and the Americas. The only real competition was among the Western Europeans themselves and this in turn simply enhanced the factors underlying their growing ascendancy over the rest of the world.

Such explanations of the historical causes of today's prevailing global economic disparities are, of course, controversial among historians and social scientists. The scholarly controversies parallel and feed into policy disputes over the extent to which countries can and should operate according to "free trade" principles in the contemporary world.

The Contemporary "Free Trade" Problematique

The demise of the European-run colonial system in the wake of World War II and the defeat of Japan left it to the United States to organize the economy of those parts of the world not under the control of the Soviet Union. This Washington attempted to do through the three-pillared structure of the General Agreement on Tariffs and Trade (GATT), the International Monetary Fund (IMF), and the International Bank for Reconstruction and Development (the World Bank).

As viewed from places like New Delhi and Acera, however, the global regime the United States was trying to install, like the global Pax Britannica England had attempted to institute in the nineteenth century when it was the economic hegemon, embodied an ideology of global economics that many of the now-emancipated nations regarded as perpetuating some of the exploitative aspects of the colonial system. Indeed, most Third World statespersons and economists rejected both the theory and the practical implications for their countries of the "neo-classical" economic philosophy underlying the U.S.-sponsored free trade regime, seeing it as more likely to worsen the post-colonial north-south disparities than to alleviate them. (Ironically, the United States, when it was a newly independent "developing country," was strongly opposed to the British-sponsored free-trade regime, perceiving that without protective tariffs U.S. manufacturing industries would be driven out of business by lower-priced British imports.)[8]

According to free-trade theory, all the world's peoples benefit from global free trade, since the universal desire to buy at the cheapest price and sell at the greatest profit will result in everyone specializing in the production of those goods and services they can produce most efficiently, thereby increasing the overall supply of desired goods and services and decreasing their costs to consumers. The prospect that inefficient producers will be driven out of the market is good, for this will induce them to find an alternative specialized niche for themselves in which they do have a comparative advantage in efficient production.

Even if valid in theory, however, the dynamics and results of such a global free-trade regime are anathema to many of the nonindustrialized countries, for their competitive niches would have to be, for the most part, in the production of primary agricultural commodities, leaving their economies highly vulnerable to the wide fluctuations in global supply (as affected by changing climate and cycles of glut and scarcities). Such specialization often turns out to mean unreliable export earnings—a condition of economic insecurity made worse by the persisting need to import finished goods which can become unaffordable when inflation and recession in the industrialized world drive up their price. The consequences, as perceived by former Tanzanian president Julius Nyerere, are that

> Tens of billions of dollars flow every year from the Economic South to the Economic North through movements in the terms of trade which have been adverse to the underdeveloped countries almost continually since the 1950s. The prices of primary commodities like, cocoa, copper, etc. etc.—which are the major export products of the Third World—go down in relation to the prices of machinery, lorries, capital investments of all kinds, and most manufactured goods. To an ever increasing extent, Third World countries sell cheap and buy dear.[9]

To make matters worse, during periods of recession in the global market for certain primary products, the countries specializing in these commodities still need to import much of the industrially manufactured goods used by their people (including the tools and vehicles used to farm and mine their basic goods). This means that in order to avoid total economic collapse, they have to borrow money from international lenders—which in turn compels these nonindustrialized countries to allocate even more of their land and labor to the production of the exportable commodities in order to pay off their international debts.

---

[8]The history of the free-trade vs. protectionist debate is well recounted by Stephen C. Neff, *Friends but No Allies: Economic Liberalism and the Law of Nations* (New York: Columbia University Press, 1990).

[9]Julius K. Nyerere, "Foreword" to Chakravarthu Raghavan, *Recolonization: GATT, the Uruguay Round & the Third World* (Penang, Malaysia: Third World Network, 1990), pp. 21–22.

Such a vicious downward spiral of relative impoverishment has indeed been the post-colonial odyssey of many Third World countries. Because of their inherited and continuing competitive handicaps, in the early 1990s the cumulative foreign debts of developing countries were running well over a trillion dollars (more than a third of the value of their combined gross domestic product), and most of them were unable to pay even the annual interest charges on these debts from their export earnings.[10] Defaulting (the international equivalent of declaring bankruptcy) is a bad option that could make it virtually impossible for the defaulting country to obtain additional credit to finance its essential imports.

What, then, are the ways available in the world polity (as currently structured) for rectifying the persisting, if not worsening, economic disparities?

Rectification Issues

It remains the position of some statespersons, moral philosophers, and social scientists that, regardless of who or what was to blame historically for the lack of economic development in many countries, the affluent countries need not regard it as their obligation to alleviate the misery of the world's poor. Frequently this position is coupled with the claim that only self-help policies can rectify the condition of the economically underdeveloped societies, and that external aid will, more often than not, prove counterproductive.

But other political leaders and intellectuals, from advanced industrial countries as well as the Third World, argue that on grounds of mutual interest, let alone moral responsibility, it is imperative for the affluent countries to help the poorer countries overcome their competitive deficiencies, and that there are many practical ways to give the poor a boost toward self-sustaining growth.

Those taking the no-obligation stance are supported with economic reasoning from market-oriented economists, neoclassical *and* Keynesian, to the effect that the reasons for the continuing economic underdevelopment of most of the poor countries lie primarily in their own policies of government intervention into their economies, which distort the natural workings of the free market. Most liberal economists, quips Robert Gilpin, seem to believe that "the poor are poor because they are inefficient."[11] The free-enterprise liberals contend that all too often in the contemporary Third World, the rigidities of the pre-capitalist feudal social order have been thrown overboard for the new rigidities of "post"-capitalist socialism, rather than allowing modern domestic economies to develop flexibly in response to the chang-

---

[10]United Nations, *World Economic Survey, 1992* (New York: United Nations, 1993)

[11]Robert Gilpin, *The Political Economy of International Relations* (Princeton: Princeton University Press, 1987), p. 269.

ing conditions of the global market.[12] The United States under the Reagan administration was the quintessential champion of this view, frequently articulated by the president himself. Typically, he reminded the Board of Governors of the World Bank and the International Monetary Fund of their mission "to facilitate individual enterprise in an open international trading and financial system." This would redound also to the benefit of the poorer countries, who should heed the lessons history has to teach about economic development: "The societies which have achieved the most spectacular, broad-based economic progress in the shortest period of time . . . believe in the magic of the market place. . . . We cannot have prosperity and successful development without economic freedom. Nor can we preserve our personal and political freedoms without economic freedom."[13]

Few Third World leaders or economists, however, have been all that eager to buy into the global capitalist free market advocated by the United States. Many, like Julius Nyerere (quoted above) contend that the free market favors those starting with a competitive advantage, particularly an advantage in developing and applying new technologies to reduce the factor costs of production. They challenge the neoclassical premise that a world free of barriers to trade and investment will bring about substantial economic betterment for all peoples, regarding it as either naive or a grand hoax. They are particularly worried about the implications for the Third World of an unfettered global free market that engenders national economies specialized in producing those goods that each particular national economy has a comparative advantage to produce more cheaply. Will this really work out to our benefit? they ask, expecting that the more lucrative product lines would be jumped into and hogged by those with the crucial comparative advantages—multinational corporations with efficient long-distance transportation and communications, ready access to investment capital, and fungible management skills—for reducing factor costs. Without the benefit of specially protected national markets, the poorer countries will be either left to specialize in the dregs of the global economy that no one else wants, or to become perpetual dependents of the rich countries and corporations. And if a Third World country does attempt to take the latter route, by providing a hospitable investment climate for multinational corporations (MNCs) for locating main-line production and marketing subsidiaries, it will have to continue to maintain a comparative advantage for attracting such investments, which usually means low-wage

---

[12]This basic market-oriented analysis of the causes and possible rectifications of economic underdevelopment is shared by economists as diverse as Milton Friedman, *Essays in Positive Economics* (Chicago: University of Chicago Press, 1953); W. Arthur Lewis, *Theory of Economic Growth* (New York: Harper & Row, 1970); and Charles P. Kindleberger, *Foreign Trade and the National Economy* (New Haven: Yale University Press, 1962).

[13]Ronald Reagan, "Address to the Board of Governors of the World Bank and the International Monetary Fund, September 28, 1981," in *Weekly Compilation of Presidential Documents*, Vol. 17, No. 40, pp. 1052–1055.

labor (often no effective unionization), regressive taxation systems, and little, if any, environmental controls.[14]

This widely shared perception in Third World countries of their competitive disadvantages and vulnerabilities produced a minimal consensus among most of them during the 1960s and 1970s on a set of demands for corrective interventions in the international market. Called the New International Economic Order (NIEO), the demands included: (1) international commodity agreements to stabilize world prices of primary-product exports at remunerative levels, preferably with built-in price increases indexed to price increases in industrial goods; (2) open access to the markets of industrial countries for goods from the poor countries (in some cases preferential access), without reciprocal access by industrial countries to the markets of the poor countries; (3) commitments by each affluent country to allocate a minimum portion of its GNP for the transfer of resources to developing countries; and (4) special debt relief, in the form of easier repayment terms, renegotiation, even forgiveness in extreme cases, for the loans extended to the poor countries by international banks and financial institutions. The Third World coalition also agitated for the elimination of weighted voting procedures favoring the affluent countries in international agencies dealing with development problems: they wanted one-country/one-vote decision rules to assure that their interests would be adequately represented.[15]

Most governments of industrial countries, advised by liberal economists (neoclassical and Keynesian alike) opposed the NIEO demands when they were first promulgated by a coalition of seventy-seven Third World countries in the 1960s. During the 1970s and 1980s, however—in large part as a reaction to the enhanced international bargaining of the Third World countries following the energy crisis generated by the Middle East oil producers—the European Community (in its Lomé Conventions with its members' former colonies) and then (begrudgingly) the United States did make some concessions in the direction of the NIEO demands. Still, it remained the dominant view among liberal economists that the contemplated interventions into the free market would create more problems than they alleviated, not only for the global economy but for the poor countries themselves.

The standard arguments by the orthodox free traders are that commodity price stabilization agreements, the maintenance by developing countries of barriers against imports from the industrialized countries, and the like retard economic development (and therefore eventual competitiveness in the global economy) by preventing the

---

[14]Rajni Kothari provides a sophisticated articulation of Third World objections to the "free market" world-order designs of the neoclassicists in his *Toward a Just World Order* (New York: Institute for World Order, 1980). For an updated reflection of Third World reactions, see Robin Broad, John Cavanagh, and Walden Bello, "Development: The Market Is Not Enough," *Foreign Policy,* No. 81 (Winter 1990–91), pp. 144–162.

[15]The basic New International Economic Order demands by the Third World coalition were passed as a resolution by the United Nations General Assembly in December 1974 as a "Charter of Economic Rights and Duties of States." General Assembly Resolution 3281 (xxix 1974).

market from weeding out inefficient producers; moreover, such market interventions artificially increase the costs of living to consumers, many of whom are poor. Objections also are raised to concessionary debt relief for the poor countries on the grounds that this tends to dry up sources of future credit and encourages even greater loan delinquency. At the same time, moratoria on outstanding debt obligations reduce the funds that otherwise would be available to the better risk borrowers—precisely those developing countries that deserved to be helped.[16]

The generally negative responses by economic experts and policymakers in the affluent countries to the global market-intervention and redistributive policies demanded by the Third World coalition have led to two important results:

First, Third World countries have become increasingly reliant on multinational corporations to bring in investment capital and other development resources. Indeed, despite the standard rhetoric still voiced by Third World politicians against the MNCs, most Third World governments are competing with each other to provide hospitable environments for the location of multinational subsidiaries. Mexico's accession to the North American Free Trade Agreement (NAFTA) with the United States and Canada is an expression of this shift in attitude. The temptations for attracting MNCs have become overwhelming. The multinational firms bring in risk capital and skilled personnel, create new centers of industry and employment, build new roads, generate electricity, harness water resources for irrigation, and set up local suppliers of goods and services. In the process the MNCs hire and train workers, technologists, and managerial personnel, thereby contributing to the diversification of skills in the host-country population required to run a modern society. Meanwhile, by creating local markets and consumer demands for new lines of goods and services, the multinationals also stimulate indigenous entrepreneurs to start their own businesses.

Second is the *reaction* on the part of many disillusioned Third World intellectuals and political leaders to the new embrace of free market ideas and particularly to the temptation to rely on MNCs as the agencies for Third World development. Even the more moderate among the original formulators of the NIEO have begun to concede the argument of the more radical, neo-Marxist *dependencia* theorists that the majority of Third World countries, by continuing to participate in the world system organized by the leading capitalist countries for their own benefit, are bound to suffer continuing exploitation. The radicalized moderates see Third World countries like Mexico succumbing to the lures of the MNCs, and thereby consigning themselves to a politically and culturally demeaning neocolonial status—even if things work out reasonably well on the economic side. This is because ownership and top management of the multinational corporations reside in individuals and groups with no

---

[16]The arguments of market-oriented economists against commodity agreements, debt relief, and other NIEO demands are well represented in Richard N. Cooper, "A New International Order for Economic Gain," *Foreign Policy,* No. 26 (Spring 1977), pp. 65–120.

compelling sense of responsibility or accountability to the host society; they might well, as they already have in many countries, develop sectors or localities in the host countries that draw talent and financial resources away from localities in greater need of development. And because the multinationals have a vested interest in preserving the cheap factor costs in the host countries (low-wage labor, tax policies allowing higher margins of profits than in the industrialized countries, and less stringent environmental and other regulatory controls), they also have compelling incentives to form covert, if not overt, political alliances with conservative groups in the host countries to suppress economic and political reform.

Accordingly, some disillusioned moderate reformers argue that the developing countries must reduce their dependence on the world capitalist system. They advocate strategies of self-reliant development, emphasizing regional multicountry economic communities of sufficient scale to generate their own balanced industrial/agricultural growth without the need of external capital investment from, or export markets in, the affluent capitalist countries. But this is a counsel of despair, for serious Third World economists understand that the entrepreneurial sectors of their societies are already too linked into the global market to retreat into a less lucrative regional market and that such a strategy would simply widen the gap between the rich and poor throughout the Third World.

An alternative view—the one to which I subscribe—holds that neither complete integration into the free global market nor Third World dissociation from the affluent countries is realistic or desirable for the poor countries; nor should these be their only choices. The affluent countries can force such a dilemma upon the Third World, in which case the world's political economy may well polarize on a rich-poor axis. But such an outcome carries severe risks to the security and well-being of the industrial as well as the economically less-developed countries.

These realizations, underscored by the global debt crisis of the 1980s,[17] have been reflected in two global summit conferences convened to deal with the predicaments of increasing global interdependence: the 1992 United Nations Conference on Environment and Development (the "Earth Summit") and the 1995 World Conference for Social Development—each attended by more than 100 heads of state.

The underlying premise of these global summits is that the affluent, for reasons of their own country's economic and ecological well-being, can no longer afford to be indifferent to the economic development or deterioration of Third World countries.

---

[17]The fear that the large debtor countries like Mexico and Brazil might have to default on their huge loan obligations to international creditors was an important source of the banking crisis in the United States and other OECD countries in the 1980s. Nine major U.S. banks that loaned over 285 percent of their capital to developing countries over the previous decade were particularly vulnerable. Financial community pressures on the loan recipients to meet their obligations, reflected in increased austerity mandates on them from the International Monetary Fund, exacerbated the economic and social instabilities of the Third World debtor countries, whereas the banks' need to correct for their previous lending binges compelled them to constrict the capital available for loans in their own societies, thus contributing to recession in the industrial world.

"Interdependence" is not simply a word created by idealistic world-order reformers but a very real condition of life bonding the fate of the rich to the fate of the poor.

The "southern" countries, although no longer colonies of the imperial "northern" countries, are still crucial to their former overlords as sources of raw materials and basic commodities and as markets for industrial and high-technology products. Even a country as well-endowed as the United States with natural resources and internal consumers for its manufactured products, is inextricably linked into global commercial relationships to such an extent that its own basic economic health has come to be dependent upon the economic health of scores of Third World countries. As international banker David Rockefeller put it in an address to the American Banking Association, "The primary direct benefits of the U.S. assisting the developing nations are simple. . . . The developing nations now provide us a larger export market than all the developed nations put together, excluding only Canada."[18] A study for the World Resources Institute (WRI) pointed out that at the end of the 1980s, U.S. trade with developing countries, exports and imports, was about one-third of total U.S. trade, with the export sector in manufactures involving over 2 million American jobs. The WRI study further estimated that 1.1 million U.S. workers lost their jobs in the 1980s due to the failure of economic growth in debt-ridden Third World countries.[19]

Especially in Western Europe, the poverty of the Third World countries is driven home by the flood of job-seeking migrants and their families and the ugly nationalistic and xenophobic backlash this is producing on the part of lower-middle-class and worker elements who fear for their own jobs.[20] This concern was stated quite succinctly by the president of the World Summit for Social Development, Danish Prime Minister Poul Nyrup Rassmussen. "Thousands and thousands and thousands of refugees are coming from various parts of the world. . . . We have a good argument now, a very concrete one, for ordinary people, which is, if you don't help the Third World . . . with a little part of your welfare, then you will have these people in our society."[21]

Help to "the Third World," however, does not necessarily translate into help for the approximately one billion people there who are living in extreme poverty. Many a Third World country features a wide internal gap in living standards between the impoverished masses and the privileged oligarchical elite—typically leading entre-

---

[18]David Rockefeller, September 22, 1984, speech, quoted by Janet Welsh Brown, "Why Should We Care?" in Janet Welsh Brown, ed., *In the U.S. Interest: Resources, Growth, and Security in the Developing World* (Boulder: Westview Press for the World Resources Institute, 1990), p. 3.

[19]*Ibid.,* p. 4.

[20]On the politics of dealing with immigrants from the Third World, see Myron Weiner, ed., *International Migration and Security* (Boulder: Westview Press, 1993) and James L. Hollifield, *Immigrants, Markets and States: The Political Economy of Immigration in Postwar Europe and the United States* (Cambridge: Harvard University Press, 1993).

[21]Prime Minister Rassmussen quoted by Barbara Crosette, "Talks in Denmark Redefine 'Foreign Aid' in Post–Cold-War Era," *New York Times,* March 10, 1995.

preneurs in the exporting and importing sectors—who control the government. Resource transfers to Third World governments (determined to protect their political sovereignty and opposed to outsiders attempting to shape their socioeconomic policies) often never reach the people most in need. As a consequence, altruistically motivated governments and nongovernmental organizations in the affluent countries are increasingly linking their assistance to verifiable commitments by recipient governments to programs that will benefit the most destitute populations. Such "human needs" conditioning was one of the most contentious issues at the 1995 World Summit for Social Development, engendering opposition not only from sovereignty-obsessed Third World governments but also from lending agencies in the International Monetary Fund nexus whose market-oriented "conditionality" programs are designed to foster export-led growth and associated infrastructure investments in the recipient countries.

Finally, if the efforts to counter the most dangerous threats to human health and well-being from disruptions of global ecologies are to have any chance of success, the poor countries will have to be induced to cooperate with the rich in changing prevailing patterns of resource use and industrialization. As will be discussed more fully in the following chapter, the industrializing sectors in the Third World as well as the high-energy consumers in the West and the post-Soviet areas are drastically abusing and overusing important resources in regional and global "commons" (the oceans, river basins, airspace, communications frequencies, the atmosphere, the ozone layer, and the earth's climatic and other essential biospheric balances). The greatest threats of population growth outpacing available resources are in the poor societies,[22] which also, because of their destitute condition, are principal sources of plant, animal, and human diseases that increasingly are being transmitted across international borders.

The peoples of the Third World are inextricably implicated in the world economy, even more than when they were colonial subjects. They are now necessary partners in its management.[23] Partners, however, need to be treated with respect and care and brought fully into the decision processes that impinge on their values and well-being—for both pragmatic and moral reasons. I will return to this imperative in Part Two.

---

[22]Donella H. Meadows, Dennis L. Meadows, and Jorgen Randers, *Beyond the Limits: Confronting Global Collpase, Envisioning a Sustainable Future* (Post Mills, Vt.: Chelsea Green, 1992).

[23]This is also the conclusion of a study directed by Ivan Head for Canada's International Development Research Center. See his *On a Hinge of History: The Mutual Vulnerability of South and North* (Toronto: University of Toronto Press, 1991).

5 The Mismatch Between
Polity and Ecology

The lack of sufficient correspondence between the legal-political structure of world society (which is built out of presumably sovereign nation-states) and the structure of the natural and artificial material environment (which is unavoidably transnational in many of its dimensions) has become a matter of widespread and urgent concern; for with the nature-altering technologies now being employed, humans are drastically affecting the conditions of life on the planet without being held accountable for the damage they are doing. The 1987 report to the United Nations by its specially appointed, distinguished persons World Commission on Environment and Development stated what is now a commonplace recognition of this planetary incongruence:

> The Earth is one but the world is not. We all depend on one biosphere for sustaining our lives. Yet each community, each country, strives for survival and prosperity with little regard for its impact on others. . . . National boundaries have become so porous that traditional distinctions between matters of local, national, and international significance have become blurred. Ecosystems do not respect national boundaries.[1]

As Jessica Tuchman Mathews noted, "The majority of environmental problems demand . . . solutions which encroach upon what we now think of as the prerogatives of national governments. This is because the phenomena themselves are defined by the limits of watershed, ecosystem, or atmospheric transport, not by national borders."[2] The fish, it has been frequently observed, refuse to read the political maps.

People attentive to international issues, however, do read the political maps; and more and more of them are concerned that the sacrosanct quality statespersons and publics have heretofore accorded to the thick lines demarcating countries may be inhibiting the kinds of cooperation needed to deal adequately with the growing environmental threats to human well-being. Reflecting these concerns, the Final Report of the April 1990 American Assembly found that

---

[1]World Commission on Environment and Development, *Our Common Future* (New York: Oxford University Press, 1987), pp. 27, 38.

[2]Jessica Tuchman Mathews, "Redefining Security," *Foreign Affairs,* Vol. 68, No. 2 (Spring 1989), pp. 162–177, quote from p. 175.

Three indivisibly linked global environmental trends together constitute an increasingly grave challenge to the habitability of the earth. They are human population growth; tropical deforestation and the rapid loss of biological diversity; and global atmospheric change, including stratospheric ozone loss and greenhouse warming. These trends threaten nations' economic potential, therefore their internal political security, their citizens' health (because of increased ultraviolet radiation), and, in the case of global warming, possibly their very existence. *No more basic threat to national security exists* [my emphasis].[3]

All nations, concluded the American Assembly report, are bound together in a new condition of "collective insecurity," which, in turn, calls for "an unprecedented strategy of international cooperation."

Agreeing with these assessments, Maurice Strong, the conference secretary of the 1992 United Nations Conference on Environment and Development, promised that "The Earth Summit will be asked to consider far-reaching reforms of the international system."[4] As it turned out, however, the Earth Summit, although adopting "far-reaching" statements of principle on ecological care (see Chapter 9 for analysis of the summit's accomplishments), gave scant attention to the implications for the structure and functioning of the world polity. This gap is both a symptom and a source of the world's most crucial ecological predicaments—which are at base failures of world society to fully face up to the new imperatives of international "commons" management.

International Commons Management: The Basic Issues

International law, diplomacy, and war have often dealt with international "commons" issues, for in the areas that are not within any country's sovereign jurisdiction, nationals of one state are likely to get in the way of nationals of other states and, not infrequently, can come into conflict over their respective rights to use the resources in particular ways. The term "commons" is applied to such areas and resources by analogy with the nineteenth-century English pattern of allowing cattle open access and free use of grazing land abutting the households of the local villagers. Some ecologists extend the analogy by warning of an international "tragedy of the commons" like that which befell the English villagers when individual households, acting out of

---

[3]Final Report of the Seventy-Seventh American Assembly, April 19–22, 1990, published in Jessica Tuchman Mathews, ed., *Preserving the Global Environment: The Challenge of Shared Leadership* (New York: Norton, 1991), pp. 325–346.

[4]Maurice Strong, "Introduction," to a report to the Trilateral Commission on the tasks of the 1992 UN Conference: Jim MacNeil, Pieter Winsemiuns, and Taizo Yakishiji, *Beyond Interdependence: The Meshing of the World's Economy and the Earth's Ecology* (New York: Oxford University Press, 1991), pp. x–xi.

perceived self-interest, kept increasing the size of their herds to the point where the commons was severely overgrazed and everyone suffered.[5]

Not every commons is fated to experience severe battles for its resources or a "tragedy" of overuse. If the valued resources of a commons are abundant, an open access, first-come/first-use regime could well be both politically and economically viable. This indeed used to be the case with many an international commons (primarily oceans and rivers) until the last half of the twentieth century.

The scientific and technological revolutions of recent decades, however, have been challenging the viability of open access, free-use regimes for major international commons. With more areas and environments increasingly accessible beyond national jurisdictions, and with their natural resources increasingly exploited for a wide array of uses, previous assumptions of abundance are giving way to anticipations of dangerous scarcity. The oceans and rivers (covering more than 70 percent of the globe), the world's interlinked plant and animal populations and food chains, its atmosphere, weather, and climate, the moon and other celestial bodies, and outer space—all of these component commons of the larger planetary commons—are being abused and overused in ways that can inflict irreparable harm to global and local ecosystems and to the human populations that they sustain. These threats point to the need to systematically reassess regime alternatives for the commons.

The ecological soundness of a regime for any particular commons is a function of the following variables: (1) the abundance or scarcity of the valued resources in the commons, (2) the mobility or stationary characteristics of these resources, and (3) the physical divisibility of the resources.[6]

Open-access, free-use regimes are theoretically the dominant solution where commons resources are abundant (meaning not vulnerable to depletion or abuse) *and* mobile or very difficult to divide. This condition, once assumed to prevail at least in the waters of the vast ocean beyond national coastal limits, can no longer be taken for granted even there as fisheries experts learn more about the ecological interdependence of deep-sea aquatic life and closer-in harvestable fish. Abundance also used to be assumed about the air in the atmosphere (presumably it would dissipate and dissolve dangerous industrial emissions), until meteorologists and medical researchers confirmed the experience of suffering citizens that the atmosphere as often as not absorbs the unhealthy substances like a sponge only to drop them later in the form of toxic ("acid") rain or snow—sometimes in neighboring countries.

Where commons resources are scarce, negotiated allocations and/or mutually agreed use rights are usually required to ensure prudent conservation and to avoid bitter conflict among rival users and allocations that are resented as inequitable. If

---

[5]Garrett Hardin, "The Tragedy of the Commons," *Science,* December 3, 1968, pp. 1243–1248.

[6]These ecological determinants of commons-regimes were formulated in Seyom Brown, Nina Cornell, Larry Fabian, and Edith Brown Weiss, *Regimes for the Ocean, Outer Space and Weather* (Washington, D.C.: Brookings Institution, 1977).

the scarce resources also happen to be essentially stationary and divisible, such allocation and use rights may be permanently assigned to particular countries, as has happened with the seabed mineral resources on the continental shelves of coastal states. But where the scarce and valued resources such as healthy air and clean water are vulnerable to contamination as they move through national jurisdictions, neither free use nor national assignment are appropriate, and some kind of authoritative international regulatory regimes are likely to be necessary.

The mismatch between polity and non-divisible commons has become especially threatening, potentially jeopardizing even the healthy survival of the human species in two Earth-enveloping features of the planet's basic ecology. I am talking of the assaults that industrial and industrializing societies are inflicting on the atmospheric and stratospheric gases and particulate matter that are the natural regulators of the Earth's unique and crucial relationship with the sun.

Authoritative scientific studies confirm that the Earth's outer protective envelope, the layer of ozone concentrated 9 to 30 miles above the Earth that shields the planet's living organisms from the sun's harmful ultraviolet radiation (a source of skin cancer), is being dangerously depleted by industrially produced chlorofluorocarbons (CFCs) and halons.[7] Although world society has bestirred itself to reduce the threat to the ozone layer, it took more than a decade from the time of the scientific discovery of this threat in 1974 for the countries most responsible for the CFCs and halons to negotiate international treaties to phase out the source activities and products (see the discussion of the Montreal Protocol and its follow-up agreements in Chapter 9). The signatories then allowed themselves until the year 2000 to complete the phase-out process—the sluggish pace of abatement dictated by corporate and short-term national economic interests, not by physical considerations. Meanwhile the concentrations of ozone-depleting substances in the stratosphere have been increasing and holes in the ozone layer have continued to widen.

The Earth's other protective envelope is made up of atmospheric concentrations of carbon dioxide and other gases that filter the sun's energy to the surface of the planet but convert much of the reflected and outgoing infrared energy into heat: the so-called greenhouse effect. This balance between incoming and outgoing energy is what has kept the planet's climate within those essentially moderate ranges of temperature consistent with the origin and survival of plant and animal (including human) life. But the moderate heat balance maintained by these atmospheric greenhouse gases is being alarmingly perturbed by human activities (especially the burning of fossil fuels and massive deforestation projects) that are thickening the global envelope of greenhouse gases to the point where too much heat is being trapped within the atmosphere—the phenomenon of global warming. If this enhancement of the greenhouse effect is allowed to proceed at expected rates over the coming

---

[7]Bernard J. Nebel, *Environmental Science: The Way the World Works* (Englewood Cliffs, N.J.: Prentice Hall, 1990), pp. 339–345.

decades it could distort the planet's climate, with potentially catastrophic consequences some time in the next century: the flooding of many coastal communities (because of the melting of Arctic ice), the desertification of already arid areas, and the proliferation of disease-bearing bacteria.[8] Although some regions might benefit from the warming (Russian Siberia, for example), the cumulative direct economic consequences and indirect political consequences (from mass migrations out of both the inundated and parched areas) are likely to convulse world society all around the globe in ways that would require draconian supranational measures to keep under control. On this much there is broad consensus in the international science community, despite disagreements over the extent to which the humans have been the cause of the long-term warming trend, and over the extent and pace of temperature increases that can be expected in the coming half century.[9]

There is intense debate, however, when it comes to what to do about the threat: Should the technologically advanced countries invest heavily now in projects for converting to energy sources that do not produce carbon dioxide (such as thermal and solar power)? Meanwhile, should overpopulated developing countries like India and China be dissuaded from petroleum and coal-based industrialization policies? Should affluent industrial countries like the United States (which by itself, with 5 percent of the world's population, produces 30 percent of the world's carbon emissions) change their lifestyles to reduce their energy consumption? Such rational correctives to the basic warming trend are typically featured in prominent *do something!* studies by ecologists and system analysts.[10] But thus far, the movers and shakers of the world polity have shied away from such socially drastic and politically risky policies (the rather innocuous 1992 Framework Convention on Climate Change, discussed in Chapter 9, being a case in point).

In all likelihood, however, human society will eventually need to choose between not exceeding the economic and ecological carrying capacity of the global commons and preserving the traditional structure and norms of the state sovereignty system.

Implications for the Functioning and Structure of the World Polity

Traditionally, where humans consumed, took possession of, or altered nature's "givens," these actions, although constrained by national or local community interests and laws, typically ignored the well-being of outsiders (human and non-human),

---

[8]*Ibid.*, pp. 336–339.

[9]United States Senate, Subcommittee on Substances and Environmental Oversight, *Global Warming: Hearing, December 10, 1985* (Washington, D.C.: Government Printing Office, 1985).

[10]See, for example, Donella H. Meadows, Dennis L. Meadows, and Jorgen Randers, *Beyond the Limits: Confronting Global Collapse, Envisioning a Sustainable Future* (Post Mills, Vt.: Chelsea Green, 1992).

especially those outside of the national community. Moreover, the international indifference was legitimized by the dominant norms and institutions of the world polity.

Despite national variations in the the amount of governmental regulation of private action and in the extent of devolution of regulatory authority to local subdivisions of government, countries the world over lodged ultimate responsibility for ensuring prudent private and community use of natural resources in their national governments. If countries got in each other's way in the use of natural resources, they would negotiate or fight to determine access or shares; and that, for the time being, would be that. But the traditional lack of continuing international monitoring and control of natural resources has become a luxury in the contemporary period, dangerous to the affluent as well as an unjust infliction on the poor.

The required international monitoring and control regimes, if they are to be congruent with the natural commons, in many cases will need to traverse the territorial boundaries of the existing nation-states. This is obviously the case for the *global* ecological commons (the Earth's biosphere, its climate and weather systems, and the great world ocean). Transborder ecology regimes will also be required for many localized biotic, geologic, and atmospheric commons.

If such ecology-protection regimes are expected to incorporate "consent of the governed" principles, the authority of the existing nation-states will in many cases have to be shared with, if not supplanted by, new transnational agencies representing ecologically defined rather than territorially defined communities.

"The political organization of the world is undergoing reconstruction," writes Lynton K. Caldwell. "The *de facto* sovereignty of the 'sovereign nation state' is being modified by new concepts of political responsibility in which environmental imperatives—changes impacting on human welfare—are becoming compelling forces."[11] Similarly, the authors of a 1991 textbook on the political dimensions of environmental problems reflected that a degree of "global governance, which seemed hopelessly idealistic only a few years ago, has been given legitimacy" in the environmental field. And they saw various UN resolutions and international covenants being prepared for the 1992 Earth Summit as marking the "development of legal concepts that . . . reduce the zone of absolute sovereignty of individual states in issues affecting the global environment." These developments pointed toward the possible future acceptance of a more comprehensive

> global governance approach [that] would . . . make the "common heritage of mankind" and "intergenerational equity" legal principles applicable to all global environmental issues that touch on threats to the global commons or natural resources affecting the interests of future generations. Such a revolutionary development in international law

---

[11]Lynton K. Caldwell, "International Response to Environmental Issues: Retrospect and Prospect," *International Studies Notes*, Vol. 16, No. 1 (Winter 1991), p. 1.

would presumably go hand in hand with the transformation of an international system by the creation of a global environmental authority.[12]

To recognize the revolutionary political implications of the growing ecological consciousness, however, is not to predict that these political implications are anywhere near being acted upon in most places nor even to say that they are widely understood. Indeed, as the larger economic and political implications become more widely understood, the likelihood is that they will generate powerful backlashes against the ecological ethos by groups emotionally and/or pragmatically attached to the existing state-sovereignty norms.

Movement toward the degree of global accountability that is needed—which may well eventually involve a revolutionary transformation of the world polity—will therefore probably take place gradually, in small steps that at the outset impinge only minimally on the legal and political autonomy of countries. Elliot Richardson (a former high official of the Nixon administration who took a leading role in the Law of the Sea Negotiations) warns against agreements whose effective implementation would require delegating to multilateral organizations the power to override national environmental policies. A global Environmental Protection Agency that deployed "a legion of inspectors and enforcers," he argues, "rather than increasing compliance, could well have the opposite effect."[13]

This much can be said with confidence: World society is entering an era of intense debate on the structure and powers of political-legal regimes for dissuading humans from unnecessarily jeopardizing their own well-being by perturbing the planet's important ecologies. Unavoidably, many of the political-legal regimes, simply because of the location of the ecologies, will have to be transnational, transregional, and global in membership and scope of authority.

The extent to which the development of such ecology-management regimes will require modification of the structure and norms of the nation-state system is assessed further in Chapters 8 and 9.

---

[12]Gareth Porter and Janet Welsh Brown, *Global Environmental Politics* (Boulder: Westview Press, 1991), pp. 155–156.

[13]Elliot L. Richardson, "Elements of a Framework Treaty on Climate Change," in World Resources Institute, *Greenhouse Warming: Negotiating a Global Regime* (Washington, D.C.: World Resources Institute, 1991), pp. 25–31.

6 Human Rights vs. State Rights

A theory of the world polity pertinent to the most intense political concerns of humans around the world must deal prominently with the issue of the rights and obligations of individuals in relation to the governments that have enforceable legal jurisdiction over them. One of the dramatic features of contemporary world politics is the emergence of powerful popular and intellectual movements challenging the three-century-old interstate norm that the relationship between a country's government and its people is to be determined predominantly, if not exclusively, *within* that country.

The foundational pillars of the traditional state-centric system—the sovereignty of each country's national government and the principle of noninterference by outsiders in any country's domestic affairs—are being assaulted by more than material forces. It is not only the increasing penetration and leaping of state borders by mobile goods, persons, and information that is undermining the strength of these state-sovereignty norms. The capacity of national governments to maintain sovereign authority over what happens within their jurisdiction is also being weakened by the worldwide popular embrace of the idea that a government is legitimate only to the extent that it rests on the noncoerced consent of the governed and secures their basic "human rights."

Ironically, many of the human rights principles that helped transform the dynastic state system into a true *nation*-state system, and that were invoked on behalf of the national independence movements that toppled the great European empires, are now playing havoc with the pluralistic world polity these principles helped to create. Almost all countries today have some ethnic or nationality groups within them who have caught the "self-determination" fever. The shape and "territorial integrity" of virtually every country is potentially up for grabs as ethnic, linguistic, and religious groups proclaim themselves to be nations deserving a state of their own. This historical irony is compounded by the fact that many of the new states in the Third World currently destabilized by separatist self-determination movements owe their existence in large measure to national self-determination demands of the kind now being used against them. And in many of these states, the leaders of the central government—in the name of national *sovereignty*—are repressing the subnational autonomy movements with no less brutality than was used against them by their colonial overlords just a few decades ago. This pattern appears to be repeating itself in quite a few of the states that, under the banner of human rights, seceded from the

Soviet Union in the early 1990s: These governments, too, show little inclination to limit their newly acquired "sovereign right" to deal with their *own* citizens in their own way, unaccountable to transnational human rights norms or agencies. The tensions—sometimes festering beneath the surface, sometimes exploding in violence—between the rights of individuals, the rights of peoples, and the rights of states will not go away. What is becoming increasingly evident is that the traditional world polity, structured as a system of presumably sovereign nation-states, cannot adequately deal with these tensions.

The Human Rights Ethos and Its Historical Antecedents

The diverse assertions and demands that in contemporary political discourse are called *human rights* are those rights and amenities that every individual is supposed to be able to enjoy simply by virtue of being a member of the human species.[1] In the works of the seventeenth-century English philosopher John Locke and in the Declaration of Independence written by his American disciples, all men (the early Lockeans were still gender biased) are "endowed" by nature or God with certain basic rights. On the European continent, these appeared as the Rights of Man, as in the French Revolution's Declaration of the Rights of Man and of the Citizen, proclaiming the liberty and equality of all persons regardless of economic class or social station. They are to be realized on a "universal" scale, as called for in the Universal Declaration of Human Rights, creating obligations in every political jurisdiction to honor and serve them.

Human rights, so conceived, are prior (in an ethical sense rather than historically) to the rights of groups, communities, or states. They inhere in individual human beings. These individual rights are derived directly from conceptions of human nature—that is, they comprise what any human, because of what are assumed to be the essential characteristics and basic needs of the human body and mind, normally ought not to be denied by other humans. For this reason they are often called *natural* rights. By contrast, the rights of collectivities are *artificial*, because the structure of human groupings, unlike the structure of groupings of animals lower on the evolutionary scale, are not given by instinct but are constructed and vary considerably across the species.

---

[1]Jack Donnelly, *Universal Human Rights in Theory and Practice* (Ithaca: Cornell University Press, 1989). See also Morton Winston, "Introduction: Understanding Human Rights," in Morton Winston, ed., *The Philosophy of Human Rights* (Belmont: Wadsworth, 1989), pp. 1–42.

The American and French Revolutions

The view that priority must be given to human rights (which by definition are natural) over the rights of states (which by definition are artificial) was given one of its most compelling political expressions in the American Declaration of Independence, where it was claimed

> that all Men are created equal, that they are endowed by their Creator with certain unalienable Rights, that among these are Life, Liberty, and the Pursuit of Happiness—That to secure these rights, Governments are instituted among Men, deriving their just Powers from the Consent of the Governed, that whenever any Form of Government becomes destructive of these Ends, it is the Right of the People to alter or abolish it, and to institute new Government.[2]

Thomas Jefferson and his co-authors, in their emphasis on "endowed" and "unalienable" rights, were reflecting a long tradition in "natural rights" philosophy, with roots extending back to the "natural law" cosmopolitanism of the Greek Stoics, its reformulation by medieval thinkers such as St. Thomas Aquinas who developed the Church's doctrine that the rulers of states were subject to a higher law, and its liberal-revolutionary metamorphosis in the hands of seventeenth- and eighteenth-century political philosophers in France (especially Montesquieu, Voltaire, and Jean-Jacques Rousseau) and Britain (most notably John Locke).

John Locke's treatises on government constituted a powerful philosophical case for the securing and enhancement of the traditional legal rights of Englishmen, enshrined in the Magna Carta (1215) and the English Bill of Rights (1689). The core of the American justification for separation from the mother country was that the American colonists were being denied what as Englishmen they were supposed to be guaranteed. Significantly, it was largely at the insistence of Locke's Jeffersonian disciples that the new Constitution of the United States of America was ratified in 1789 with ten amendments modeled closely on the English Bill of Rights. Supporting the campaign to amend the proposed Constitution, Jefferson, then the American ambassador in Paris, wrote back to congressional leader James Madison that a "bill of rights is what people are entitled to against every government on earth."[3] But foreshadowing the pattern seen in later movements for "national self-determination," the newly instituted American government, bent on consolidating its power, soon passed its own Alien and Sedition Acts against subversive internal dissent. Moreover, the newest nation-state, while shunning entangling alliances, was

---

[2]*A Declaration by the Representatives of the United States of America*, in Congress Assembled, July 4, 1776.

[3]Jefferson's letter to Madison quoted by Richard Pierre Claude and Burns H. Weston, eds., *Human Rights in the World Community: Issues and Action* (Philadelphia: University of Pennsylvania Press, 1989), p. 4. Weston's lead essay in this volume provides a succinct overview of the historical development of human rights ideas.

content to take its place in the society of nation-states and to endorse the interstate society's norms of sovereignty and mutual noninterference in one another's domestic affairs.

The post-independence recrudescence in the United States of public philosophies giving legitimacy to the claim that the rights of individuals can only be realized in a well-ordered state, and therefore reasons of state must often override the claims of individuals, was consistent with the general reaction among philosophers and states-persons worldwide against the "reign of terror" perpetrated in the name of the Rights of Man by the revolutionary French government. Reacting, too, against Napoleon Bonaparte's incitement of antigovernment liberal/nationalist uprisings throughout Europe (which Napoleon used as a pretext for French imperialist aggression), the United States, by default if not by participation, joined in the nineteenth-century restoration of conservative statecraft. Once again, mutually respectful relations among sovereign governments was supposed to be the hallmark of the legitimate world order.

From Post-Napoleonic Conservatism to World War I

In post-Napoleonic Europe and America the theory and practice of international law again rediscovered its essence in the state-sovereignty–protecting classics of Hugo Grotius, Christian Wolff, and Emmerich de Vattel. International legal scholar Louis Henkin characterizes the restored statist worldview in a form that shows its mockery of its Jeffersonian antithesis:

> All states are [created] equal. They are endowed [by their Creator] with certain [unalienable] *inherent* rights. Among these are [life] *existence,* [liberty] *independence/autonomy,* and the pursuit of [happiness] *national interest.* To secure these rights [governments] *law* is instituted among *states,* deriving *its* [just powers] *legitimate authority* from the consent of the [governed] states. (Brackets and italics provided by Henkin.)[4]

Still, human rights battles, fueled by republican, democratic, and socialist ideologies of the nineteenth century, continued to pervade the post-Napoleonic nation-states—sometimes exploding into revolutionary violence (France in 1839; throughout Europe in 1848) and civil war (the United States in 1861). But according to the reaffirmed Westphalian ideology of *inter*national relations the turmoil was to be confined within the recognized jurisdictions of the sovereign states. Statespersons might meet, as provided for in the post-Napoleonic Concert of Europe, to discuss and assist one another in dealing with situations of domestic insurrection, but they solemnly pledged in rhetoric and treaties not to interfere in one another's domestic affairs.

---

[4]Louis Henkin, "Law and Politics in International Relations: State and Human Values," in Robert L. Rothstein, ed., *The Evolution of Theory in International Relations: Essays in Honor of William T. R. Fox* (Columbia: University of South Carolina Press, 1991), pp. 163–188, quotation from p. 165.

There were, to be sure, some departures in the nineteenth century from the Concert statecraft of mutual respect and mutual restraint and mutual help among governments to put down radical domestic uprisings. The opportunities to weaken a rival imperial power in its sphere of control, particularly when the dissidents demanding their rights were of the same ethnic grouping as one's own citizenry, were sometimes too tempting to resist. Yet for most of the century the prevailing *realpolitik* norms (reinforced by orthodox scholarly writing of international law and diplomacy) were by and large observed: Governing elites remained either indifferent to how their counterparts in other countries dealt with rights issues or actively assisted their fellow conservatives to preserve law and order.

By the turn of the century, however, the disintegration of the Turkish-ruled Ottoman Empire juxtaposed with the declining power of the neighboring Austro-Hungarian Empire gave an unprecedented opening for the Slavic peoples in the Balkans (themselves divided among diverse ethnolinguistic groups) to demand their basic human rights—preeminently the right of national self-determination. When the autocratic Tsar of Russia, perceiving a great opportunity to expand Russia's sphere of influence under the banner of pan-Slavism, began to aid and abet secessionist wars against the Austrians and the Turks, Austria (fearing a radical disintegration of its imperial realm) enlisted the help of Germany in countering the independence movements in the Balkans. Thus was created the combustible cauldron that was ignited into World War I by the assassination of the Austrian Archduke Ferdinand during his July 1914 visit to Sarajevo, a hotbed of Serbian nationalism.

The League of Nations, National Self-Determination, and the Onset of World War II

One of the lessons that President Woodrow Wilson and other liberals around the world drew from the terrible destruction of World War I was that the elemental tension between the rights of peoples and the rights of states could no longer be left to the balance-of-power mechanisms of the nation-state system to control. If new orgies of violence were to be avoided, imperial states that were losing legitimacy with their subjects would have to be induced to allow genuine national self-determination in their realms.

Various minorities treaties and a system of mandates and trusteeships requiring the preparation of some of the world's colonized peoples (most of them formerly under the control of the defeated Central Powers) for self-government were instituted under the League of Nations. But the League's mechanisms for managing national self-determination proved no more effective than its collective security mechanisms, for the League itself was too deeply imbedded in the state-sovereignty system. No individuals, *sub*-state groups, or *trans*-state groups had "standing to sue," as it were, for their rights. Participation in any of the relevant agencies of the

League—deliberative, executive, and judicial—was accorded only to official representatives of recognized national governments. No League agency could have access to any part of the territory of a country or a segment of its population unless such access was officially permitted by the national government of that country. Nor could the Permanent Court of International Justice hold any state accountable to the terms of a treaty it had not signed. Moreover, states could refuse to accept the jurisdiction of the Court.

Given this historical context, it is not at all surprising that World War II was precipitated by powerful states cynically exploiting "human rights" issues: the anticolonial, antiracist themes in the Japanese expansionary power plays in Asia; the national self-determination justifications employed by Hitler for his Anschluss of Austria and his absorption of the Sudetenland in Czechoslovakia.

The Nuremberg and Tokyo War Crimes Tribunals

It took the monstrous acts of genocide perpetrated by Nazi Germany upon civilian populations under its control, particularly the Holocaust against some six million Jews, to generate popular acceptance of the idea that nation-states, even within their jurisdictions, can commit crimes against world society and that some agencies of humankind must be created to hold state officials accountable for such crimes. Claiming that they were acting on behalf of humankind, the governments of the victorious coalition in World War II constituted a postwar tribunal that convicted the top political and military officials of the German and Japanese wartime governments of committing and conspiring to commit "war crimes," "crimes against the peace," and, in the case of most of the Nazis, "crimes against humanity." The legally controversial nature of the trials was underscored by Britain's unwillingness to associate itself with the charge of "crimes against humanity." The British government agreed that "war crimes" and "crimes against the peace" could be derived from treaties on the laws of war and from peace pacts to which the German and Japanese governments had been parties; but the British found no "laws of humanity" from which to derive crimes against humanity. The U.S. and French jurists, however, invoked *natural* law and "just war" concepts (proscribing disproportionate destruction and attacks on noncombatants) in support of the Nuremberg findings that the Nazi death-camp murders of millions of Jews, for example, constituted a gross crime against humanity.[5] In the words of the tribunal's charter,

CRIMES AGAINST HUMANITY . . . [include] murder, extermination, enslavement, deportation, and other inhumane acts committed against any civilian population, before or during the war, or persecutions on political, racial or religious grounds in execution

---

[5]Donald A. Wells, *War Crimes and Laws of War* (Lanham: University Press of America, 1991), pp. 109–126.

of or in connection with any crime within the jurisdiction of the Tribunal, whether or not in violation of the domestic law of the country where perpetrated.[6]

The Nuremberg and Tokyo tribunals went further than any international agency had ever gone in subordinating the actions of nation-states to a presumed higher law of the human community—a law comprising enforceable rights and obligations for *all* individuals by virtue of their being members of the human community.

Other controversial issues of world law and justice also were raised by the Nuremberg and Tokyo trials, not the least of which was the worrisome precedent of victors prosecuting and judging the vanquished. Not surprisingly, the victors failed to subject their own arguably disproportionate acts of war—the firebombing of German and Japanese population centers and the U.S. use of atomic weapons against Hiroshima and Nagasaki—to an international judgmental process analogous to the trial they imposed on their defeated enemies.

The Convention Against Genocide

Although the international legal fraternity continues to debate the legitimacy of the Nuremberg and Tokyo tribunals and their verdicts, one of their legacies was adoption in 1948 by the United Nations General Assembly of the Convention on the Prevention and Punishment of the Crime of Genocide. The Convention outlaws "acts committed with the intent to destroy, in whole or in part, a national, ethnic, racial or religious group." Such genocidal acts include not only killing members of the group, but also causing "serious bodily or mental harm" or deliberately "inflicting on the group conditions likely to bring about its physical destruction."[7]

The Genocide Convention is a uniquely strong international instrument when it comes to enforcement. It obligates all signatories to punish through their own national legal systems persons who have committed any of the enumerated acts, whether the guilty persons are "constitutionally responsible rulers, public officials or private individuals." But signatories are also obligated to submit disputes concerning application of the Convention to the International Court of Justice "at the request of any of the parties to the dispute."[8] It was largely because of the provision for compulsory ICJ jurisdiction that the U.S. Congress, worried about the erosion of national sovereignty, was unable until 1988 to mobilize a majority to approve the Convention.

---

[6]The text of the Nuremberg "Crimes Against Humanity" account is from Victor H. Bernstein, *Final Judgment: The Story of Nuremberg* (New York: Boni & Gaer, 1947).

[7]*Convention on the Prevention and Punishment of the Crime of Genocide,* 78 United Nations Treaty Series 277 (adopted December 9, 1948; entered into force January 12, 1951), Article 2.

[8]*Ibid.,* Articles 4 and 9.

The United Nations Human Rights Regime

It was a foregone conclusion, even before the full extent of Nazi atrocities was exposed at Nuremberg, that the post–World War II order would give unprecedented emphasis to human rights. The anti-Axis coalition, under the leadership of the United States, claimed to be fighting Germany and Japan not simply out of the geopolitical motive of preventing these aggressor states from becoming imperial hegemons but also—indeed primarily, in its public articulation of war aims—to allow all peoples to enjoy the freedoms proclaimed in the Atlantic Charter by Franklin D. Roosevelt and Prime Minister Winston Churchill. The claim surely exceeded the reality. Neither the Soviet Union nor the European colonial members of the coalition had any intention of extending such freedoms as a matter of right to all the peoples within their jurisdictions. And there is considerable evidence in the diplomatic record that FDR was more of a *realpolitik* international statesperson than his democratic rhetoric suggested. But the expectations, once raised, could not be treated lightly after the war.

Thus the Charter of the United Nations, although primarily a pact between countries to collectively oppose aggressors who would threaten the independence or security of any of them, gives preambular prominence to the signatories' determination "to reaffirm faith in fundamental human rights, in the dignity and worth of the human person, [and] in the equal rights of men and women. . . ." And one of the basic purposes of the United Nations enumerated in Article 1 is "To achieve international cooperation in . . . promoting and encouraging respect for human rights and for fundamental freedoms for all without distinction as to race, sex, language, or religion."

Lest anyone get carried away by the Charter's good human rights intentions, however, Article 2, Section 7 provides the sobering caveat: "Nothing contained in the present Charter shall authorize the United Nations to intervene in matters which are essentially within the domestic jurisdiction of any state or shall require Members to submit such matters to settlement under the present Charter." Notably, the reiterated obligation in Article 55 to promote "universal respect for, and observance of, human rights and fundamental freedoms for all" is presented as a means of assuring the conditions of stability and well-being necessary for peace and security, not as an end equal in value to peace and security. And in the provisions establishing the UN trusteeship system, where the states overseeing the trust territories are held to the objective of promoting respect for human rights in these areas, Article 79 reassures member governments that "The terms of trusteeship for each territory to be placed under the trusteeship system, including any alteration or amendment, shall be agreed upon by the state directly concerned."[9]

---

[9]*Charter of the United Nations* (signed at San Francisco, June 26, 1945; entered into force October 24, 1945).

These circumscriptions around the Charter's commitment to human rights are the product of the fact that the United Nations, like the League, was still basically an interstate institution constructed of, by, and for national governments jealous of their sovereign prerogatives. International legal scholars point out that the delegates to the founding conference in San Francisco rejected a Charter provision that would have given the United Nations the mandate to *protect*, not simply to promote, human rights.[10]

The Charter's carefully hedged legitimation of human rights considerations still lagged behind the growing popular support for rights-based democracy as a universally valid public philosophy—an emerging *Zeitgeist* (spirit of the times) with the potential of displacing the traditional Westphalian principles of state sovereignty and noninterference as the normative basis for world law. The spreading ethos of political liberalism could not be denied by statespersons accountable to popular pressures and was given *its* "charter" within the UN system in the form of the Universal Declaration of Human Rights passed by the General Assembly in 1948.

The Universal Declaration constituted an omnibus enumeration, without clear prioritization, of virtually all the demands being made by citizens of their governments around the world—demands that governments not interfere with their civil liberties and guarantee basic amenities like jobs, education, and health care. Unwieldy, cumbersome, and often self-contradictory in its specific provisions, the Declaration was not a treaty requiring ratification by member governments. Being only a resolution of the UN General Assembly it was not, in a formal sense, international *law*. But as pointed out by Louis Henkin,

> Adoption of the Declaration confirmed that the international political system had accepted human rights as a systemic value, and had given it prime place on its political agendas. The international agenda was mainly promotional, as the U.N. Charter had projected, but occasionally, and increasingly, it became also normative and "judgmental."[11]

With the Universal Declaration as their imprimatur, the transnational human rights constituency was able to press ahead with a new aura of legitimacy to translate their demands into binding international and domestic law. Four such instruments, legally binding on their signatories, were adopted by the General Assembly in the mid-1960s and received the requisite number of ratifications by national governments to come into force in the mid-1970s: the International Covenant on Civil and Political Rights (ratified at the time of this writing by some ninety countries); the International Covenant on Economic, Social, and Cultural Rights (ratified by some 100 countries); the International Convention on the Elimination of All Forms of

---

[10]Burns Weston in Claude and Weston, *Human Rights in the World Community,* p. 21.
[11]Henkin, "Law and Politics in International Relations," p. 177.

Racial Discrimination (ratified by some 150 countries); and—the most innovative of all—the Optional Protocol to the International Covenant on Civil and Political Rights (ratified as yet by only thirty-seven countries).[12] The Optional Protocol created the United Nations Human Rights Committee and empowered it to consider written petitions directly from *individuals* who claim that their rights enumerated in the Covenant on Civil and Political Rights have been violated—with the proviso that the claimants must first "have exhausted all domestic remedies."[13] The committee may hold hearings and issue findings, but these findings are informational only and do not have the force of law.

Since their adoption by the UN General Assembly in the mid-1960s, this cluster of basic covenants, increasingly referred to as the "international bill of rights," has in turn spawned a multitude of specialized and auxiliary human rights conventions and forums—further challenging the traditional norm that how a government treats the people in its jurisdiction is its own business.[14]

The European Human Rights Regime

The most progress toward subjecting national governments to international standards of human rights has taken place among the twenty-one member states of the Council of Europe, all of whom are parties to the European Convention for the Protection of Human Rights and Fundamental Freedoms. Signed in 1950, the European Convention (and subsequent protocols) has served as a model for the human rights covenants of the United Nations and other regional groupings, but none of these has gone as far as the European regime in giving individuals the chance to obtain human rights redress from forums outside of their own national systems. The key operational provision of the European Convention is Article 25, which gives the European Commission on Human Rights (established by the Convention) the authority to receive petitions "from any person, nongovernmental organization or group of individuals claiming to be the victim of a violation by one of the High Contracting Parties of the rights set forth in this Convention, provided that the High Contracting Party against which the complaint has been lodged has declared

---

[12]*International Covenant on Civil and Political Rights,* and *Optional Protocol to the International Covenant on Civil and Political Rights,* 9 United Nations Treaty Series 171 (both adopted 1966; entered into force 1976); *International Covenant on Economic, Social and Cultural Rights,* 993 United Nations Treaty Series 3 (adopted 1966; entered into force 1976); and *International Convention on the Elimination of All Forms of Racial Discrimination,* 660 United Nations Treaty Series 195 (adopted 1966; entered into force 1969).

[13]*Optional Protocol,* Article 2.

[14] Myers S. McDougal, Harold D. Lasswell, and Lung-chu Chen, *Human Rights and World Public Order: The Basic Policies of an International Law of Human Dignity* (New Haven: Yale University Press, 1980).

that it recognizes the competence of the Commission to receive such petitions."[15] (Most of the members of the Council of Europe have signed such declarations.) In such cases, the petitioner and the involved governments are obligated to cooperate with the Commission's investigation.

If the European Human Rights Commission is unable to secure a settlement among the parties to a dispute, it draws up a report stating "its opinion as to whether the facts found disclose a breach by the State concerned of its obligations under the Convention,"[16] and proposes next steps to the Ministers of the Council. These next steps may include referring the case to the European Human Rights Court, also established by the Convention. Only states or the Commission (which can represent individual petitioners) have standing before the Court as plaintiffs. But an individual or nongovernmental group that can persuade the Commission or a friendly government to back its complaint can usually obtain a hearing by the Court, in view of the fact that most of the member governments have accepted the Court's compulsory jurisdiction. The seven-judge tribunal has the authority to find a member government to be in conflict with its obligations under the Convention. Moreover, according to the Convention, "the decision of the Court shall, if necessary, afford just satisfaction to the injured party."[17]

An authoritative study of regional human rights regimes published in 1989 found "that the European regime has been genuinely receptive to processing human rights grievances." But the study also reported that over 95 percent of all petitions are screened out during the process and concluded that even in this comparatively progressive system "statist imperatives [still] tend to outweigh the values of human dignity."[18]

An opportunity for expanding the Council of Europe's human rights regime would appear to have emerged out of the post-1989 collapse of the Soviet empire in Eastern Europe. The disintegration of the Communist sphere of control was in large part the accomplishment of reform groups operating in the name of the human rights provisions of the 1975 Helsinki Accords (the 1975 Final Act of the thirty-five-country Conference on Security and Cooperation in Europe), which had been signed, but not honored, by the Kremlin and its satellite governments in Eastern Europe.[19] But any formal broadening of membership in the Council of Europe to

[15] *European Convention for the Protection of Human Rights and Fundamental Freedoms,* 213 United Nations Treaty Series 221 (signed 1950; entered into force 1953), Article 25.

[16] *Ibid.,* Article 46.

[17] *Ibid.,* Article 50.

[18] Burns H. Weston, Robin Ann Lukes, and Kelley M. Hnatt, "Regional Human Rights Regimes: A Comparison and Appraisal," in Claude and Weston, *Human Rights in the World Community,* pp. 209–211.

[19] *Conference on Security and Cooperation in Europe, Final Act,* Department of State Publication 8826, General Foreign Policy Series 298,1975, especially Article 7 ("Respect for Human Rights and Fundamental Freedoms, Including the Freedom of Thought, Conscience, Religion or Belief"), and Article 8 ("Equal Rights and Self-Determination of Peoples").

include the non-Communist Eastern European governments, like the broadening of membership in the European Community contemplated for post–cold war Europe, is controversial, for it could dilute the degree of consensus on various issues that has been achieved in the twenty-one-member Council. Then, too, there is uncertainty over whether the legacy of the 1989–1991 anti-communist revolutions, which were in substantial part nationalistic revolutions against Soviet imperialism, will feature an atavistic return to intercommunal hostilities or a new flowering of cosmopolitan individualism. The outcome of this intensifying post–cold war struggle for the political minds of the peoples of Eastern Europe will depend on the strength and interaction of many of the other trends discussed in this book.

World Society, Human Rights, and the Future of the World Polity: Toward a New Paradigm

A central argument of Charles Beitz's 1979 book, *Political Theory and International Relations,* was that the trends making for an increasingly interdependent world society require a shift in discourse in both domestic political theory and international relations theory—in the former, away from its tendency to confine considerations of justice to what happens *within* nation-states; in the latter, away from its almost exclusive preoccupation with what happens *among* nation-states. It was time to develop a new discourse, and perhaps a new political philosophy, at the intersection of traditional political theory and international relations. The new discourse was to be

> concerned with the moral relations of members of a universal community in which state boundaries have a merely derivative significance. There are no reasons of basic principle for exempting the internal affairs of states from external moral scrutiny, and it is possible that members of some states might have obligations of justice with respect to persons elsewhere.[20]

Beitz's call for a new discourse was reflected in a series of lectures by the distinguished international relations analyst and theorist Stanley Hoffmann (published under the title *Duties Beyond Borders*). One of the most historically informed and philosophically erudite scholars in the "realist" school, Hoffmann now granted that the growing interdependence of peoples was inconsistent with the traditional view that nation-states are self-contained moral communities, immune from the criticism of outsiders for how they deal with their own citizens. He challenged the argument of Henry Kissinger that the best one can do for human rights is to establish moder-

---

[20]Charles R. Beitz, *Political Theory and International Relations* (Princeton: Princeton University Press, 1979), pp. 181–182.

ate interstate relations. Rather, in the human rights field, said Hoffmann, we are increasingly experiencing "the collision between man as a citizen of his national community and what could be called an incipient cosmopolitanism, or man as a world citizen." When we deal with human rights, he observed, "we are in the typical problem of the in-between—moving toward Kant's notion of cosmopolitan law, yet held back by the fact that the chief actors in world affairs are the states, frequent violators of human rights."[21]

Hoffmann's modified "realist" view finds support in the assessment from British international political theorist R. J. Vincent that because political power remains concentrated at the level of the state, "any scheme for moral improvement has to find its way in this world of states."[22] But, like Hoffmann, Vincent does not therefore retreat into the traditional statist model. It does not mean, he says, "that we simply bump up, finally, against the buffer of the state."

> For we have observed the reality of a transnational world from which proposals about the rights of humans come. . . . Individuals and groups other than states have forced themselves on the attention of international society, and the international law of human rights has been both the response to this and the handle for further progress.[23]

Professor Vincent's balanced and sober assessment includes a striking conjecture of a kind that I have been encountering rather frequently in recent years on the part of historically knowledgeable international relations scholars: "'Realists' . . . may be missing a transformation from international relations to world politics as significant as that which established the society of states, and for which the idea of human rights is a kind of midwife."[24]

---

[21]Stanley Hoffmann, *Duties Beyond Borders: On the Limits and Possibilities of Ethical International Politics* (Syracuse: Syracuse University Press, 1981), pp. 95–96.

[22] R. J. Vincent, *Human Rights and International Relations* (Cambridge: Cambridge University Press, 1986), p. 124.

[23]*Ibid.*, pp. 151–152.

[24]*Ibid.*, p. 128.

7 The Incongruity of
Society and Governance
in the Nation-State System

In Chapters 1 through 6, I attempted to explain the emergence and persistence of some of the most problematic features of contemporary world society: global anarchy; insufficient cooperation among peoples across national borders; the prominence of war as a means of dealing with international conflict; gross maldistributions of economic amenities; threats to the health of essential planetary ecological systems; and the large area of contradiction between the quest for human rights and the norms of the nation-state system.

I have found that much of the explanation lies in the basic institutions and norms of the world polity itself rather than in nature, in science and technology, or in the economy. And there is often a common source of trouble: an insufficient correspondence between the world's overall political anarchy and other aspects of world society that are becoming more integrated. Looked at as a whole, the world polity—still rather rigidly structured as a nation-state system—lacks congruence with the human groupings that are increasingly determining who gets what, when, and how in world society.

A well-functioning polity normally features an essential congruence between, on the one hand, the effective authority possessed by society's governing institutions and, on the other hand, the behavior that must be constrained by government in order to maintain or further society's values. By contrast, where behavior escapes needed governmental constraints—as it so often does today in the global nation-state system—we do not have a well-functioning polity.[1]

---

[1]My use of the term *congruence* as an analytical concept is similar to its use by Robert C. Johansen in his groundbreaking book, *The National Interest and the Human Interest: An Analysis of U.S. Foreign Policy* (Princeton: Princeton University Press, 1980). "Rapidly changing technology and patterns of interaction," writes Johansen, "are making societies inseparable from one another, but the present pattern of international political participation remains unchanged. . . . As this incongruity between political institu-

Congruence, in this sense, does not imply institutions of governance that, on the model of "statist" regimes, intervene heavily to control human behavior throughout the society: Governance/society congruence can exist in sufficient measure in relatively permissive or laissez-faire regimes—which in many locales and realms of human activity may well be the type of polity most conducive to the realization of societal values. But the concept does imply at least a *capacity* of government to mobilize and apply sanctions and incentives to constrain the behavior of relevant elements of society as required to maintain society's essential structure and norms. Indeed, the lack of capacity for authoritative self-governance, especially if this deficiency is widely perceived throughout the society, is one of the conditions conducive to political violence; because without enforceable rules for managing conflict, those whose interests clash have little to rely on besides raw power to constrain their adversaries from simply grabbing and taking.

The Traditional Sovereign State System

For three centuries the world polity has been premised on a particular pattern of governance/society congruence: the expectation that the most intensive patterns of human interaction would take place within territorially defined jurisdictions, each having its own regime of governance (or "state") whose supreme authority over what happened in its jurisdiction would be recognized and respected by the other states. Attempts to intervene in another's jurisdiction would be considered illegitimate, and grounds for war.

Each of the presumably sovereign states would control interpersonal and intergroup behavior within its jurisdiction so as to provide at least the minimum personal and institutional security necessary for the performance of basic societal functions: the protection of persons and property from physical attack; the enforcement of laws and contracts; the orderly exchange of goods and services; the husbanding of resources essential to the healthy survival of the population; and the maintenance of the society's cultural, moral, and legal norms, including the rights and obligations of individuals and standards of distributive justice.

Because these basic functions of society and governance in the traditional world polity were to be provided *within* each of the sovereign "nation-states," international or transnational interactions could be relatively sparse and could be managed for the most part by negotiation or periodically (in cases of conflict unresolvable through

---

tions and social needs is allowed to deepen, self-government will be undermined . . . because it will be unable to respond to citizens' needs" (p. 11). He finds the source of many U.S. foreign policy problems in "the incongruity between the *functional unity* and the *political disunity* of the globe" (p. 17).

peaceful bargaining) by war. Looking at the world from this perspective, there was no crucial incongruence between the configuration of global society and the anarchic structure of global governance, for global society itself was compartmentalized into national enclaves of human interaction. Most countries would be willing to take their chances in the anarchic world polity when it came to handling international relations, in preference to subordinating the sovereignty of their territorial unit to "supranational" governing bodies purporting to act on behalf of some larger inchoate international community, let alone a nonexistent worldwide community of humankind.

The Contemporary Pattern

Obviously, today's world polity departs considerably from the traditional picture of a global society of sovereign nation-states interacting with each other only at the margins of their existence. Indeed, the contemporary world exhibits a growing incongruence between the dynamic trans-jurisdictional mobility of persons, things, and information and the comparatively static institutions of national governance—to the point where, without hyperbole, the anarchically structured nation-state system can be characterized as being in crisis. This systemic crisis is an expression of the increasingly perceived (and very real) incongruities worldwide in society/governance relations along five dimensions: (1) the protection of community values vs. the destructiveness of warfare; (2) the behavior of the economy vs. the structure of the polity; (3) the location of ecological systems vs. political boundaries; (4) pluralistic cultural identities vs. loyalty to a given nation-state; and (5) human rights vs. state sovereignty norms.

The Incongruity of War with Community Values

The nation-state system, being essentially of anarchic structure, has compelled each country (acting on its own, or with assistance from allies) to be able to credibly threaten military action to protect its independent existence and highly valued interests. To be sure, countries not able to marshall such military capabilities can survive as sovereign states, but only at the mercy of those with the power to violate their autonomy. To the extent that the nation-state system is pervaded by such highly vulnerable states, its basic foundations are severely undermined; for the system's essential norms of national sovereignty and nonintervention are sustained ultimately by mutual military deterrence, not mutual mercy.

But when going to war involves placing the national community at high risk of virtually total destruction—which today's military technology makes all too likely—an intolerable disproportion arises between the ends and means of foreign policy: No foreign interests, save perhaps those essential to the defense of the homeland itself, are worth the destruction of one's entire national community. As the disproportion grows between the values that are supposed to be protected by the exercise of military power and the values that must be risked in a big war, the international system of presumably sovereign nation-states is fundamentally undermined in its principal sustaining mechanism. Countries lacking sufficient military force of their own to deter provocations from a great power armed with awesome destructive capabilities are no longer able to count on allies to redress the threatening imbalance of power. Formal "mutual security" pacts are coming to be widely regarded as hollow commitments, unlikely to be honored at moments of truth. NATO and the Warsaw Pact, under the impact of Mutual Assured Destruction capabilities, were experiencing this profound crisis of credibility just at the time that the demise of the U.S.-Soviet rivalry rescued them from facing up to their strategic obsolescence.

In parallel with the crisis of confidence over the viability of alliance commitments, there is a growing worldwide understanding that a war on the dimensions of either World War I or World War II fought with the weapons now in the arsenals of the great powers could put the survival of the entire human species in jeopardy. Accordingly, a global "community" does now exist (in both elite and popular perceptions) with respect to at least the shared vital interest in avoiding such a war. But there is still no effective institutionalization of that global community interest. The United Nations organization is the closest the world has come to such institutionalization, yet the UN clearly lacks the power to constrain the behavior of the actors in a position to catalyze the species-threatening holocaust. (The Security Council's authorization of members' use of military force in 1991 in response to Iraq's invasion of Kuwait was not an adequate test of the UN's capacity for collective security actions against great powers.) Unlike the nation-states themselves, whose governments are assumed to monopolize the legitimate violence capabilities of the national community, the putative global survival community has no comparable monopolization of violence capabilities.

In short, contemporary world society still operates with a growing incongruity at the most fundamental level: (1) the inherited political/legal forms for securing the physical survival of national communities; and (2) the vulnerability of these communities to virtually total destruction at each other's hands—a mutual vulnerability that (despite some flirtation with the fantasy of strategic population defense systems) the inherited political/legal entities, as long as they maintain their sovereign autonomy, have no real power to overcome.

The Incongruity of Economy and Polity

Whereas at the level of individual countries we can observe substantial congruence between the economy and the polity (and often talk about the political economy of a country), at the trans-country level, the economy is increasingly functioning at cross purposes with the polity—the nation-state system and its legal norms of national sovereignty and noninterference by foreigners into a country's domestic affairs. This is an incongruence with fundamental implications for the durability of the nation-based structure of the world polity. When a country's policies for regulating national markets can be avoided or overwhelmed by transnational buyers, sellers, and investors, the national polity is eroded at its very essence: the capacity to sustain, at least within the country's borders, public safety and health, orderly commerce, social justice, and integrity of the national culture.

This growing incongruence between transnational economy and national polity is a basically irreversible trend, emanating from the irrepressible efforts by humans to increase the range and ease of exchanging goods, services, and ideas. The intelligence and inventiveness of the human species, in enhancing the mobility of persons, things, and information, has been radically transforming the meanings of both natural geographical space and artificial political borders.[2]

In the 1790s it took a few years to circumnavigate the globe. In the 1990s jet aircraft can fly around the world in less than a day, and spacecraft can orbit the Earth sixteen times each twenty-four hours. Communications technology has effectuated even more dramatic compressions of time-distance relationships. By bouncing signals off of Earth-orbiting satellites, electronically processed sounds and visual imagery can be sent almost instantaneously from any point on Earth to any other point. And photographic and heat/energy sensing devices on observation satellites can obtain and transmit data on the geology, weather, crops, and other resources of any locale on the planet.

Countries, corporations, and even individuals in possession of (or with rights to use) the advanced transportation and communication systems—particularly when combined with capabilities for sophisticated information processing and data analysis—are often able to "access" (a new verb of the times) the markets and economic information of others worldwide, leapfrogging, as it were, controls on ingress and egress at national borders and other traditional legal mechanisms by which countries have attempted to maintain sovereignty over their own economies.

More than ever before, in fields central to the economic functioning and well-being of a country, investors and producers and sellers and buyers are thickly linked in networks of interdependence with their customers or suppliers in other countries. In some of these fields (for example, telecommunications broadcasting, oceanic shipping, air transport, international banking) the networks of interdependence have given rise to formal organizations representing governments and private industry groups, with the latter frequently playing the most influential roles. In other fields (for example, petroleum, basic agricultural commodities, electronics hardware and software) the relations between producers and consumers—sometimes involving negative interdependencies—are intensely bargained out through cooperative negotiations or coercive threats, with transnational interests often colluding in price, sup-

[2]Lester R. Brown, *World Without Borders* (New York: Praeger, 1974).

ply, and market-share arrangements and to bring pressure on their respective national governments.

Multinational/multiproduct firms are both the creatures and exploiters of the new mobility and interdependencies. Manufacturing as well as sales of the products of these corporations takes place worldwide, making the boardrooms of some of these multinationals today's functional equivalents of the imperial chambers of previous centuries: By their unilateral "sovereign" decisions to invest capital here or there, to build roads and seaports, or to pull up stakes for a more congenial locale, these *neo-imperialists* can drastically affect the life chances of people the world over (positively or negatively), often with less political, let alone legally enforceable, accountability than even the old mercantilist imperialists.

The technologically sophisticated movers of capital—whether they be goods-producing firms, banks, investment houses, or money brokers—have become the powerful movers and shakers in the new global economy. As put by the chairman and chief executive officer of the Unisys Company,

> In the financial marketplace . . . the ability to develop and gain access to vast data bases, to handle complex computing with lightning speed, and to communicate instantaneously, has had a profound impact. . . . First, information is now universally available, in real time, simultaneously, in every financial center of the world. Second, technology has tied all the principal countries and world financial and banking centers together into one integrated network. Few countries or parts of the world can any longer remain insulated from financial shocks and changes, wherever they may occur. Third, technology has made possible the establishment of a new, comprehensive system and highly efficient world market to match lenders and borrowers, to pool resources and share risks on an international scale without regard to national boundaries.[3]

The new transnationalism in the global economy is producing, willy-nilly, a new transnational axis of political alignment—often more tacit than explicit. The new alignment not only cuts across the post–World War II East-West, North-South groupings of countries but also is cutting across political party and interest-group alignments within countries that heretofore have focused primarily on the roles government should play in the domestic economy. On the one side of the new alignment are those entrepreneurs, professionals, farmers, and blue-collar workers who see themselves benefiting from the increasing mobility of persons, goods, information, and money and are willing to take their chances in the larger markets this is creating; they stand for global free trade and the removal of domestic barriers to transnational commerce. On the other side are those most likely to lose from a fully open international economy (again, in all sectors of the economy): those who have

---

[3]W. Michael Blumenthal, "The World Economy and Technological Change," *Foreign Affairs*, Vol. 66, No. 3 (special issue on "America and the World 1987/88," 1988), pp. 529–550, quote from pp. 537–538. (Blumenthal was secretary of the U.S. Treasury, 1977–1979.)

found a niche in the domestic market as a result of special governmental protections and subsidies that give them a competitive advantage over foreign competition.

The much lamented lack of "party discipline" in the domestic politics of most countries, as well as the disintegration of some of the most important interstate coalitions of recent decades—the North Atlantic economic community, the Soviet-led COMECON grouping, the Organization of Petroleum Exporting Countries (OPEC), and the Third World "Group of 77"—are all attributable, at least in part, to this growing incongruence between the new transnational relationships in the emergent global economy and the dominant associational bases of the polity in the traditional nation-state system.

Efforts to achieve a new congruence between economy and polity on a regional basis, most prominently thus far in the European Union, are also in danger of being overwhelmed by the rapid globalization of economic interdependencies and the transnational/trans-regional political alignments this is spawning.

The Incongruity of Ecology and Polity

The planet Earth's natural ecological patterns—the interdependencies among plant and animal life and the geological and meteorological environment—have often directly influenced the location and form of organized human communities; but ignorance, short-sighted indifference to the long-term effects of their current disruptions of nature, and territorial conflicts between human communities have just as often made for a substantial lack of match between the spatial dimensions of human communities and the world's basic ecological patterns. Indeed with our growing technological capabilities (and conceits) for altering nature's "givens," most territorially specific political jurisdictions, originally formed in part to harness an area's natural ecologies, are becoming less and less congruent with dimensions of the ecologies that are being perturbed.

Some of the perturbed ecologies are global in scope; and nature's reactions to the assault on these ecologies—cancer-producing sun rays flooding through the depleted ozone layer; excessive global warming from the thickening of greenhouse gases in the atmosphere—threaten to punish the human species for its arrogance and indifference toward the other living and nonliving inhabitants of the planet.

Some of the most tangible and immediately visible disturbances are against natural ecologies that, while transnational in scope, are still local and regional. The resulting disputes among neighboring countries are of the kind that historically have been least susceptible to noncoercive diplomatic resolution in the anarchic world polity. To the traditional war-provoking conflicts over rights to navigate, fish, or divert the waters of rivers, lakes, or seas used in common by various countries we now have added conflicts over the pouring of effluents into such bodies of water that can degrade their value for other users. Similarly, the growing awareness of how the injection of industrial byproducts into the planet's other highly mobile medium—the atmosphere—can severely injure agricultural productivity as well as cause life-threatening human illness in neighboring populations has multiplied the opportunities for nations to get angry at one another. In addition, trans-border injuries caused by mega-accidents such as nuclear power-plant meltdowns and oil-tanker spills further expose the inadequacy of the existing international political/legal order to handle the interdependencies and mutual vulnerabilities of peoples across national lines.

"Put bluntly," writes Jessica Tuchman Mathews, vice president of the World Resources Institute,

> our accepted definition of the limits of national sovereignty as coinciding with national borders is obsolete. The government of Bangladesh, no matter how hard it tries, cannot prevent tragic floods [without] . . . active cooperation from Nepal and India. The government of Canada cannot protect its water resources from acid rain without collaboration with the United States. Eighteen diverse nations share the heavily polluted Mediterranean Sea. . . . Indeed, the costs and benefits of alternative policies cannot often be accurately judged without considering the region rather than the nation.[4]

Although the impact of new technologies, *and* scientific awareness of the ecological implications, has widened and heightened both the fact and perception of the incongruities among ecologies and existing national polities, it has not yet engendered sufficient collateral motivation to mobilize communities transnationally to deal effectively with the implications. Relatively speaking, therefore, the political/legal lag behind the material realities of ecological interdependence is greater than ever.

The Incongruity of Nation and State

Although commonly referred to as a "nation-state system," the world polity has never been in a condition in which virtually all nations have states of their own or all states are essentially congruent with the nations they purport to represent. To be sure, each of the world's recognized countries—unless in the throes of a civil war—normally comprises both a state and a nation congruent with its territorial jurisdiction: a country-wide set of institutions and officials with at least the legal writ (if not actual power and authority) of supreme governance throughout the territory; and a collateral country-wide set of symbols, rituals, and myths reflecting (or designed to create) a common and distinctive cultural identity among the inhabitants of the territory. But in any slice of time, some of the world's many ethnic groups who consider themselves to be culturally distinct "nations" will have members that are a significant portion of the population of more than one country; and almost every country will contain some such ethnic groups who are not substantially assimilated into the dominant culture, perceiving themselves to be a distinct nation within the

---

[4]Jessica Tuchman Mathews, "Redefining Security," *Foreign Affairs*, Vol. 68, No. 2 (Spring 1989), pp. 162–177, quotation from pp. 174–175.

larger nation-state, and in some cases even alienated from the country's dominant ethnic groups.

These incongruities, on the one hand, between the shape of countries that purport to be the dominant focus of national loyalties for their populations and, on the other hand, the living spaces occupied by peoples with alternative national loyalties, have played havoc with established political boundaries throughout modern history. One of the principal precipitants of war has been the effort by one or another of the nations that have been fragmented by existing boundary lines and/or compelled to adopt the cultural ways of the dominant ethnic group of their state to redraw existing political jurisdictions so as to match their strongest national loyalties.

Some world-order reformers have proposed that this cause of war could be largely eliminated through "national self-determination" plebiscites (a dream of President Woodrow Wilson). But unless such plebiscites include arrangements to allow the losers to obtain citizenship in a jurisdiction in which *they* would be in the majority, this determination by vote of the basic national identity of each nation-state could still leave about just as many alienated minority subnations within states as before. Plebiscites might eliminate some regimes in which an ethnic or religious minority previously lorded it over a majority of different ethnic or religious makeup; but, assuming the perpetuation of the state-sovereignty system, there would be no guarantees against the newly installed majorities tyrannizing the now-deposed minorities unless such guarantees were specifically provided in the constitutions of particular countries.

Contrary to conventional expectations, neither democratization nor modernization has, in the aggregate, forged greater congruence between the nations and the states of the world. Indeed, some of the bitterest communal conflict has occurred in democratic polities: Catholics against Protestants in Northern Ireland; the Flemish-Walloon rivalry in Belgium; and separatist agitation by the Francophone Quebecois of Canada. And concurrent with the dismantling of the Soviet state in the late 1980s and early 1990s came a flare-up of fanatic separatist nationalism in the Baltic states, the Ukraine, and Kazakhstan, bitter communal strife among rivalrous ethnic groups in the southern Soviet republics of Azerbaijan and Georgia.

Modernization and democratization, rather than assimilating diverse ethnic groups into a homogenized greater nation, have put previously dispersed or repressed members of ethnic subcultures in touch with their "brothers" and "sisters" and provided communal leaders with both the technical wherewithal and the philosophical justification to mobilize such groups to assert their collective "rights." Increased literacy, mobility, and exposure to the standards of living enjoyed by other groups often generate feelings of relative deprivation,[5] which are translated into

---

[5] See Ted Robert Gurr, *Why Men Rebel* (Princeton: Princeton University Press, 1970); and Samuel P. Huntington, "Civil Violence and the Process of Development," *Adelphi Papers*, No. 83 (London: International Institute for Strategic Studies, December 1981).

demands for rectification—either through redistribution of society's privileges and amenities, or by granting political autonomy to the aggrieved ethnic group.

In sum, nations (being states of mind more than territorial entities or tangible institutions of government) are constantly in the process of forming and reforming in response to changes in the interaction and dependency patterns among human groups—patterns that under the impact of new technologies are being altered more dramatically and swiftly than ever before. The national identities by which the peoples of the world differentiate themselves at any point in time may give way in subsequent periods to alternative national groupings, making the latter intensely uncomfortable with governments premised only on the salience of the older national identities. More and more, the congruence of nation and state, where is does exist, is fortuitous; and nation-states are becoming increasingly unstable as foundational units of the world polity.[6]

The Incongruity of Basic Human Rights and State-Sovereignty Norms

The idea that every human being, simply by virtue of being human, has certain basic rights vis-à-vis all other human beings and that governments are created to secure these rights—in other words, that all individuals are "naturally" endowed with rights, but governments and other collectivities possess merely artificial and recallable powers—is at tension with the normative foundations of the nation-state system. This "rights of man" theory (an impetus for and mobilizer of the eighteenth-century American and French revolutions, the twentieth-century decolonization movements, and the 1989–1990 "revolution" in Eastern Europe against Marxist-Leninist regimes) contradicts the philosophy, still dominant among statespersons and international relations theorists, that human rights have no independent existence outside of well-ordered states.

The established state-centric view—with roots extending back to Plato and Aristotle, and elaborated variously by St. Thomas Aquinas, Edmund Burke, and John Stuart Mill, with contemporary expressions as diverse as Walter Lippmann, Michael Walzer, and Mikhail Gorbachev—holds that a stable and durable political community is at least the necessary context for, if not the source of, individual rights. The implication (sometimes made explicit) is that the existing governing institutions of the recognized national polities must be respected as the agencies for making the sometimes painful trade-offs and allocations among various rights claimants within each country. For each country is assumed to comprise a people

---

[6]I have elaborated on this volatile and subjective nature of nationhood in chapter 12 in *New Forces, Old Forces, and the Future of World Politics* (New York: HarperCollins, 1995).

with a special history and evolved culture, even if multiethnic, which is embodied in its political system, and which it is the state's role to nourish and protect against outsiders. Unless the government in power forfeits this trust by extreme (virtually genocidal) measures against its citizenry or by so trampling on the rights of significant minorities that it provokes civil war or secession, foreigners (including those who purport to represent the "international community") have no grounds for intervening. Additionally, according to this view, international stability and peace require that national governments forbear from supporting rights claimants within another state's borders. (Here we have the "realpolitik" justification for the Bush administration's aloof stance toward the Chinese government's massacre of student demonstrators in Tiananmen Square in the summer of 1989.)

The traditional state-centric view, however, has come under increasing assault in recent decades. The biological and social sciences confirm the commonality, despite cultural differences, of the basic human needs of subsistence, security, love, and (in varying manifestations) dignity of the person. The proposition that all of us, by the fact of being human, have a right to at least minimal satisfaction of these needs has come to command nearly universal assent. The intellectually derived correlative that servicing such basic human rights is the principal task of human polities, and that the worth of any polity is a function of how well it performs this task, has put the legitimacy of all extant polities up for grabs, so to speak. Whether particular nation-states, and the prevailing territorial demarcations, do indeed merit the badge of political legitimacy is, according to this view, subject to continuing assessment; accordingly, neither today's governments nor today's borders are sacrosanct. Moreover, those currently located outside of existing jurisdictions may well have a claim to be part of the relevant community of human rights assessors; this is particularly the case where ethnic, religious, ideological, class, occupational, and professional "brothers" and "sisters" are in intense communication with each other across national borders.

Thus, the increasing mobility of persons and ideas, along with the mobility of economic goods and services, is creating more than societies of material interdependence incongruent with the political/legal jurisdictions of the nation-state system; it is also creating (or re-creating) transnational, trans-border community identities and political loyalties. At best (for the persisting primacy of the nation-state system), the transnational human rights constituencies will be expressed merely in cross-cutting associations of individuals and groups who, when it comes to determined assertion of their claimed rights, nevertheless will be inclined to accept the dispensations rendered by the national legal and political system in which they reside. At worst, the transnational human rights constituencies will openly challenge and defy the authority of the nation-state–based political systems to render legitimate dispensations; and through civil disobedience or violence, perhaps organized transnationally, they will prevent the established polities from functioning effectively.

The worst-case scenario of a de-legitimation of nation-state authorities is increasingly plausible, and may be the most probable outcome over the next few decades of the spread of the individualistic human rights ethos, unless there is considerable institution building in the world polity to create political and legal authorities that will be more congruent with various human rights constituencies than are the existing nation-states and that will be regarded as legitimate arenas for mediating and adjudicating conflicting human rights claims.

Part Two

Toward Normative Theory

8 The Normative Framework

The shape of the contemporary world polity, and the way it will be transformed in the years ahead, is not simply given to us by natural laws of political evolution. The choices political leaders and their constituents make at any point in time can profoundly affect the evolution of the world polity, and these choices are, at least in part, the result of preferences for particular ways of life as opposed to others.[1]

I am talking here of judgments that are substantially the result of beliefs about the moral worth of the object or condition preferred, and not simply judgments about practicality, utility, feasibility, and the like. Such "normative" judgments typically include ideas about what is fair and equitable, what is just, and what constitutes ethical behavior; in the political realm these evaluations are applicable to the substance of public policy as well as to the decision-making process, institutions, and distributions of power that produce policy.

Useful normative discourse is, of course, bounded by preliminary assessments of what is or is not plausible. The range of realistic choice now facing us has surely been limited or expanded by choices made in previous historical eras. In other words, Part Two of this book is grounded in Part One. But since our understanding of the multifarious connections between past choice and future options of human society (and how these are constrained by nature's givens) remains at best only rudimentary, we must operate under the assumption that the alternative paths along which the world polity can develop are still quite open. Indeed, the evolution of the world polity may be more open than ever, and more than ever subject to conscious human volition.

---

[1] See Gabriel A. Almond and Stephen J. Genco, "Clouds, Clocks, and the Study of Politics," *World Politics,* Vol. 29, No. 4 (1977), pp. 489–522. My recognition of the way changing normative preferences can alter presumably constant political realities is consistent with, although not identical to, the post-"realist" school of thought in international relations scholarship called "constructivism." See especially Nicholas Greenwood Onuf, *World of Our Making: Rules and Rule in Social Theory and International Relations* (Columbia: University of South Carolina Press, 1989). Although I give emphasis to the fact that what we call political reality is in substantial part shaped by our view of it, I do not embrace the "constructivist" claim that virtually all politically relevant facts of life are "socially constructed" out of the ideas prevailing in the society at hand. From my perspective, certain facts are indeed realities that constitute (or shape) the political facts of life, independent of anyone's mind-set about them—for example, the death and destruction that would be inflicted by the detonation of a one-megaton nuclear warhead on a populous city, or the existence of some six million AIDS cases in Africa in early 1995.

If anything, the growing problem for the human species as we continue to enlarge our powers for altering nature is having so much power to choose, even at the extremes of living, dying, and extinguishing the conditions required for the survival of the species itself, let alone alternative quality-of-life arrangements. We cannot remain innocent of the fact that our various current preferences (or indifferences) can powerfully influence the shape of both domestic and world politics in the years ahead.

The normative considerations (influenced in part by subconscious and inherited predispositions), in conjunction with considerations of feasibility and practicality, will affect the extent to which any of us—the constituents of the world polity—commit our minds, bodies, and material assets to certain courses of action and attempt to convince others to make similar commitments. This interplay among value-driven individuals and groups (including their impact on relatively passive individuals and groups) will be one of the powerful determinants of the essential character of the world polity.

Accordingly, the normative framework set out below is meant to contribute to public debates over what is desirable or undesirable, and consequently to affect the prospects of various developments, in the world polity. To the extent that these arguments are persuasive with leaders of thought and others with political influence, they will affect the way decision makers (including voters) evaluate the costs and benefits of the practical choices facing them. In turn, such changing assessments can also affect academic theories about which features of the world polity are relatively fixed and which are relatively malleable.

The Concept of World Interests

Any framework for assessing world political structures and behavior in the world polity must include assumptions about what is good (or bad) for the world as a whole—particularly its human inhabitants. Just as much of the foreign and domestic policy discourse within countries assumes that there are "national interests" (meaning conditions that are desirable for the whole country viewed as an entity), there is ample reason to think of "world interests" as those conditions that are desirable for the entire planet Earth viewed as an entity.[2]

---

[2]Again, as with the analytical concept of "congruity" developed in Chapter 7, the normative concept of "world interests" developed in this chapter resembles ideas earlier advanced by Robert C. Johansen in *The National Interest and the Human Interest: An Analysis of U.S. Foreign Policy* (Princeton: Princeton University Press, 1980). Johansen proposes a value framework called "global humanism" that "rests on the assumption that the human race is the important constituency to consider" when making foreign policy. The guiding principle for major economic and political decisions would be "the service of human needs, . . . rather than the maximization of national power or corporate profit." With respect to natural resources and ecologies, Johansen would have policymakers give prime concern to the care of "the *entire* planet, the atmosphere around it, and the high seas . . . for both present and unborn generations," in contrast to the national interest approach of valuing the condition of only that part of the planet that lies within (or can directly affect) the country's sovereign territory (pp. 21–22).

Whether and to what extent world interests should override national, regional, or other particular interests and rights—like the question of the priority to be accorded national interests over local or special interests within a country—is left open. The integrity of the whole is not, by definition, of greater value than the integrity of the parts. Unitary states break up into separate sovereign states, sometimes with morally compelling justifications. National interests do not prima facie supersede individual rights. Indeed, in the world polity, traditionally the interests and rights of all presumably sovereign countries have had greater moral and legal standing than claims on behalf of the entire "world community."

What is claimed here, as a minimum, is that there are world interests that have moral value in their own right; and that such world interests, *in addition to* established national and special interests, need at least to be taken into account in evaluating different configurations of the world polity and the behavior of states and other actors in world society.

The World Interests of Highest Value

Once we undertake to specify the substantive characteristics of particular world interests, the issue of the priority to be given any of them over other world, national, or special interests is bound to arise and is appropriate to debate. I have no hesitancy in arguing for and rank-ordering certain world interests and presenting this valuation as an integral part of my proposed theory of the world polity.

The following are my candidates for highest-value world interests. My reasons for nominating them and ranking them vis-à-vis one another and in relation to various national and special interests are indicated. In proposing them as the foundational normative imperatives of the good world polity, I hope to stimulate others to participate in this norm-building effort and to come forward with their candidates for highest-value world interests.

The next chapter elaborates a set of corollary norms structures and conditions that, on the basis of my understanding of how the world works developed in Part One, appear to be necessary for the realization of these normatively imperative world interests.

1. Survival of the Human Species.   Clearly, this is the cardinal world interest. Putting aside the issue raised by some Eastern religions as to whether the survival of the human species is more important than the survival of other living things,[3]

---

[3]Some contemporary ecological philosophies also challenge the idea that human survival is necessarily to be accorded higher value than the survival of other aspects of the natural world. See, for example, Lawrence E. Johnson, A *Morally Deep World: An Essay on Moral Significance and Environmental Ethics* (Cambridge: Cambridge University Press, 1991). The embrace of such a "deep ecological" ethic by politi-

humankind's survival is without doubt the necessary condition for the realization of any and every other human value (except, perhaps, salvation in the afterlife). "Survival" here should be taken to mean in a reasonably healthy condition of body and mind (we might debate what this means in fact) so that reproduction of healthy offspring can be sustained into future generations.

This world interest now requires assertion because humans have developed and deployed weapons of war that cumulatively have the potential for turning most of the world's cities into radioactive waste, and these weapons may well be used if past habits of heart and mind and militarized diplomacy persist into the future.

The survival of the species is also placed at risk by nature-altering agricultural and industrial processes and technologies capable of severely disturbing the meteorological and ecological conditions of the Earth's biosphere that sustain human life. These biosphere-disturbing activities are undertaken by national societies, corporate firms, or other special entities in the service of their particular interests, usually with no hostile intent whatsoever toward outsiders, but also with little if any reference to larger community interests. The "external" negative effects often do not in a directly calculable way hurt those who produce them, even though, cumulatively, they may eventually degrade or reduce the value of the entire human population's essential life-sustaining resources.

2. Reduction in the Amount of Killing and Other Extremely Brutal Treatment of Human Beings.

I feel no hesitation in asserting this as a world interest—a priori, as a self-evident good requiring no other justification, mindful, of course, that its pursuit, like the pursuit of any good, may on occasion have to be constrained in order to avoid greater value losses.

Killing and torture of one's fellow nationals is regarded as evil *within* most countries, except during periods of civil war, unless justified by the necessity of preventing at least as great an evil (usually also killing or torture), and the prohibitions are usually backed up by stringent legal sanctions. There are a few communities in which simple reprisal killing not required for deterrence of future violence is still condoned, but this older retributive standard is disappearing.

A universal extension of the imperative of reducing physical violence to encompass actions that would inflict death and pain on people with whom one has no ethnic or other primordial bonds would represent a further stage in the evolution of humankind. According to some analysts, this has been happening. The historian John Mueller, for example, sees a process already well under way "in which the insti-

---

cally active environmentalists is analyzed (and endorsed) by Robert C. Goodin, *Green Political Theory* (Cambridge: Polity Press, 1992). I, for one, am not ready to abandon a human-centered value system, nor, do I believe, are most human beings. Indeed, it would be quite a large step in the moral development of most people for them to accept moral responsibility for the survival and well-being of humankind as a whole. Thus, respect for the planet's natural ecologies, although appearing in my list of important world interests, is ranked behind five humanistic interests.

tution of war [at least among the industrialized great powers] has gradually been rejected because of its perceived repulsiveness and futility."[4]

Yet, obviously, not everyone is ready to apply this norm to their own (or their country's) international behavior. For some, the obligation to refrain from all but absolutely necessary violence stops at the borders of their national jurisdiction. Others continue to assert the legitimacy of international military intervention to service various ideational goals (especially the liberation of their ethnic or religious "brothers and sisters" from regimes that deny them their human rights).[5] Moreover, among those who might subscribe to the ideal of a warless world, there are many who consider effective military deterrence—even if it requires the threat to initiate nuclear warfare—as still the most reliable guarantor of peace, short of the establishment of a centralized world government capable of monopolizing the instruments of violence.[6] But to the extent there is a putative world community forming whose constituents are willing to assert their bonds with one another across national and ethnic lines, we may find increasing numbers of influential people bringing pressure on their national and ethnic communities to find alternatives to the traditional "normal" resort to violent means of asserting and defending their group's particular interests.

3. Provision of the Basic Conditions for Healthy Subsistence to All the World's Peoples. This includes, first of all, an obligation to eliminate pockets of starvation and eradicable life-threatening disease. It also includes the elimination of avoidable unhealthy degradation of global and local ecological systems. It starts from the premise that the most basic human right is the right to life (the sine qua non of all other rights), and recognizes that this right can be negated not only by physical violence but also by the denial of the requisites for human survival: uncontaminated and adequate water, food, and air, shelter against climatic extremes, and protection against disease.[7]

My argument for tending to these basic subsistence needs universally is primarily normative and, as with the argument for reducing the amount of killing in the world, a priori in its major premise rather than utilitarian. Utilitarian grounds can be invoked, but they are insufficient. Thus, an argument can be made that some of the

---

[4]John E. Mueller, *Retreat from Doomsday: The Obsolescence of Major War* (New York: Basic Books, 1989), quotation from p. 264.

[5]On the various justifications for military intervention, see Chapter 9.

[6]The American Catholic bishops in their 1983 pastoral letter on war and peace unequivocally condemned the *use* of nuclear or other weapons for mass destruction but still conceded the necessity, under the cold war conditions of the time, of continuing to rely on nuclear *deterrence* while working toward substantial disarmament. National Conference of Catholic Bishops on War and Peace, *The Challenge of Peace: God's Promise and Our Response* (Washington, D.C.: United States Catholic Conference, 1983).

[7]Henry Shue, *Basic Rights: Subsistence, Affluence, and U.S. Foreign Policy* (Princeton: Princeton University Press, 1980).

most lethal diseases (for example, AIDS) cannot be reliably quarantined, and therefore extreme poverty anywhere threatens the well-being of even those who would confine themselves to enclaves of affluence. A parallel argument is that it is in the interest of the relatively affluent to make a good faith effort to ameliorate the suffering of the desperately poor, lest the latter become so alienated and angry at those better off that they organize revolutionary movements and wars to forcibly rectify the maldistribution of resources and wealth. But these propositions about the possible indirect global consequences of local poverty must contend against the reluctance of those who are relatively well off to make current real sacrifices in their standard of living to assure against speculative threats. Accordingly, my argument for a globalized subsistence policy rests ultimately on the deontological grounds that it is simply unjust for some members of the human community to be denied the basic requirements of physical survival while others exist with substantially more than they need. (The issue of devising practical policies to significantly alleviate this inequity will be addressed in Chapter 9.)

4. Protection of Individual Citizen Rights. This category includes the exercise of the standard civil, political, and economic rights—beyond mere survival and subsistence—now claimed by persons all around the world simply by virtue of being human. (The demands for such entitlements put forward by ethnic and religious *groups* on behalf of their collectivity do not always coincide with the individualistic human rights claims, though frequently they are the product of claims that the members of one's group, being discriminated against as a group, are being denied the birthright of equal treatment as individual members of the larger society. The group claims that are primarily for collective rather than individual rights are dealt with under point five below.)

In asserting that the protection of the standard rights of individuals is a highly valued, albeit fourth-ranked, world interest I am deliberately taking issue with the traditional Westphalian normative basis of the nation-state system that puts a higher value on the sovereign autonomy of the recognized nation-states than on the rights of individuals vis-à-vis one another or vis-à-vis governments.[8] And I am challenging the associated rule against interference by outsiders in the domestic affairs of countries.

The Westphalian system, reinforced by Grotian principles of international law (emphasizing mutual respect and sociability among states), originated as a pragmatic requirement for avoiding the total breakdown of civic order in Europe during the seventeenth-century wars of religion. It was a reaction against the unbridled violent intervention of Protestants and Catholics against one another across state boundaries. In the context of the bloodshed and chaos of the time, a codification of an

---

[8]I analyze this tension between "human rights" and "states' rights" in Chapter 6.

anarchic structure among henceforth totally sovereign jurisdictions was clearly preferable to the trans-state anarchy then tearing apart European society.

In the twentieth-century nation-state system, however, an equally important source of bloodshed and violation of elementary standards of human decency has been the lack of international accountability by governments for how they treat the people within their jurisdictions. Whereas the rudiments of interstate civic order might still require a presumptive mutual respect by peoples of one another's systems of governance, that presumption of mutual interstate respect—for both moral and practical reasons—should be accorded legitimacy only to the extent that a national government is not the cause of below-subsistence conditions among its people and to the extent that it rests on the uncoerced consent of the governed.[9]

The universalization of the *claim* to basic human rights is now an unavoidable fact of life. Governments or ruling elites ignore this claim at their peril, at least over the long run. Moreover, the increasing mobility of persons and information assures that, like it or not, human rights conditions in all countries will be globally monitored; and governments known to be gross violators of widely shared standards of physical well-being, political democracy, and due process of law will be subject to exposure and political pressure from other governments, international agencies, and transnational associations to reform their behavior.

5. Preservation of Cultural Diversity. Both as an end in itself and on utilitarian grounds, world society should allow distinct cultural communities (who desire it) considerable autonomy to practice their own ways of life—provided they grant *their* minority communities the same privilege, and provided the exercise of such cultural self-determination does not fundamentally undermine the other highly valued world interests.

The human species, only recently evolved, and still evolving the characteristics that the larger natural system and human volition selects as the traits worth preserving, has yet to find *the* way of life most conducive to the realization of basic human needs and wants. Even those who accept the premises of theistic causality can find ample evidence, in the form of the variety of religions, that the gods are not in complete agreement on the best design of human communities.

Such "communitarian" concepts are often invoked by champions of the state-sovereignty system. In a highly centralized political order—it is argued—cultural diversity would be only that which was permitted by those in control of the world state; and if the ruling world authorities decided to interfere with the way of life of a particular cultural group, that group would have no place else to go. In the decentral-

---

[9]R. J. Vincent, in *Human Rights and International Relations* (Cambridge: Cambridge University Press, 1986), advances a similar argument that the authority of national states ought to be respected, but that this respect should be conditioned in part on their human rights performance. Following Shue, Vincent emphasizes basic subsistence rights performance as the primary criterion and is more equivocal about political rights than I am.

ized world polity, by contrast, if those in control of a country repress the minorities in their midst, the repressed minorities presumably at least have the option of migrating to another country where they will be better treated, or perhaps even constitute the majority culture. Indeed, the opportunity to emigrate has at times provided a safety valve in the nation-state system, allowing for the deflation of dangerously combustible domestic situations that otherwise could lead to full-scale civil war and intervention on behalf of the warring parties.

6. Protection of the Planet's Basic Natural Ecologies and Environment. In addition to protecting those features of the planet's makeup and environment that natural scientists have found are (or may be) essential to the survival of the human species in a healthy condition, my sixth-ranked normative imperative asserts that humans should themselves deeply respect, if not stand in awe of, nature's givens. We are still very primitive in our understanding of the connections in the universe—what causes what, both concretely and transcendentally in space and time—and therefore ought to be highly reluctant to cause avoidable large perturbations in the natural order (or disorder).

The objective should be to serve these ecological values without major sacrifice to the other, higher-priority, world interests and, vice versa, to serve the other normatively imperative ends with minimum sacrifice of ecological values.

7. Expansion of Accountability. All of these world interests imply a greater willingness than in previous historical eras by statespersons, powerful private interests, and general publics around the world to treat the inhabitants of the planet Earth as citizens of a global community. The globalization of economic and ecological relationships has already created a highly interdependent world society; but a society cannot be deemed to be a community unless there is considerable mutual accountability among its members for how they deal with the community's resources and for how they treat one another.

The accountability principle can be stated simply: *Those who can or do substantially affect the security or well-being of others (especially by inflicting harm) are assumed to be accountable to those whom they affect.* Such accountability should apply both "horizontally" (to relations *among* communities) and "vertically" (to relationships *within* communities and institutions).[10]

The need to pay attention to accountability, so defined, was foreshadowed by the diagnosis of the crisis of the world polity in Part One where I argued that world soci-

---

[10]I borrow the concepts of *horizontal* and *vertical* accountability from Robert C. Johansen, "Building World Security: The Need for Strengthened International Institutions," in Michael T. Klare and Daniel C. Thomas, eds., *World Security: Challenges for a New Century* (New York: St. Martin's Press, 1994), pp. 372–397.

ety is experiencing an increasing incongruence between its patterns of material interaction and its political and legal arrangements for controlling these interactions in the general interest. In other words, world society has reached the stage in its evolution in which its polity, like domestic polities, needs to be based on at least the rudiments of community; and this means that the world polity's traditional dominant norm of national sovereignty needs to be accommodated to, if not eventually supplanted by, structures and norms of international accountability.

Dealing with the Tensions and Trade-offs

My prioritization of this set of seven highly valued world interests does not eliminate the problem of managing conflicts among them. The rank-ordering cannot by itself provide the basis for determining how much of any of the lower-ranking, but also—in their own right—highly valued interests (for example, individual property rights or communal autonomy) should be sacrificed in the service of world interests that may be more highly valued (for example, the worldwide elimination of pockets of starvation or the prevention of threats to ecologies that are essential to healthy human survival).

My general prescription is that we should choose courses of action that will involve the least cumulative value loss, when all the highly valued interests are taken into account. This means that, case by case, additional moral reasoning and pragmatic analysis of the consequences are still needed for the tough choices; but we should not expect either philosophy or social science to provide sufficient bases for resolving all the conflicts.

Managing such inevitable difficulties is, after all, the essence of *politics*. In addition to standard international political bargaining, the evolving world polity (if it is to serve the world interests effectively) may well require considerable institution building—that is, the enhancement of the legitimacy and authority of judicial and parliamentary bodies (new ones, if need be) with memberships that are congruent with and representative of the affected communities. This leads to the subject of Chapter 9: the public policy and institutional implications of the normative imperatives.

9 Implications for Public Policy and Institutional Development

This chapter outlines important policies and institutions implied by the normative imperatives set forth in the previous chapter. Given the way the present world system works (as analyzed in Part One), the normative imperatives are likely to remain largely unrealized statements of principle unless their actualization is strongly encouraged by policy initiatives and institutional developments of the kind indicated in this chapter.

Such policy and institutional objectives can be viewed as a second tier of world interests, derived from the other highly valued world interests. This does not mean that the derived objectives are without value in their own right. But their overall importance resides primarily in their function as instruments for achieving the normatively imperative world interests more than in their intrinsic value.

The needed policies and institutions can be grouped under four categories:

- *Policies and institutions designed to keep conflict from escalating to levels of belligerency that could jeopardize the most highly valued world interests* (survival of the human species; reducing violence among humans; healthy subsistence; human rights; cultural diversity; and ecological protection).
- *Policies and institutions designed to prevent major threats to the planet's life-sustaining biospheric environment.* Such policies and institutional instruments are also of great importance, because biospheric destruction, too, whether it occurs in wartime or from peacetime activities, can prevent the realization of most of the other highly valued world interests.
- *Policies and institutions designed to alleviate poverty around the world and ensure that all societies will have the opportunity for sustainable economic development.* Where minimum healthy subsistence is denied, the remaining world interests (human rights, cultural diversity, and ecological protection) have little meaning. Nor are countries harboring large populations of the abjectly poor, and unable to rectify their condition, likely to be good "citizens" of the world polity when it comes to conflict control, biospheric protection, and other fields where mutual international accountability is needed.
- *Policies and institutions designed to foster intercountry and trans-country accountability.* These are needed to bring the world polity into congruence with contemporary social and material relationships.

130

The particular policies and institutions discussed in this chapter are only illustrative of the *kinds* of developments needed to bring a just world polity into being. My selection of items and their capsule analysis are not meant to be definitive, let alone exhaustive. The intention is to stimulate practitioners, policy analysts, and scholars to enter into dialogue on how to translate the public philosophy of the world polity into public policy.

Conflict Control

The increasing availability of weapons of mass destruction requires special vigilance to prevent conflicts from enlarging and intensifying to levels that could precipitate another world war. The required policies and institutions are of two basic kinds: (1) those that deal with the *substance of issues* that are likely to propel opponents into confrontations with a high potential of drastic escalation; and (2) those directed toward controlling the *means of coercion and destruction* employed in ongoing conflicts.

Conflict Moderation Through Dealing with Substantive Issues

The substantive sources of conflicts with the potential of large-scale violence can be handled noncoercively through either, or some combination of, (1) skillful bilateral or multilateral negotiation of outcomes acceptable to the contending sides, (2) acceptance by the parties to the conflict of outcomes proposed by noninvolved, presumably neutral, persons or institutions, or (3) a willingness by the parties to be bound by legislation voted in institutions to which they belong. (These means of handling disputes are discussed under the category of conflict *moderation* rather than the more familiar "conflict resolution" or "dispute settlement" to emphasize the fact that in cases of intense conflict, particularly where the sources are deep and persistent, efforts to moderate the conflicts are often more likely to succeed than are efforts to solve them.)

In well-developed domestic polities, most intense conflicts are handled by one or more of these three methods. Often direct negotiation of differences is conducted within substantive and procedural guidelines already prescribed by legislation and previous adjudication of similar conflicts; yet, such negotiations—even in the domestic arena—are rarely unaffected by mutual perceptions of the power of the parties to get their way in tests of economic or political strength. Where direct negotiations fail to produce mutually acceptable outcomes, parties are enjoined to litigate their disputes through the society's official judicial agencies and to refrain from attempting to violently impose their wills on one another. But the acceptance of the outcomes of such adjudicatory processes, particularly when contending parties are expected to accept substantially less than they were demanding, requires in turn that the parties regard their society's judicial system as legitimate (in the sense of applying just law and applying the law justly) and not simply "the instrument of the ruling class." Finally, if contending groups are to accept as legitimate the outcomes of their society's basic political process of law-making—that is, to agree to be bound by electoral mandates or parliamentary decisions whether or not the votes on particular issues are in their favor—they must experience some successes for their side from these processes so as not to feel that "the system" is fundamentally stacked against them.

These means of conflict management have evolved in domestic polities as pragmatic alternatives to the intolerable disruptions of civic life caused by violent modes of determining who gets what, when, and how. For the reasons adumbrated throughout this book, and specifically elaborated in the following sections, the world polity has attained a condition in which international functional equivalents of the domestic means of conflict management have become equally necessary to the preservation of civic life and, with sufficient political leadership, such pacific means can become practicable.

Negotiation. Within societies, and international society is no exception, negotiation may or may not be heavily relied on as a method of dealing with intense violence-prone conflicts. The dominant normative culture may vary in time and place, with some societies holding up their great negotiators as exemplars and some societies glorifying their macho confronters and warriors. If international society is to experience a major normative shift away from the culture of war heroics and toward the culture that rewards the more creative diplomatic skills, much of the responsibility for helping to effectuate this shift must be borne by scholars, other intellectuals, artists, and people in the media generally.

Negotiation implies a willingness to compromise on some of one's interests in order to achieve an outcome that, balancing advantages and disadvantages, is perceived by each of the sides to be better for them than would be a continuation of the conflict in the absence of such compromises. Successful negotiation, therefore, requires that the parties be able to distinguish between their primary (or "vital") interests and their secondary interests, and that they be adept at bargaining over their secondary interests.

To the extent that the avoidance of war (because of the high risk of mutual devastation) becomes a vital interest of international adversaries, not only the incentives to negotiate but also the prospects of successful negotiation are enhanced—provided that one or more of the adversaries resist the temptation to exploit the rival's fear of war by pretending (bluffing) to be willing to fight rather than compromise even on secondary interests. Thus if the recognition that in a war among heavily armed adversaries there can be "no winners" is to be translated into successful negotiation, their leaders and publics must learn how to be internationally empathetic: Each side must be able to look at conflict situations from the other's point of view and to understand the opponent's definitions of its vital interests. Otherwise, rivals are likely to miscalculate how much they can challenge each other short of intolerable provocation and to misperceive when the opponent's threat to use force is only a bluff or real.[1]

Successful negotiations to defuse war-prone conflicts also require diplomats wise in knowing when to "fractionate" disputes into discrete issues, so that nonnegotiable issues do not hold back agreement on negotiable ones and, conversely, knowing when to "link" the satisfaction of an opponent's enthusiasm for a particular negotiating result that is readily achievable to the opponent's cooperation in achieving a positive outcome in less tractable matters.[2] Again, home-country understanding of and support for this crucial art of diplomatic bargaining can spell the difference between success or failure in conflict-moderation negotiations.

Mediation, Arbitration, and Adjudication. Parties to a conflict are often more willing to moderate their demands on each other if their compromises do not seem to be primarily responses to the opponent's pressure but rather are responses to proposals from a neutral and/or authoritative source. A noteworthy example was Jimmy Carter's mediation in 1994 of the conflict between Washington and Pyongyang over North Korea's threat to renounce its Nuclear Nonproliferation Treaty obligations. The need for national governments to utilize such "third party" services to facilitate compromises in war-prone international conflicts has increased with democratization of domestic polities. Democratic national governments, requiring popular approval in order to make credible threats of military action, usually find it necessary to focus passions of patriotism and national honor on the issues in dispute—passions which are then difficult to quell and which can be mobilized against leaders who appear too willing to concede to an enemy's demands in order to avoid a fight. But for these very reasons, there is a need (from the perspective of the world interest in moderating conflict) to legitimize and enhance the authority of international processes and agencies to deflect the political risks of concession away from insecure national leaders.

The Covenant of the League of Nations went so far as to mandate that all signatories must rely on such third-party mechanisms "if there should arise between them any dispute likely to lead to a rupture." Articles 12 through 15 stipulated that parties to disputes of this sort must submit them either to the Council of the League, to the Permanent Court of International Justice, or to other League-certified international tribunals or commissions for resolution. Countries were prohibited from waging war

---

[1]Seyom Brown, *The Causes and Prevention of War* (New York: St. Martin's Press, 1994), pp. 193–197. See also Hans J. Morgenthau, *Politics Among Nations: The Struggle for Power and Peace,* 5th edition revised (New York: Knopf, 1978), pp. 550–560.

[2]For the theory and practice of the conflict "fractionating" strategy, see Roger Fisher and William Langer Ury, *Getting to Yes: Negotiating Agreement Without Giving In* (Boston: Houghton Mifflin, 1981). An exposition of the "linkage" approach is provided by Henry Kissinger, *White House Years* (Boston: Little, Brown, 1979), pp. 129–130.

against members who complied with the awards or decisions of these bodies; and even in cases of noncompliance, League members were to refrain for at least three months before waging war against violators—the so-called cooling off period.[3] Like the collective security provisions of the League, however (see discussion of "collective security," below), these provisions were rendered irrelevant by the massive aggressive acts of Japan, Italy, and Germany in the period between World War I and World War II.

The United Nations provisions for "Pacific Settlement of Disputes" (Chapter VI of the Charter) revive the League concepts, but in more permissive language:

> The parties to any dispute, the continuance of which is likely to endanger the mainte-nance of international peace and security, shall, first of all, seek a solution by negotia-tion, enquiry, mediation, conciliation, arbitration, judicial settlement, resort to regional agencies or arrangements, or other peaceful means of their own choice.[4]

The most used, and easiest to arrange, third-party process in international society is *mediation* (usually called "conciliation" when the third party is an international commission or board), with the mediator making proposals for compromise, which the parties to the conflict are free to either accept or reject. Especially when conflicts have reached a brink-of-war condition, the potential belligerents are likely to have already convinced themselves that the stakes to the nation are too high to subject to authoritative binding dispensations by presumably neutral international authorities. Usually, the most that can be expected from a national government in such a crisis situation is that it allow international mediators to offer suggestions which it will seriously consider.

The *arbitration* of disputes, relied on heavily in domestic societies for controlling labor-management, interpersonal, and intergroup conflict, is harder to come by in international society because it requires the disputants to accept the formal authority of the arbitrator to issue findings and awards that will be binding on them. Typically such international arbitrators will be panels of judges or arbitrators provided for in special arbitral treaties (or clauses in treaties) that the contending countries have negotiated to cover disputes in particular fields. In the absence of preexisting arbitra-tion arrangements, disputants can agree on the spot to appoint a special arbitrator whose findings they will accept.

When an official court handles a dispute, issuing authoritative findings and bind-ing awards, the process is called *adjudication*. This function is performed among countries by the International Court of Justice (sitting at The Hague, Netherlands) and for intra-European disputes by the European Court of Justice.

Despite the fact that international arbitration or adjudication implies some erosion of the sovereignty of the national governments who agree to submit their disputes to

---

[3]*Covenant of the League of Nations,* signed at Versailles, June 28, 1919.
[4]*Charter of the United Nations* (1945).

authoritative third-party panels, there has been a substantial increase in reliance on such international mechanisms in the last half of the twentieth century that are at least quasi-supranational. Examples of this trend are the proliferation of multinational technical commissions to monitor adherence to intergovernmental agreements on the use or disruption of "commons" resources—in particular oceanic and riparian fisheries, and air and watersheds subject to pollution.

Realistically, the enforcement of adjudicatory or quasi-adjudicatory findings of international bodies (particularly where enforcement involves awarding and denying tangible privileges) still must be expected to remain almost entirely the responsibility of the national governments of the involved parties. As such, international arbitral or adjudicatory findings might seem to carry no more supranational authority than the recommendations offered by international mediators. The difference, particularly for relatively democratic states, lies in the publicly offered acceptance—prior to submission to the international authority—of the obligation to adhere to the authority's findings. National governments that renege on such solemn obligations run the risk of losing legitimacy with their own constituents—unless, of course, there is an overwhelming popular consensus for violating the obligation.

Policy-making by International Bodies.   The third basic approach to conflict moderation is to convene representatives of the concerned states to establish what rules and allocations will prevail in particular fields of contention. The convening of representatives can be in the form of regular meetings of more or less permanent international institutions, such as those of the United Nations system and its sister agencies like the World Bank and the International Monetary Fund. Or ad hoc meetings of groups of countries can be convened to make or revise a set of rules for a particular field, such as the Law of the Sea Conference. Although convened for a special task and then disbanded at the completion of their work, conferences of this type may remain in session for a period of years to complete their work.

Simply by becoming members of such international policy-making bodies, countries are indicating a willingness to be bound by the results of the deliberative processes of the agencies they have joined, even if decisions on particular issues go against their preferences ("You win some, you lose some"). Although member countries still retain the sovereign prerogative of refusal to accept a particular outcome and can withdraw from an international body that too frequently acts against their interests, and although the enforcement of the decisions of any such international body still must be accomplished primarily through and by the legal systems of its members, the presumption of membership is that on balance there is more to be gained than lost by processing one's conflicts with other countries in particular fields through a deliberative international body than by direct might-makes-right confrontations or direct international bargaining only once removed from coercive power relationships. Certainly, the world interest in conflict moderation would favor more countries adopting this presumption in more and more issue areas.

To the extent that world society does come to rely more heavily on global and regional deliberative institutions to define the rights and obligations of governments and to mandate the essential terms of compromises in war-prone international conflicts, their charter provisions concerning membership, representation, voting, and other decision-making rules become matters of major political import. Whereas some world interest norms—especially those premised on equal citizenship rights of individuals—might seem to imply giving substantial legislative powers to general membership assemblies representing numbers of people (not individual countries), it is highly unlikely that the most powerful actors in the existing world system (national governments and multinational corporate enterprises) are anywhere near ready to countenance such a revolutionary transformation of the world polity. So if the enhancement of the role of international deliberative bodies is indeed to service the world interest in conflict control, more acceptable constitutional designs of such bodies need to be advanced. Acceptable designs probably will have to continue to accord substantial authority to national governments, even while granting some representation to important non-state groupings. And voting arrangements, on different issues and in different agencies, will give weight to particular kinds of actors and capabilities whose support is essential for the implementation of the policies voted.[5] As in the current United Nations and its auxiliary agencies, considerable compromise with both the democratic ideal of one person/one vote and the international law ideal of the sovereign equality of states (one country/one vote) continues to be the political price of powerful-actor support for the effectuation of the needed policy-making by world institutions.

Escalation Control Via Controls on the Use of Military Force

Insofar as the intensity of a high-stakes international conflict has not been reduced by finding substantive outcomes acceptable to the parties, war remains an ever-present possibility; and each side, even if not itself inclined to initiate military hostilities, will suspect the other side of inclinations to settle the conflict by war. The tendency on both sides of a conflict, therefore, will be to pay close attention to the military balance of power and to attempt to redress perceived imbalances in their disfavor; the resultant competitive arming and alliance-building can easily exacerbate mutual suspicions of hostile intent, converting mere opponents into deadly enemies, obsessed with the need to deter one another and to be in a position to prevail militarily if deterrence fails.

---

[5]Richard Falk's "preferred world polity" in his *A Study of Future Worlds* (New York: Free Press, 1975), while contemplating a radical centralization of power in a global institution, features a multihouse legislative body with voting rules to assure that any binding world law produced by the global institution must be based on a very widespread and solid consensus.

Realistically, therefore, in the absence of a fundamental reform in the structure of the world polity that would accord a global supranational authority a monopoly over the most powerful instruments of violence, the world interest in preventing conflicts from escalating into wars of species-threatening dimensions requires special controls on the deployments and uses of the military forces that remain dispersed among the nations.

These controls include ideational, material, and institutional restraints on the resort to military force—some of which can be implemented unilaterally, some of which require multilateral agreement and enforcement. The available menu of such controls features the reassertion of "just war" principles, non-provocative redeployment of weapons and troops, arms control agreements on the size and characteristics of national military forces, international peacekeeping units, and collective security arrangements.

Just War Principles and Prohibitions. Fortunately, there is a rich tradition of "just war" concepts, embraced by moral philosophers in most of the world's cultures and reflected in international covenants on the rules of war, that can be drawn upon to buttress efforts to prevent or control the violent escalation of conflict. But unfortunately, the just war tradition, although philosophically robust, has had too few defenders in positions of political power during the twentieth century. The gap between the strong consensus among ethicists and international lawyers on the one hand, and the practices of states and revolutionary movements on the other hand, underscores the need to freshly reassert, propagate, and popularize the just war principles.

The just war principles, as they have evolved in the discourse among ethicists, apply to two kinds of decisions about the use of lethal force: the legitimacy of decisions to go to war (*jus ad bellum*); and the legitimacy of decisions about the conduct of war (*jus in bello*).

On the Resort to War. The traditional *jus ad bellum* concepts, adapted to contemporary circumstances, should be accorded a prominent place in high councils of decision to help ensure that the threshold between tough bargaining and the actual outbreak of military hostilities will never be crossed cavalierly, as it used to be when war could be regarded, in Carl von Clausewitz's formulation, as "a continuation of political commerce by other means." (See discussion of the cultural determinants of war in Chapter 3.) Domestic decision-making routines requiring wide concurrence across society's interest groups and publics before war can be undertaken; international covenants committing signatories to utilize dispute settlement processes and to consider threats of force only as a last resort—all such controls against mindlessly sliding into war as conflict intensifies—need reaffirmation and enhancement to generate awareness of, and give operational meaning to, the profound differences between war and nonviolent conflict.

The leading principle of just war is that war must not be undertaken unless it is for a *just cause.* The just causes—that is, legitimate reasons—for war have narrowed as the destructiveness of war has increased. Today the legitimate reasons still include, preeminently, responding to military attack on one's own country or coming to the defense of another country that has been the victim of military attack. In other words, interstate "aggression" (defined as the first use of destructive force) is presumptively wrong; and it is legitimate, and at times even obligatory, to go to war to counter acts of aggression, either to stop the aggressors from going further or to undo or retaliate for the wrongs that have been committed. But the philosophical-legal tradition strongly opposes preemptive attacks in anticipation of impending aggression and even more strongly proscribes preventive war to reverse an enemy's buildup of forces that would change the military balance of power. In this it is at odds with much modern strategic thinking and practice, in which the vital interest in reducing one's losses in an impending (and presumably unavoidable) war overrides the moral obligation not to initiate the hostilities.[6]

Unlike in some historical periods, notably the era of European overseas imperial expansion, going to war in order to *enhance* the power or wealth of the nation is not considered to be a just cause. But using force to *protect* one's power or wealth is held to be legitimate in many quarters.[7]

Similarly, since the Peace of Westphalia ended seventeenth-century wars of religion, ethicists and statespersons have generally held that it is wrong to start a war to *spread* a particular way of life. Yet this proscription has not prevented governments from invoking way-of-life justifications as part of their array of reasons for forging military alliances and fighting in support of another country or revolutionary movement. Napoleon Bonaparte marched his armies across Europe ostensibly in support of the "rights of man" (nationalist-liberal uprisings against monarchies); Woodrow Wilson told the Americans they were entering World War I to "make the world safe for democracy." Winston Churchill and Franklin Roosevelt claimed that they were prosecuting World War II on behalf of the "four freedoms." The United States

---

[6]The fragility of the prohibition of preventive war was exhibited in the Cuban missile crisis of 1962, when the Kennedy administration seriously contemplated attacking the Soviet missile bases in Cuba and invading the island if Khrushchev did not remove the nuclear missiles. President Kennedy himself, however, although not ruling out these military options, was determined to find a diplomatic resolution to the crisis.

It was also the primacy of security interests over moral rectitude that prompted Israel, in the opening blow of the 1967 Six-Day War, to preemptively attack Egypt's warplanes on their bases. In 1981, a strict interpretation of the just cause criterion would have led to a condemnation of Israel's destruction of Iraq's fledgling nuclear reactor; but the Reagan administration, privately appreciative of Israel's action, issued a mild and ambiguous public rebuke. Similar considerations led some prominent U.S. strategists to advocate a preventive "surgical" strike to destroy North Korea's nuclear weapons–producing potential in 1994 (a proposal that was made moot by Pyongyang's agreement to modify the offending facilities under substantial international inspection).

[7]Thus Secretary of State Henry Kissinger warned in 1974 that the United States might be compelled to use force against the Arab oil producers if their supply-restrictions and pricing policies threatened to "strangulate" the United States.

fought for ten years in Vietnam in a futile effort to prevent it from going commu-nist. Khrushchev transported Cuban troops into Angola to support "wars of na-tional liberation" (meaning Marxist-led insurgencies) in southern Africa.

The flareup of nationality and ethnic self-determination movements in the post–cold war period—many of them involving communities with members in more than one country—has once again catapulted the issue of using military force to suppress or assist groups asserting their independence to the top of the international agenda. This in turn has raised the issue of the legitimacy of international military interven-tion (unilateral or multilateral) for any of a wide range of "human rights" causes. The result is that the morality and legality of military interventions across state lines for altruistic reasons have become one of the most contentious issues among ethicists as well as statespersons.

Much of the contemporary debate over the legitimacy of military intervention uses as a starting frame of reference the restrictive principles articulated by moral philosopher Michael Walzer in his influential treatise, *Just and Unjust Wars*. Adapting a formulation originally set forth by John Stuart Mill, Walzer argues that for military intervention across state lines to be considered legitimate, at least one of the follow-ing conditions must prevail in the country that is the target of intervention:

- a large-scale military struggle by a political community for independence must be well under way; that is, "what is at issue is secession or 'national liberation'";
- the country's boundaries have already been crossed by the armies of a foreign power; that is, "what is at issue is counterintervention";
- the violation of human rights within the country is so terrible that it negates the normal sovereignty rights of the national government; that is, what is at issue is "enslavement or massacre."[8]

Walzer, it should be noted, is not arguing that external military intervention is obligatory in these situations, only that military intervention in such cases is not excluded by the "just cause" principle. I agree and, along with Walzer, am very reluc-tant to endorse a more permissive set of conditions. The international consensus in support of the Mills/Walzer's restrictive criteria has been breaking down, however, especially with respect to how terrible violations of human rights must be before out-side intervention is warranted. The proposition that outsiders must refrain from intervening in cases of ethnic conflict until a full-blown secessionist war has broken out is also coming under increasing challenge.[9]

---

[8]Michael Walzer, *Just and Unjust Wars: A Moral Argument with Historical Illustrations* (New York: Basic Books, 1977), pp. 89–90.

[9] The current intellectual and policy ferment over the intervention issue is well reflected in Laura W. Reed and Carl Kaysen, eds., *Emerging Norms of Justified Intervention* (Cambridge: American Academy of Arts and Sciences, 1993).

The emerging pressures for a more flexible interpretation of what constitutes a "just cause" for military intervention puts a greater burden on other *jus ad bellum* principles in cases where further deliberation is needed to put the brakes on the mad momentum toward war—in particular, the principles of last resort, proportionality, and competent authority.

The principle of *last resort* holds that even where there is a "just cause," all means other than war must have been tried to reverse the wrong (or prevent what would otherwise be inevitable) before it is justifiable to start a war. These other means typically include the conflict moderation devices discussed in the previous section and the interjection of international peacekeeping forces between potential belligerents (as discussed later in this chapter). They may also include coercive measures short of war, such as the withdrawal of diplomatic recognition, economic embargoes and boycotts, the freezing of financial assets, the denial of travel visas to the nationals of the offending country, and the denial of access rights to international airports and seaports.

The principle of *proportionality* permits going to war only if the damage that the fighting is likely to produce is less than the harm that would be sustained if force were not used. This formal criterion is obviously very elastic, being subject to the estimates of likely damage, which, in any event, will involve considerable guesswork. But insofar as decision makers have every reason to believe that the war they are contemplating *will* produce levels of destruction grossly disproportionate to any realistic fruits of victory, the principle enjoins them to refrain from initiating hostilities. Consistent with the world interest philosophy expounded in Chapter 8, the calculus of destruction should include not only what will be suffered by one's own country and one's allies, but also what will be suffered by the enemy.[10]

The final principle of the *jus ad bellum* tradition applicable to contemporary circumstances is the requirement that war be conducted or legitimized by a *competent authority.* A conservative application of this principle would preserve the norm that only national governments are permitted to wage war, with the possible exception of self-determination movements aspiring to achieve recognition as nation-states. A reformist application—prompted by the breakdown of congruence between nation and state in many parts of the world—would attempt to lodge the legitimizing function in the international peace and security institutions of the world polity (namely, the UN Security Council, or perhaps an enhanced International Court of Justice) that are mandated to serve world interests as distinct from national or particular

---

[10]The requirement of assessing damage to all parties is also consistent with the original meaning of the proportionality principle as propounded by the medieval church theologians. It should be noted, however, that they applied this and other just war principles only to wars among Catholic princes; in wars against the infidels, especially the Muslims, and later, even the Protestants, good Catholic princes could let all hell break loose.

interests.[11] This would not deny national governments the prerogative of acting quickly to defend their countries in advance of appropriate international authorization; but if an emergency prompts a unilateral decision, the government that felt compelled to resort to an early use of force out of self-defense would be obligated to seek such international legitimation immediately after the start of hostilities.

On the Conduct of War. Despite efforts to restrict the circumstances under which the resort to war will be considered legitimate, we must expect and prepare for the fact that wars will continue to break out, whether by inadvertence or design. Thus, the world interest in sustaining the conditions for healthy human existence on the planet in addition to elementary moral considerations also requires a strengthening of the rules and practical controls on the way wars are fought. Without minimizing the profundity of the step from peace into war, it has become more important than ever to maintain and reinforce as many moral and physical thresholds as possible between the different kinds and dimensions of warfare that are now possible.

Paradoxically, the traditional *jus en bello* principle that has become the most problematical with respect to implementation is the one that is universally regarded to be the most important—namely, the *prohibition against attacking noncombatants.* This and the corollary prohibitions (against the bombardment of undefended civilian facilities and the like) were subscribed to by virtually all countries in the Hague conventions and protocols on the rules of war codified in the early part of the twentieth century; but they were grossly violated by the belligerents on all sides during World War II, culminating in the incineration of Hiroshima and Nagasaki in August 1945. As the war progressed, the companion *jus in bello* principles of *military necessity* and *military proportionality* (requiring that only such force should be used as is necessary to accomplish the military objective and that the destruction permitted must be proportionate to the importance of the objective) were stretched into presumed license to destroy the enemy's military-industrial infrastructure. Accordingly, ports, transportation hubs, and key industrial facilities became legitimate targets. It was an easy

---

[11]This variant of the competent authority principle is consistent with Morton Halperin's argument in "Guaranteeing Democracy," *Foreign Policy,* No. 91 (Summer 1993), pp. 105–122. Halperin proposes that "the United States should explicitly surrender the right to intervene unilaterally in the internal affairs of other countries by overt military means or by covert operations. Such self-restraint would bar interventions like those in Grenada and Panama, unless the United States first gained the explicit consent of the international community acting through the Security Council or a regional organization" (p. 120). Similarly, a leading Catholic theologian, concerned about the contemporary stretching of the criteria permitting interstate intervention, argues that "a revised ethic must restrict the category of 'proper authority' to undertake intervention. Some multilateral forum should be an intrinsic necessity for justifiable intervention, at least at the level of authorization (as distinct from the operational level of carrying out intervention)." J. Bryan Hehir, "The Politics and Ethics of Intervention," *Centerpiece* (Newsletter of the Center for International Affairs at Harvard University), Vol. 8, No. 2 (Autumn 1994), pp. 4–5.

additional step to attack population centers, the objective being to destroy the enemy's will to fight—the end presumably justifying the means.

The principle of noncombatant immunity also has been eroded from below in the post–World War II period by the tactics characteristic of insurgency and revolutionary wars. Some aspects of insurgencies or revolutions have been conducted by uniformed soldiers against the military personnel and facilities of the government they are trying to overthrow, and counterblows by government forces have been directed at paramilitary units of the revolutionaries. But in many cases, the violence has been inflicted by nonuniformed insurgents against national and local officials and collaborators of the regime, and the government's counterviolence has been targeted broadly at elements of the population assumed to be participating in or even simply supporting the revolutionary movement.

The fact that the industrialization and totalization of warfare has prompted belligerents to distort *jus in bello* principles from limitations into license, from prohibitions into permission, can lead to three very different responses. One is to throw away the rule book, recognizing that war *is* hell—and simply concede to the evil ethic that defeat of the enemy overwhelms all other values. Another response is pacifism: the rejection of the possibility of just wars. (Pacifist philosophies have experienced a revival among ethicists and laypersons since World War II, but have little chance of being embraced by governments.) The third response, which I advocate here, is to reaffirm and sharpen the *jus in bello* principles to make it unambiguously clear that the burden of justification, at every step of the escalation process, lies with those who would expand the scale of death and destruction, and that those responsible for intentional killing of noncombatants have presumptively committed a crime and are subject to prosecution by international tribunals. Such a strengthening of the just war principles, however, needs to be reinforced with military deployments and use-of-force doctrines that make deliberate choice by accountable decision makers both possible and necessary before any new threshold of violence is crossed in an ongoing conflict.

Unilateral Deterrence and Firebreak Strategies. Some military deployments and strategies are more war-prone than others, and some are highly likely to result in automatic escalation once war starts. World interests, therefore, require that countries scrupulously refrain from military deployments and strategies that are provocative and have uncontrollable escalation potential.

Three fundamental problems inhere in attempting to rely on military deployments and strategies to prevent the outbreak and escalation of major war: (1) Some of the very deployments and strategies that seem efficacious for preventing major wars can obliterate efforts to control and terminate lesser wars once they start. (2) Deployments and strategies designed to limit the pace and intensity of military escalation and to provide opportunities for war termination may convince potential aggressors that they can control their risks and therefore undermine their inhibitions against aggression. (3) Deployments and strategies motivated entirely by the goals of deterring or defending against major aggression can appear to the other side as menacing indications of an intention to attack—the paradox often referred to as "the security dilemma." I call the recognition of the need to avoid all three of these dangers simultaneously "the security *tri*lemma."

Although difficult, military deployments and strategies can be constrained so as to avoid all three horns of the trilemma. The principal means for this are the maintenance of well-defined "firebreaks" separating different degrees of battle escalation, by agreement (either tacit or explicit) between adversaries whenever possible, but in any event as a matter of national policy. The imperative of battle control is sustained by national decision routines and command-and-control systems to assure that the crossing of any of the established firebreaks (or thresholds, if you will) between different levels of violence can never happen automatically, but always requires fresh "moment of truth" decisions on the part of the highest political decision makers. The imperative of deterrence is sustained by the existence of capabilities for higher levels of violence and by the announced willingness of political leaders to decide to employ such capabilities if lesser capabilities are unable to induce a satisfactory termination of a conflict.

The first, and most crucial threshold of all, is the threshold between the exchange of threats of war and the actual outbreak of military hostilities. This threshold should never be crossed cavalierly, as it used to be when war could be regarded, in von Clausewitz's formulation, as "a continuation of political commerce by other means." (See discussion of the cultural determinants of war in Chapter 3.) The reaffirmation of "just war" principles, although important, is insufficient. Domestic decision-making routines requiring wide concurrence across society's interest groups and publics before war can be undertaken; international covenants (field-specific, region-specific, and universal) committing signatories to utilize dispute settlement processes and to consider threats of force only as a last resort—all such controls against mindlessly sliding into war as conflict intensifies—need enhancement to generate awareness of, and give operational meaning to, the profound differences between war and nonviolent conflict.

Once war erupts (military planning must acknowledge, prudentially, that this may happen despite anyone's best efforts to stop it or obtain an immediate cease-fire), salient firebreaks can be maintained to control the location and kinds of targets that can be attacked and types of weapons that can be employed. Through the design of weapons, their deployments, and command/control procedures zones of belligerency can be restricted to designated territorial areas and sanctuaries established (even within the territories of belligerents) so as not to provoke additional countries into a war. Consistent with traditional "just war" principles of proportionality and discrimination, belligerents must refrain from destroying primarily civilian sites, such as schools, hospitals, residential districts, and other locales containing large numbers of noncombatants. To adhere to such restrictions it is essential to be able to keep control, during active belligerency, over which types of weapons are used and withheld from use, particularly being able to maintain special restrictions on the use of nuclear, chemical, and biological weapons.

A standard objection to efforts to maintain such a firebreak regime is that by giving would-be aggressors the impression that they can control the risks to themselves in warfare it will undermine deterrence. But, in reality, there should be little to fear on this account. The *capacity* of defenders against attack to respond at different levels (including the most awesomely terrible) still faces potential aggressors with the prospect of costs that will outweigh their sought gains; moreover, this capacity of defenders to control their own level and pace of involvement lends credibility to their threats to impose unacceptable costs on the aggressors. The alternative—the threat of virtually automatic escalation to all-out war—can paralyze defenders no less than aggressors; and the anticipation that this might be the case could well tempt aggressors to stage sudden, *fait accompli* power plays against vulnerable victims, under the assumption that at the moment of truth the victims and their allies will settle for the new status quo rather than assure their own destruction by going to war against the aggressors. At least for conflicts between the major military powers, the credibility of threats to counter aggressors with whatever level of force is required to deny them their anticipated gains cancels out the assumed loss in deterrent clout that some abstract theories hold would be the result of maintaining the capacity to fight in a limited and controlled way.

The overriding consideration justifying firebreak strategies, however, is the supreme world interest (which, presumably, also would be the supreme national interest of massively armed countries involved in war against one another) in terminating any escalating hot war short of global holocaust. This requires salient stopping points along the course of military escalation, while there is still something of value left to negotiate about and there are still competent authorities left to undertake such negotiation.

Firebreak strategies can also serve the normative imperative of reducing the amount of killing even in those cases where war appears justified by supreme national interests. They provide *possibilities*—in contrast to strategies of virtually automatic escalation—for belligerents to adhere to the traditional moral and legal "just war" strictures of proportional damage and noncombatant immunity.[12]

Arms Control. Notwithstanding efforts to control the course of escalation once war starts, each crossing of a threshold (the step from crisis into war, the crossing over the firebreak between conventional war and chemical or nuclear war, the entry of additional countries into the war) reduces the chances for preventing further escalation up to the level of global holocaust. Realizing that the kind of conflict escalation no one wants could occur anyway because of mistaken fears that one's opponent was about to strike first (or to cross a major threshold first in an ongoing war), gov-

---

[12]Support for continuing to adhere to the rules of proportionality and discrimination, despite the immense difficulties of doing so in contemporary warfare, is found in the 1983 pastoral letter of the National Conference of Catholic Bishops on War and Peace, *The Challenge of Peace: God's Promise and Our Response* (Washington, D.C.: United States Catholic Conference, 1983).

ernments can agree to verifiable mutual limits on the types of weapons in their arsenals and their deployments that will reduce the likelihood of such miscalculations. The two primary ways of doing this are (1) to reduce the advantages from striking first and (2) to develop reliable means of demonstrating that a first strike is not being prepared.

Ironically, the very technological trends that have made war a threat to the entire planet have conspired with the dominant trends in nuclear-age strategic thinking to virtually negate the advantages of striking first against a great power armed with advanced weaponry. This condition, prevailing between the United States and the Soviet Union by the late 1960s, achieved widespread recognition as Mutual Assured Destruction (MAD), and its positive value was endorsed and reinforced in the principal strategic arms limitation agreements of the 1970s: SALT I (including the Anti-Ballistic Missile Treaty) and SALT II. Thus, the irony produced the correlative paradox of rival superpower strategists agreeing not to deploy "defensive" forces (meaning counter-weapon weapons) that could substantially reduce the capability of the opponent to inflict intolerable destruction on one's own country. The MAD basis for strategic force planning and arms control got equated in the popular imagination with strategies for destroying cities rather than military installations (it was acceptable to kill people, but not weapons). In the 1980s, this presumed "mutual hostage" basis for deterrence earned the condemnation of the U.S. American Catholic Bishops and provided President Ronald Reagan with a moral justification for pursuing his Strategic Defense Initiative ("Star Wars").

The popular understanding of assured destruction confused the *capacity* to exterminate cities with actual war plans. War plans since the early 1960s have included options of major strategic attacks on a wide range of purely military targets away from centers of population (with the latter still "held hostage" to deter the enemy from attacking one's own cities). Whether any such high-level firebreaks could be sustained in fact during strategic nuclear war is, of course, debatable.[13] The arms control rationale for both superpowers maintaining MAD capabilities, however, was still valid in any case: namely, that the capacity to retaliate with devastating effect after having suffered the worst attack the enemy could deliver would *reduce* the incentives on either side to strike first.

Unfortunately, the condition of Mutual Assured Destruction (which still exists between the United States and Russia, despite the post–cold war reduction in their strategic arsenals) is unable to overcome two problems inherent in the peace-through-deterrence approach, which make it unwise to *rely* on the threat of assured retaliatory destruction as a strategy—either to prevent a World War III or to stop a war between great powers from escalating into a world-destroying holocaust.

---

[13]The most prominent skeptical view of the likelihood of controlling strategic war is Desmond Ball, "Can Nuclear War Be Controlled?" *Adelphi Papers,* No. 169 (London: International Institute for Strategic Studies, 1981).

The first problem is the old "security dilemma" of one side's intendedly deterrent military posture being read by the opponent as a preparation for aggression: contemporary strategic "second strike" weapons (especially those capable of discriminating targeting) are indistinguishable from "first strike" weapons (those designed to knock out the enemy's retaliatory forces). If such multiple-mission weapons are put on high alert during an extreme crisis to assure they are not destroyed on their bases, the enemy could easily interpret the alerting measures as a first-strike preparation and decide to launch his most lethal forces preemptively to prevent their being incapacitated in the first exchange of blows. (Mutual alerting, by the same dynamic, could produce a mutual incentive to preempt.) A suspicion that the enemy has targeted one's command centers would only heighten the perceived need to get in the first blow.

The second interrelated problem is that to the extent war plans include options for early military campaigns short of holocaust levels of warfare, the advantages of surprise and launching the first blows at these lower levels are hardly eliminated. Indeed, the fear of escalating to higher levels of warfare can even put a premium upon a swift *fait accompli,* which presumably will leave the opponent no rational military options for reversing it. In the ensuing event, however, the opponent's "rational" acceptance of the *fait accompli* may not materialize, and "irrational" considerations of not being humiliated (or having one's "credibility" undermined) may drive the violence to higher and higher levels.[14]

An innovative arms control approach for countering the misperceptions and miscalculations that can lead massively armed adversaries into unwanted war goes under the rubric of confidence building measures (CBMs). CBMs agreed to in the 1980s by NATO and the Warsaw Pact (many of which are still valid in the post–cold war era) included, for example: procedures for signatories to inform each other in advance of military exercises involving large contingents of troops or weapons, or missile firings, and to provide opportunities for adversary countries to observe these exercises; and escalation control centers (sometimes called "nuclear risk reduction centers") staffed by multinational contingents of military officers, including particularly those from adversary countries, in the military command headquarters of potential belligerents to assure continuous direct communication with each other. Such measures to be most useful depend on a shared modicum of trust that the participant countries are not engaged in systematic deception as to their military deployments. But they may even be of some value in countering efforts at systematic deception through the discovery of telltale departures from normal routines, or through demands by suspicious parties for evidence (such as taking crucial force components off of alert status) that would contradict their suspicions.

---

[14]Richard Ned Lebow explores the risks of nuclear preemption, escalation miscalculation, and loss of control in his *Nuclear Crisis Management: A Dangerous Illusion* (Ithaca: Cornell University Press, 1987).

International Peacekeeping Forces. Another important means available to antagonists who have not yet resolved an intense dispute but do not want to go to war (or continue fighting) is a *neutral "military" presence* in the immediate zone of war-prone confrontation. Such "soldiers without enemies," typically (but not necessarily) organized under the auspices of the United Nations, are composed of military contingents contributed by a number of countries not allied with either side in the particular conflict. Their functions can range from monitoring the adherence to the terms of a truce agreement, which require them to be equipped with little more than vehicles and binoculars, to providing a military buffer against anticipated attempts to violate a cease-fire line or demilitarized zone, in which case they could be armed with tear gas, rifles, machine guns, even light artillery.

Such peacekeeping forces are uniquely *inter*national not only in their composition but in the basis of their authority: Their presence, composition, and basic missions are approved in advance by those countries on whose territory they will be deployed.[15] This essential feature is a source of both their effectiveness and their weakness.

They are most effective in monitoring and reinforcing truces and cease-fires that include demilitarized zones between the belligerents (for example, those established at the end of the 1973 Arab-Israeli war, in the Sinai desert between Israel and Egypt, and on the Golan Heights between Israel and Syria). International peacekeeping forces stationed in such military disengagement zones need not be heavily armed even to accomplish their buffering function, which is provided by simply being there in sufficient numbers to require those who would violate a disengagement agreement to run into the international force as if it were a plate glass window wired to set off a loud alarm.

They are least effective when deployed into civil conflicts to help reestablish law and order among interspersed feuding groups (as in Lebanon in the early 1980s). For in such situations the international contingents run the risk of being identified with the domestic political factions of coalitions currently responsible for governance and, therefore, also a target of dissident violence whenever it flares up.

International peacekeeping forces are also not really appropriate for active international conflict suppression in the absence of a truce among belligerents—a problem complicating the deployment of UN forces in Yugoslavia in the early 1990s. In such cases they have to be heavily armed fighting units, and if their military missions are not precisely circumscribed and then rigidly implemented with scrupulous discipline by the participating units—an extraordinarily difficult requirement for units in a

---

[15]Margaret P. Karns and Karen A. Mingst, "Maintaining International Peace and Security: UN Peacekeeping and Peacemaking," in Michael T. Klare and Daniel C. Thomas, eds., *World Security: Challenges for a New Century* (New York: St. Martin's Press, 1994), pp. 118–213.

multinational command—they can end up fighting on one side or the other in the war (as happened in the Congo in the early 1960s). Such military participation will almost certainly de-legitimize the neutral status and good offices of the international institution or group that created the peacekeeping force, and reduce its capacity to arrange and oversee a cessation of violence, not only in the immediate conflict but also in subsequent conflicts among other sets of antagonists.

The post–cold war era seemed at the outset conducive to the institutionalization of a framework for a UN peacekeeping command and supporting infrastructure. As proposed in 1992 by UN Secretary General Boutros-Ghali, a permanent command framework would allow for rapid assemblage and deployment of forces from members of military contingents made available and trained especially for peacekeeping operations.[16] The combined national forces would be periodically exercised under a supranational command organization so that they would be able to function with dispatch and efficiency as a UN peacekeeping force whenever needed. Such a permanent structure would have to be highly modular in design—at the command as well as the national contingent levels—to ensure that its personnel were indeed sufficiently neutral with respect to the belligerent sides in particular conflicts requiring its presence.

Support for UN-organized and -commanded peacekeeping forces has since lost favor in the United States, however, following some confused and badly bungled UN operations in Somalia in 1993 involving U.S. contingents. In the face of rising domestic opposition to putting U.S. soldiers under UN commanders, the Clinton administration, which took office championing an enhanced peacekeeping role for the United Nations, soon dampened its enthusiasm. "Our nation has begun asking harder questions about proposals for new peacekeeping missions," President Clinton told the United Nations General Assembly in September 1993: Is there a real threat to international peace? Does the proposed mission have clear objectives? Can an exit point be identified? How much will the mission cost? What will be its command and control?[17] (Fending off threats of congressionally imposed restrictions, administration spokespersons let it be known that the new policy precluded putting U.S. troops under the command of foreign officers.)

Other countries, in the face of declining U.S. political and financial support for UN peacekeeping operations, are following suit, reversing a trend that from 1988 to 1995 showed UN peacekeeping troops around the world growing from 9,570 to more than 62,300 under a UN peacekeeping budget that increased from $230 million to $3.6 billion. Reluctantly adapting to the new reality, Secretary General Boutros-Ghali has been talking of the need to "contract out" more peacekeeping

---

[16]Boutros Boutros-Ghali, *An Agenda for Peace: Preventive Diplomacy, Peacemaking, and Peace-keeping* (NewYork: United Nations, 1992).

[17]President Clinton's Address to United Nations General Assembly, September 27, 1993, *Department of State Dispatch,* Vol. 4, No. 39.

responsibilities to multinational forces led by major powers with special interests in particular disputes—like the operations of France in Rwanda, the United States in Haiti, and Russia in Chechnya. This represents a backsliding to a traditional "spheres of influence" approach to world order, about which the secretary general is most unhappy. His appeal, rather (and rightly so), is for a renaissance of political will on the part of UN members to cooperate with one another worldwide to counter the rising tides of international instability and violence.[18]

Collective Security. The most ambitious method of escalation control developed within the nation-state system—being premised on the obligation of all countries to preserve the security of all of them against transborder military aggression—is an effort to collectivize (if possible to universalize) deterrence. Reflected in the core peace and security provisions of the Covenant of the League of Nations and the Charter of the United Nations, the collective security approach is targeted on the threshold between nonviolent and violent means of international conflict prosecution and is designed to prevent any country from taking the first step across that threshold. Collective security as such does not concern itself with the substantive merits of the issues over which countries are ready to fight, nor does it attempt to deflect countries from war by facilitating compromise. Rather, it comes close to delegitimizing the unilateral initiation of war (there may be cases of impending war where striking the first blow could be justified), and backs this up by mechanisms to assure that the aggressor will be countered not only by the direct victim and its political allies but by the combined sanctions of all the countries in the collective security system.

Thus, Article 16 of the League covenant stated that war by any country in disregard of the dispute-resolution provisions of the covenant (Articles 12 through 15; see above) was "*ipso facto* . . . an act of war against all other Members of the League." The members were obligated to immediately sever all trade and financial relations with the aggressor and, severally, in accord with recommendations of the League Council in the particular case, to contribute armed forces to international military actions that might be undertaken against the aggressor.[19]

Despite the failure of the League system to put down the aggressions that led to World War II, collective security was again given pride of place among the purposes of the United Nations as enumerated in the Charter. Chapter I, Article 1, Section 1, defines this as "To maintain international peace and security, and to that end: to take effective collective measures for the prevention and removal of threats to the peace, and for the suppression of acts of aggression or other breaches of the peace." Chapter VII of the Charter accords the Security Council the role of determining the existence of aggression or other breaches of the peace and deciding what countermeasures shall

---

[18]Barbara Crosette, "U.N. Chief Ponders Future of Peacekeepers," *New York Times*, March 3, 1995.
[19]*Covenant of the League of Nations.*

be taken by members of the United Nations, severally or jointly under the UN flag—including military action under direct control of the Security Council itself, operating through the UN Military Staff Committee (composed of the chiefs of staff of the five permanent members of the Security Council).[20]

In the reasons for having available such collective security mechanisms for deterring and (if deterrence fails) suppressing military aggression we also find the reasons why this method of controlling escalation often may not work. By sharing the responsibility among all members of the system for opposing the aggressor, not only is there a reduction in the sacrifices that would have to be borne in lives and material resources by those few who would be acting out of considerations of direct and tangible self-interest, but there is also a sharing of the political risk of alienating the aggressor nation and its friends over the long term. This risk-sharing among all members can induce those who otherwise might be fearful of reprisal by the aggressor to participate in threatening and applying sanctions. And the promise of such a concerted response might well deter the would-be aggressor. But if effective counteraction to an aggressor *depends* on the willingness of all or most members of the collective security system to act in concert (put another way: those with the power to put down the aggressor would not act unilaterally), then conniving aggressors—such as Tojo, Mussolini, and Hitler in the 1930s—may be tempted to bank on the very existence of such a system to slow down or paralyze timely and effective counteraction to their moves.[21]

The framers of the UN Charter attempted to anticipate and hedge against a potentially paralyzing overdependence on international consensus by endorsing, in Articles 51 and 52, the continuing right of *self*-defense by individual countries or groups of countries in cases where the Security Council has not yet been able to act. Indeed, it was only under the cover of Articles 51 and 52 that the United Nations was able to survive the cold war, for in the absence of these provisions, the major defense alliances on which countries felt compelled to rely for protection during the 1950s and 1960s (NATO and the Warsaw Pact) would have been contradictory to the Charter.[22]

In the post–cold war period, with an operating consensus among all five permanent members of the UN Security Council now quite plausible with respect to breaches of the peace and corrective action, as happened in 1990 in response to Iraq's invasion of Kuwait, the use of collective security processes and institutions to deter

---

[20]*Charter of the United Nations.*

[21]The strengths and weaknesses of collective security are explored in Inis L. Claude, Jr., *Swords into Plowshares: The Problems and Progress of International Organization* (New York: Random House, 1984).

[22]The only instance of "collective security" action by the United Nations during the cold war is its role in authorizing the U.S.-led military response to North Korea's invasion of South Korea in 1950. This would not have been possible, however, had the Soviet Union not been absent from the Security Council when the key votes were taken. See Brown, *The Causes and Prevention of War*, p. 183.

or suppress military aggression by lesser powers is a real option. But as the Gulf War demonstrated, there is a declining probability for maintaining the required Security Council consensus as we move up the scale from condemnatory resolutions, to economic embargoes, to military deployments, to the actual use of military firepower against the aggressor.

Still, in order to deter or put down the resort to military force on the part of any of the five permanent members of the Security Council (or an ally of any of the five), the more traditional means of applying countervailing power—unilaterally or through alliances—will need to be used. This only underscores the imperative of enhancing conflict moderation structures and policies, as distinguished from military countermeasures, to deal with world-interest-threatening confrontations between the great powers.

The various instrumentalities and policies for conflict control discussed above are logical derivatives from the world interest imperatives of sustaining healthy human existence on the planet and reducing the amount of violence in human society. But objective necessity is an insufficient determinant of human choice, if the requisite habits of heart and mind are not also present. The ability of responsible decision makers and their constituencies to *perceive* how near-term "national security" policies (that may appear cost-effective on the basis of established power-maximizing criteria) can increase or decrease the likelihood of conflicts spiralling out of control requires training in psychology and intercultural empathy as well as political economy and military strategy. And the ability to *act* on the basis of such more enlightened perceptions requires, in addition, a kind of "moral" training: strengthening the capacity of peoples and statespersons to subordinate near-term material and power payoffs to the longer-term species-survival imperatives of community building.

Biosphere Protection

Ecology and environment-protection undertakings that have a presumptive claim to the status of world interests are those that appear to be required in order to maintain the basic biospheric conditions that sustain healthy human life on earth. I say "appear to be required" because respectable minorities among the relevant scientific authorities contest some of the findings of their peers on the extent to which various human activities are disturbing essential biospheric patterns. Yet elementary prudence requires that policies be instituted to reduce the likelihood of at least those scientifically plausible dire consequences that the majority among the relevant scientific authorities believe could indeed be irreversible.

At the time of this writing, there is a basic (even though far from universal) scientific consensus on the proposition that irreversible dire disturbances to the Earth's life-sustaining ecologies are likely to result from a continuation of certain agricultural and industrial processes.

This basic scientific consensus has provided the rationale for United Nations mandates for countries to institute domestic policies and negotiate international agreements to protect the biosphere. The most important progress on the international front thus far has been with respect to ozone depletion, global warming, and threats to the planet's biological diversity; but for each of these realms much more still needs to be accomplished.

Preventing Ozone Depletion

The trace gas, ozone, is found throughout the earth's atmosphere. At lower levels it can be noxious; but in one of its locations—the stratosphere six to thirty miles in altitude—it performs the crucial life-sustaining function of absorbing certain wavelengths of the sun's ultraviolet radiation that can cause cancer and other profound damage and mutations in plant and animal cells. It is now known that various gases produced on earth by humans have been migrating up to this stratospheric region where they are dangerously thinning the protective ozone layer. The principal culprits are chlorofluorocarbons (CFCs), one of modern industry's wonder chemical compounds, that have been widely used as coolants for refrigerators and air conditioners, in insulating and packaging materials, and as spray propellants.

Understandably, scientific findings about the dangerous properties of CFCs as well as proposals to prevent their production were initially opposed by powerful industry groups and governments representing them. Yet a majority of countries have signed on to the Montreal Protocol of September 1987 and follow-on international instruments committing themselves to stringent CFC abatement policies.

The way the international obligations to protect the ozone layer materialized can be instructive to other efforts to achieve cooperation among nation-states in the service of world environmental and ecological interests. The alarming results of a succession of investigations by respected international panels of scientists in the 1970s and 1980s generated popular pressures that resulted in CFC-abatement legislation in the United States and a few other industrial countries—this despite the fact that no government wants to impose extreme CFC prohibition measures on its own industries without a reliable commitment by other countries to similar measures, considering the costs of developing substitutes for the CFC-producing items could reduce the ability of home industries to compete in key sectors of international commerce. But having to bear the costs of the new controls, and determined to rectify their competitive disadvantages, some 500 of the affected U.S. companies formed the Alliance for Responsible CFC Policy to lobby for *international* controls on CFCs. Following suit, the United States government changed from an opponent of international abatement treaty to a supporter. In 1986 and 1987 the U.S. Department of State disseminated information worldwide through all of its embassies on the threat CFCs posed to the ozone layer. A similar dynamic operated in other countries where strong environmental movements were bringing on anti-CFC legislation. The affected industries became champions of international controls on CFCs and induced their governments to apply major diplomatic pressures on those countries without domestic controls. Meanwhile the United Nations Environmental Program conducted an intensive program of international scientific and policy workshops on the issue, at which the groundwork was laid for negotiating the formal control protocol.[23]

Countering the Greenhouse Effect

Although at least as compelling as the need to prevent ozone depletion, it has been more difficult to obtain the international cooperation required to prevent a dangerous warming of the planet from the buildup of concentrations of carbon dioxide (CO_2) and other gases in the atmosphere. This is because adequate correctives would involve drastic, and very expensive, changes in the energy production and consumption patterns of most countries—in particular, a conversion from energy obtained from the burning of fossil fuels (principally petroleum and coal) to clean sources such as solar energy. Such a conversion is understandably strongly opposed by many powerful domestic and transnational interests and, in any event, could not occur without government subsidies. Nonetheless, and despite initial resistance by the Bush administration, 154 of the 178 countries participating in the 1992 Earth Summit at Rio de Janeiro obligated themselves by signing the Framework Convention on Climate Change, to work toward the objective of "stabilization of greenhouse-gas concentrations in the atmosphere at a level that would prevent dangerous . . . interference with the climate system." Environmental lobbies plus most of the countries in the European Community wanted the convention to bind signatories to rapid and specific percentage reductions in their emissions; but the United States, threatening not to sign, was able to water down any such specific commitments to no more than a *goal* to restore greenhouse gas emissions to 1990 levels by the year 2000.[24] But this was only a symbolic, if not self-deceptive, gesture with no real prospect of reversing the threat, for even if the goal were to be met, the absolute buildup of greenhouse gas concentrations would continue at the 1990 rate—which was already alarming to most climatologists.

This means that the objective of stabilizing the greenhouse effect will have to be pursued through subsequent negotiations or national legislation on the part of the largest producers of carbon dioxide emissions. Some of those whose cooperation is essential if the threat is ever to be effectively contained are populous developing countries; in the midst of industrializing their economies, they are reluctant to take kindly to environmentalist imperatives that could slow down and increase the costs of their economic development. The framework convention made a start toward

---

[23]Richard Elliot Benedick, *Ozone Diplomacy: New Directions in Safeguarding the Planet* (Cambridge: Harvard University Press, 1991).

[24]For an analysis of the United Nations Framework Convention on Climate Change see Edward A. Parson, Peter M. Haas, and Mark A. Levy, "A Summary of the Major Documents Signed at the Earth Summit and Global Forum," *Environment,* Vol. 34, No. 8 (October 1992), pp. 12–13.

dealing with this predicament by establishing funding mechanisms that, if adequately provisioned by the affluent countries, could subsidize the adoption of more efficient energy systems by the poor countries. At least this much can be said for the Rio summit's initiatives on global warming: They charted the direction toward a stabilized climate and legitimized the need to restrict fossil fuel emissions. The next steps are technologically and economically feasible, but they will require political commitment and leadership.

Preserving Biodiversity

Finally, the least understood characteristic of the biosphere, but likely to be the most crucial ultimately to the healthy survival of the human species, is the enormous diversity of the biological organisms that link the multiple ecologies of the Earth to one another. Most biologists agree that it is the diversity of the planet's species that maintains the crucial ecologies of the biosphere (visibly illustrated by the way plants are pollinated by birds and insects). Health scientists have only in recent decades become cognizant of the great potential that a large proportion of the millions of unique micro-organic species may have applications in medical science to combat deadly diseases like cancer and AIDS. Yet with seeming indifference, humans are destroying their nonhuman co-inhabitants of the biosphere at an ever-accelerating rate: Authoritative studies estimate the current rate of such human-inflicted species loss to be several dozen a day and climbing, which could mean a species loss of 50,000 a year by the year 2000; and if the trend continues, perhaps only about half the species now alive (roughly 30 million, but no one really knows) might be lost by 2100.[25] Major sources of this tragic ecocide ("tragic" because it is the unintended consequences of otherwise justifiable economic development policies) include the spread of cities and agro-industrial developments that fragment the natural habitats of interdependent species, deforestation, and the destruction of coastal wetlands.

The growing scientific concern about the consequences of biodiversity loss to the planet's overall ecological health was reflected in draft agreements formulated in international meetings leading up to the 1992 Earth Summit. But ignorance and short-sightedness at the political levels diluted the provisions by the time they were ready for signing by the heads of state.

Still, one of the Earth Summit agreements does constitute an advance over the previous indifference to species loss and provides a basis for more enlightened policies: The Convention on Biological Diversity combines (1) admonitions to national governments to develop plans for protecting biologically rich habitats and extinction-threatened species within their jurisdiction with (2) obligations by countries to allow access to key habitats by commercial firms and institutes that are engaged in legitimate medical research and medical product development. (The Bush adminis-

---

[25]A. J. McMichael, *Planetary Overload: Global Environmental Change and the Health of the Human Species* (Cambridge: Cambridge University Press, 1993), pp. 238–243.

tration declined to sign the Biological Diversity Convention because of a clause giving "prior consent" for such access to the source countries; but the Clinton administration has indicated a readiness to sign.)

The Summit's Authoritative Statement of Principles on the World's Forests, however, turned out to be a hollow shell (or trunk). Third World countries that earn considerable foreign exchange from marketing lumber and wood products decimated the statement with amendments that eliminated most of the language that would have made national governments internationally accountable for how they managed their forests. The result, as characterized by the Environmental and Energy Study Institute, was "a set of principles which emphasizes sovereign rights to exploit forest resources and thus tends to legitimate existing policies of some countries that imperil those resources."[26] There has to be another way, for the tropical rainforests of the developing world contain about two-thirds of the Earth's species.[27]

It has become even more clear since the Rio Summit that the very real fear of many developing countries that they would suffer economically under an effective global regime to preserve the forests is unlikely to be relieved by lecturing them on their moral obligation to give priority to the future of the planet's biosphere. World society can overcome this dilemma only by fashioning a "global bargain" on deforestation and biological diversity that would commit developing countries with tropical forests to refrain from significant deforestation in exchange for debt forgiveness by their major international creditors and increases in development assistance from the more affluent countries.[28]

Poverty Alleviation and Sustainable Development

International obligations to help the destitute people of the world are, of course, considerably more difficult to come by than are domestic obligations. Even within well-ordered domestic communities, policies to effect the necessary financial and resource redistributions are often highly contentious.

If the economically and politically powerful actors in world society were to find a way of skimming 5 percent off the world's gross annual product of $20 trillion to transfer to the welfare of the one billion people the World Bank finds are living in abject poverty, all human beings could live substantially above the subsistence threshold.[29] The annual dollar amounts involved would be approximately equal to

---

[26]Gareth Porter with Inji Islam, *The Road from Rio: An Agenda for U.S. Follow-up to the Earth Summit* (Washington, D.C.: Environment and Energy Study Institute, 1992), p. 6.

[27]McMichael, p. 253.

[28]Various means of pursuing such international development/ecology bargains are described by Gareth Porter and Janet Welsh Brown in their *Global Environmental Politics* (Boulder: Westview Press, 1991), pp. 148–151.

[29]International Bank for Reconstruction and Development/The World Bank, *World Development Report* (New York: Oxford University Press for the World Bank), issued annually.

the amount being spent each year on military arms during the last decade of the cold war. But even if only half of the cold war era's military budgets were treated as a "peace dividend" and redistributed to the people in greatest economic need, human starvation could be virtually eliminated.[30]

The assumption of this global *economic capacity* to transfer the economic resources needed to bring and sustain all the world's peoples above the subsistence threshold informs the reports of various prominent international development commissions (the two Brandt Commission reports and the Brundtland Commission report, for example).[31]

Realistically, however—in view of the lack of a traditional normative base or major structural apparatus for effectuating and managing global financial and resource redistributions from rich to poor people—efforts to institute global distributive justice obligations on the world's affluent countries will have to proceed gradually. This was confirmed in March 1995 in Copenhagen by the circumscribed commitments approved by the leaders of national governments at the World Summit for Social Development. Long on statements about the shared imperative of eliminating poverty and social injustice, but short on specific obligations, the final Summit "Declaration" called for:

- Priority to be given to programs to accelerate economic and "human resource" development in the least developed countries;
- The "equitable" global and domestic distribution of the benefits of global economic growth;
- Commitments by the affluent countries to allocate 0.7 percent of their GNP to development assistance for the poor countries "consistent with countries' economic circumstances and capacity to assist";
- Commitments by "interested developed and developing partners" to allocate 20 percent of the donor country's development assistance and 20 percent of the recipient country's national budget to "basic social [poverty alleviation] programs" (as distinct from the kind of "structural adjustment" programs typically mandated by the International Monetary Fund).
- International lenders to "substantially reduce" the debts of the least developed countries, particularly in Africa, and to explore "innovative approaches to manage and alleviate" the debt burdens of other developing countries.[32]

---

[30]Ruth Leger Sivard, *World Military and Social Expenditures 1993* (Washington, D.C.: World Priorities, 1993).

[31]Independent Commission on International Development Issues (chaired by Willy Brandt), *North-South: A Program for Survival* (Cambridge: MIT Press, 1980); the Brandt Commission 1983, *Common Crisis North-South: Co-operation for World Recovery* (Cambridge: MIT Press, 1983); and World Commission on Environment and Development (chaired by Gro Harlem Brundtland), *Our Common Future* (New York: Oxford University Press, 1987).

[32]International Institute for Sustainable Development, "Summary Report on the World Summit for Social Development," transmitted over the Internet by the Institute as a part of its *Earth Negotiations Bulletin,* Vol. 10, No. 44, March 15, 1995.

Again, the Brandt and Brundtland commissions are a source of useful ideas: As a minimum, even before it became plausible to expect major reductions in arms budgets, they suggested that revenues for this purpose could be raised by taxes on the exploitation of the international "commons" (deep seabed mining, fishing beyond national economic zones, Antarctic resource exploitation, parking satellites in the geostationary orbit, and the use of the broadcasting frequency spectrum), and taxes on international trade and transportation (particularly arms sales, the shipping of petroleum, and air travel). Almost imperceptible levels of excise or surtaxes on such international activities would raise revenues far larger than the cumulative foreign aid budgets of industrialized countries. The taxes, collected mainly from the affluent countries (national governments would administer the tax collection), would go into internationally managed funds for priority distribution to the peoples most in need.[33]

But even if such resources could be extracted from the world's affluent, there is no guarantee that the recipient governments of the poorer countries would transfer the resources to the *people* most in need. Indeed, many of the Third World countries with the worst poverty are run by oligarchical dictators or a small elite class of wealthy entrepreneurs who, while advocating *international* distributive justice in global arenas, have no intention of instituting economic redistributive policies at home. Their governments are the first to invoke the sovereignty norms of the nation-state system against any efforts to vest international aid-giving agencies with the authority to oversee the way transferred resources are put to use by the recipient governments. Thus, efforts at the 1995 World Social Summit to obligate countries to institute internal redistributions of wealth and power to rectify traditional or market-produced inequities ran into strong opposition, mainly from Third World delegations.

In the global war against poverty too, then, a principal impediment to mobilizing the needed resources and getting them delivered on target is the traditional nation-state system itself—its state sovereignty structure and norms. Given the reality that world society has not been able as yet to devise an alternative world order, global constituencies who want to accomplish their objectives need to work through the system, and this means appealing to the interests of and striking bargains with those who run the system in various parts of the world.

The leaders of Third World countries, as a part of their determination to hang on to their sovereign prerogatives, do have an interest that can be appealed to that is consistent with genuine distributive justice: their interest in achieving sustainable economic development for their countries. This means reducing the demeaning dependency on handouts from the rich countries; it means being able to feed their own people—across generations—largely out of their own nationally generated

---

[33]International Commission on International Development Issues, pp. 244–245; World Commission on Environment and Development, pp. 340–342. See also E. B. Steinberg and J. A. Yager, *New Means of Financing International Needs* (Washington, D.C.: Brookings Institution, 1978).

resources; it means diversifying their economies so as to be able to escape from the vulnerable niches they have been compelled to occupy in the global economy in order to earn the foreign exchange to finance essential imports. Sustainable development of this sort also requires, as emphasized in the Brundtland report, precise, locally tailored and culturally appropriate applications of scientific knowledge and technological tools to the tasks of economic development.

Sustainable development thus must involve at least a three-way cooperative relationship among (1) international community provisioners of scientific knowledge and technological tools, (2) the indigenous people who will be adapting these inputs to their own cultures, and (3) the national governments who will be providing the material and public-order infrastructure and financing (in cooperation with external funding sources) for supplying these resources to the people who will be actually using them. These requirements for sustainable development have been derived in large part from the "brainstorming" among development and ecology experts that led to the 1992 Earth Summit and were reflected in its key documents. Thus, "Agenda 21," the comprehensive set of action imperatives developed at Rio, calls for the adoption of "community-based approaches to sustainable development" that will involve locally affected groups, including indigenous peoples, in the determination of land and water rights and natural resources management rules. The underlying philosophy was aptly articulated in the Brundtland report's insistence that sustainable development policies must be designed "to assure that growing economies remain firmly attached to their ecological roots and that these roots are protected and nurtured so that they may support growth over the long term."[34] What is being asked for is not altruistic noblesse oblige but *accountability*—both laterally (among countries) and vertically (by governments to the peoples they are expected to serve). The institution of such arrangements is the final policy imperative to which we now turn.

Accountability[35]

The international structures and procedures needed to assure that those who can negatively affect the well-being of others are accountable to those whom they may harm range across a wide spectrum. At one end are ad hoc meetings between those

---

[34]World Commission on Environment and Development, *Our Common Future*, p. 40.

[35]The analysis in this section is informed by recent scholarship on international "regime" creation and maintenance in particular fields; but I find the conglomerate concept of *regime* itself too amorphous—in its fusion of norms, policies, and institutions—as a guide to thinking about the policy and institutional instruments needed to implement world interest norms. The recent literature on international "regimes" collects under the definition articulated by Stephen Krasner: "Regimes can be defined as sets of implicit or explicit principles, norms, rules, and decision-making procedures around which actors' expectations converge in a given area of international relations." Quoted from his overview essay for the symposium on

who can affect one another (when information and/or threats are exchanged and/or behavioral adjustments are negotiated, after which the parties go home); at the other end are permanently sitting decision-making institutions. Accountability arrangements can also vary across another spectrum, intersecting the first one, that ranges from obligations to keep the affected or potentially affected informed of what is being (or will be) done to them to agreements not to act without the approval of the affected parties.[36]

At the most rudimentary level, those negatively affected by others would be given an opportunity to express their grievances, and those allegedly responsible for the harms and injustices would be expected to explain the reasons for their actions. In the human rights field, as shown in Chapter 7, there already has been some movement in recent decades to institutionalize this kind of informational accountability through granting limited investigatory responsibilities to the United Nations Commission on Human Rights in cases that appear to reveal a consistent pattern of gross violations of human rights. Parties to the International Covenant on Civil and Political Rights (about half of the world's countries) are obligated to submit biennial reports on human rights conditions in their countries to a Human Rights Committee of eighteen independent experts. The Human Rights Committee conducts public questioning of the state representatives of countries submitting these reports.[37]

In the related field of labor-management relations, the International Labor Organization (ILO)—composed of delegates from worker organizations as well as governments—is the auspice for formulating universal standards for the rights of labor (including collective bargaining, nondiscriminatory practices, equality of remuneration, health and safety standards, etc.) that are submitted to governments as covenants for their adoption. The ILO's Committee of Experts on the Application of Conventions and Recommendations receives periodic reports from the participating governments and issues "observations" on the failures of countries to live up to the labor conventions they have signed.[38]

More substantial international accountability is provided in the Council of Europe's human rights system; the European Commission on Human Rights, backed up by the European Court of Human Rights, is empowered to hear complaints from private parties as well as governments.

"international regimes" published in *International Organization,* Vol. 35, No. 4 (Fall 1981) and Vol. 36, No. 2 (Spring 1982) and subsequently published as Stephen D. Krasner, ed., *International Regimes* (Ithaca: Cornell University Press, 1983).

[36]For a parallel discussion of the need and opportunities for international accountability, see Robert C. Johansen, "Building World Security: The Need for Strengthened International Institutions," in Michael T. Klare and Daniel C. Thomas, eds., *World Security: Challenges for a New Century* (New York: St. Martin's Press, 1984), pp. 372–397.

[37]Jack Donnelly, *Universal Human Rights in Theory and Practice* (Ithaca: Cornell University Press, 1989), pp. 206–210.

[38]*Ibid.,* pp. 219–220.

Arms control is also a field for enlarging international accountability, and there are some useful precedents to build upon. Even before the end of the cold war, East-West agreements for mutual monitoring of potentially threatening movements of armed forces were becoming standard fare under the rubric of confidence building measures; and provisions in arms limitation treaties are allowing for mutual inspection to verify compliance.

Some arms control treaties contain formal accountability procedures for handling complaints of noncompliance, as, for example, the obligations undertaken by the United States and the Soviet Union in the Anti-Ballistic Missile Treaty of 1972 to be answerable to one another in a Standing Consultative Commission for any alleged violation of the treaty provisions. Other examples are the mutual on-site inspection provisions of the Intermediate Nuclear Force Treaty of 1987 and the verification provisions that are part of the various late–cold war arms reduction treaties negotiated between the Soviet Union and the United States and their erstwhile military allies.

The Treaty on the Non-Proliferation of Nuclear Weapons (NPT) is thus far the most ambitious undertaking in the arms control field in that it provides for institutionalization of international accountability at both the information and approval levels. The "Safeguard" provisions of the NPT mandate the International Atomic Energy Agency (IAEA) to operate a global accountability system, albeit a highly imperfect one, in the form of IAEA inspections of the nuclear power facilities of Non-Proliferation Treaty signatories to assure their adherence to their obligations not to acquire nuclear weapons. If a country is found to be in violation of the NPT/IAEA Safeguards, the nuclear-capable countries, acting on behalf of the world interest in restricting the spread of nuclear weapons, are supposed to stop transferring even peaceful nuclear technologies and equipment to the offending country. The NPT obligates the nuclear-armed signatories to pursue negotiations leading toward even their nuclear disarmament, and makes them accountable in this to the other signatories in the form of periodic treaty review conferences during which the nuclear-armed countries must report on their accomplishments or lack of them in pursuing the goal of nuclear disarmament.[39]

Not surprisingly, it is in the trade and monetary fields that international accountability is already quite prominent, for national governments and powerful nongovernmental economic actors need such accountability arrangements to assure the durable and predictable terms of trade and reasonably stable monetary values on which flourishing international commerce depends.

Mutual accountability is clearly the foundational norm of the General Agreement on Tariffs and Trade (GATT) and the World Trade Organization (WTO) and is

---

[39] *Treaty on the Non-Proliferation of Nuclear Weapons;* text in U.S. Arms Control and Disarmament Agency, *Arms Control and Disarmament Agreements* (Washington, D.C.: U.S. Government Printing Office, 1984), pp. 91–95.

reflected in their centerpiece rule of *reciprocity:* namely, that national policies affecting international trade are to be internationally coordinated so that they are "mutually advantageous." Members of the WTO agree to submit their disputes with one another concerning adherence to this reciprocity rule and other provisions to WTO panels of experts and to bring their policies in line with the findings of these panels. Members are obligated to participate in a series of international negotiations (called "rounds") to effect continuing reciprocal reductions of tariffs and other barriers to free trade across national borders. Membership in the organization does not require countries to relinquish their ultimate sovereign right to refuse to sign or implement a particular WTO agreement. In any event, enforcement of GATT/WTO rules is through the administrative agencies and courts of member governments. But internationally decentralized enforcement, far from negating the mutual accountability obligations, gives them strength and durability in the inevitable contest against short-term and more narrowly selfish pressures.

A parallel set of mutual accountability obligations that are enforced largely through national finance ministries has been instituted in the field of monetary, banking, and currency relations—again, out of the perceived mutual interest of countries in maintaining stable arrangements for paying for goods and services across national lines. If countries must severely constrict normal international commerce because of temporary national treasury or trade payments deficits or drastic currency exchange-rate fluctuations (the latter sometimes deliberately instituted by a national government to counter an adverse balance of trade), then in the aggregate everyone loses. The recognition that these common interests cannot be adequately attended to on the basis of unilateral national decision-making and require sustained international consultation, coordination of monetary and banking policies, and some international pooling of financial reserves for disbursement to countries with severe deficits is what led to the creation of the International Monetary Fund after World War II. The IMF has become the principal auspice for negotiating the elaborate web of multilateral agreements and consultative arrangements now subscribed to by the major industrial countries to avoid repeating the unilateral "beggar thy neighbor" monetary and fiscal policies that brought on the disastrous world depression of the 1930s. These mutual accountability arrangements include agreements to refrain from unilateral currency devaluations and to limit market-determined currency exchange-rate fluctuations within stipulated ranges, and commitments to at least consult multilaterally (and as much as possible to coordinate) on national fiscal policies, particularly interest rates charged by central banks, that can have a major impact on international patterns of trade and investments.

These needed supranational constraints often run up against the inclination of democratically elected governments unilaterally to pursue fiscal, monetary, and trade policies in the service of the relatively short-term economic concerns of their electoral constituencies. But this difficulty only points up the need for enlightened political and intellectual leadership with a capacity to compellingly articulate to resistant constituency groups the extent to which their particular interests are dependent upon the health of the global economy, and to devise policies that minimize the negative impact of the globally accountable policies on vulnerable domestic groups.[40]

The accountability relationships needed to give voice to the distributive justice claims of the world's poor are thus far found mostly outside of the GATT and IMF arenas, in institutions and negotiating forums—such as the United Nations Conference on Trade and Development (UNCTAD), periodic "global negotiations" on world development, and various commodity price-stabilization systems—set up largely at the insistence of the developing-country coalition. The World Bank, although responsive to the development needs of the poor countries, is (like the IMF) run primarily by the donor countries. There has been some effort in both the World Bank and the IMF to provide enlarged representation to the developing countries in the formulation of criteria for financial assistance; but, understandably, those who contribute the financial resources want to keep dominant control over how the resources are disbursed. In UNCTAD and related arenas the "voice" of the disadvantaged countries is heard more loudly (resolutions are usually passed on the basis of one-country/one-vote rules), but the advantaged are obligated to do little more than *listen*.

It is in the realm of shared environments or "commons" that political and legal accountability norms and structures congruent with the patterns of material interdependence show the greatest promise of the kind of institutionalization that would presage the development of a community-based world polity. This hope rests less on any growth of international altruism than it does on the premise that powerful actors will increasingly see where their self-interest lies. No matter that some of the users and abusers of the planet's biosphere and other common "airsheds" and bodies of water are small or poor countries; because their independent actions can significantly degrade the usability of such commons, they are in a position to bargain with non-negligible weight when it comes to setting rules of use and the design of organizations to implement these rules. Thus, the Law of the Sea treaty of 1981, negotiated and signed by most of the countries of the world, reflects the fact that the large maritime countries must navigate through straits and along coasts often under the control of small countries, and the fact that overfishing or water pollution by upstream countries can degrade the living resources depended on by downstream countries. Taking advantage of their crucial role in the ocean commons, the developing countries were able to get the technologically advanced maritime powers to agree to the principle of world ownership of the minerals on the deep seabed and to an International Seabed Authority, with voting and other decision-making rules largely

---

[40]Robert B. Reich, "Beyond Free Trade," *Foreign Affairs*, Vol. 61, No. 4 (Spring 1983), pp. 773–804, presents a well-reasoned case for the desirability and feasibility of such "industrial policies" by governments to help those who would otherwise lose out in the international economic competition convert to more competitive professions and enterprises.

in accord with Third World preferences, that will oversee the deep seabed mining operations and the distribution of revenues.[41]

Similarly, as argued in Chapter 5, it will be impossible to adequately protect the world's essential biospheric balances if the developing countries engaged in large-scale deforestation/industrialization projects fail to participate in the new international regimes to reverse the planet's CO_2 buildup and ozone depletion. Accordingly, the developing countries, aware of their new bargaining clout, are becoming more successful—and legitimately so—in negotiating special technology-transfer or financial concessions for themselves in order to facilitate their conversion to development strategies responsive to global environmental imperatives.

Other domains in which both safety and efficiency considerations have already compelled acceptance of the logic of international accountability are broadcasting and aerospace transportation. The frequency bands and communications satellite parking slots on the geostationary orbit would become so congested as to prevent the international transmission of clear telecommunications signals if international broadcasters were not required to obtain International Telecommunication Union (ITU) approval before using these resources. The life-threatening congestion in the air transportation field has made for universal acceptance of international accountability arrangements: Standardized navigational, signaling, and equipment rules, which aircraft are expected to follow in using international air corridors and airports, are formulated by the International Civil Aviation Organization (ICAO); and all governments and private carriers are required to notify ICAO of any differences between their practices and its rules—information that is disseminated by ICAO to all members. Although ICAO lacks direct enforcement powers, any carrier that refuses to adhere to the organization's rules is very likely to be denied airspace and landing rights by other members.

The Realism of Global Community

The apparent vast disjunction between what humankind must do to survive on the planet in a reasonably decent condition (the normative imperatives outlined in Chapter 8) and the way world society has typically worked throughout history (Chapters 1 through 7) point to the need to modify the world polity at least along the lines suggested in this chapter. These relatively marginal modifications in international political behavior, if substantially achieved, would add up to a substantial evolution of world society in the direction of world community. To the extent that

---

[41]Seyom Brown et al., *Regimes for the Ocean, Outer Space, and Weather* (Washington, D.C.: Brookings Institution, 1977). For a pessimistic and disparaging assessment of the efforts by the Third World coalition to enhance their bargaining power in commons issues, see Stephen D. Krasner, *A Structural Conflict: The Third World Against Global Liberalism* (Berkeley: University of California Press, 1985).

humans around the world do indeed begin to perceive of themselves as members of a global community, other more substantial reforms of the world polity—those capable of bringing the governance of world society into basic congruence with evolving material, cultural, and basic power relationships—also become feasible.

It should be noted that the analysis here comes nearly full circle to embrace ideas articulated more than four decades ago by the father of the "realist" school of international politics, Hans Morgenthau—my mentor during my graduate years at the University of Chicago. Doubting that human civilization could survive a nuclear world war, and predicting the inevitability of such a war on the basis of the behavioral characteristics of the anarchic nation-state system, Morgenthau concluded that the only way human civilization could be saved from destruction was by the establishment of a world government. The problem—and it was a real *problem* for Morgenthau, not just the "given" it has become for some of his disciples—was that world government would remain a utopian dream in the absence of world community, and the world (during the cold war era when Morgenthau wrote) was nowhere near becoming a community. Accordingly, Morgenthau counseled, there was one rational grand strategy left for constructive statecraft: *Work toward the evolution of world community through patient diplomacy* designed to steer the great powers away from challenging each other's vital interests while building habits of mutually respectful bargaining over secondary interests.

Today, with the demise of the cold war and the disintegration of the bipolar division of the world system having removed for the time being the prospect of war between any of the great powers, human civilization has an additional lease on life during which to attempt to implement Morgenthau's wise counsel. And, as I have indicated above, there are many arenas within which great and lesser powers can through patient diplomacy further the construction of the mutual accountability relationships that are the essence of community.

The new, world community–building diplomacy proposed in this chapter is not inconsistent with the realistic analysis in Part One of how the world works. The needed statecraft, however, will not emerge automatically out of the inherited *system*—even on the basis of some of the constructive courses of action already established. The evolution of world society into world community, in other words, is not systemically determined. It will require active and extraordinarily skillful leadership on the part of those committed—dare I say *morally* committed—to help in this further evolution of humankind.

The final chapter deals with the relative influence of systems, subsystems, states, and individuals in effecting (or preventing) the needed reforms of the world polity.

Conclusion: The Case for a Normatively Oriented Theory of the World Polity

The basic structure and behavior of the world polity, unlike the world's physical, chemical, and biological systems, is not predominantly given to us by the history of the natural universe. Rather, the world polity (like all political systems) is largely an artifact—founded and sculpted out of human values and learned skills, more than by nature's givens—that can be remodeled, maintained, or demolished. The structure and norms of the world polity are the products of policies *chosen* by the states and other actors that make up the world system and its various subsystems. At the same time, the structure and norms of the world political system influence the behavior of the subsystems comprising it.

Change or stability can be generated at any level (from micro to macro) in the world polity. Such change or stability-generating forces can also come from or be processed through structures and behavioral fields not fully encompassed by the political system—namely: ethnic/cultural/religious groupings, the economy, the ecological environment, and the physical universe. Developments in any of these "nonpolitical" fields will affect, sometimes profoundly, the conditions of life, perceptions, and values of the same persons who construct, operate, and transform the world's political system and subsystems.

Such a complex and tangled web of possible relationships between so many different kinds of phenomena might seem to defy efforts to develop a coherent theory of the world polity. But if we conceptualize about the world polity as an analytically discrete system (itself comprising discrete subsystems)—adopting Kenneth Boulding's broad definition of a system as "any structure that exhibits order and pattern"[1]—we do have a basis for formulating theory about the important cause-effect and constancy-change relationships in the world polity. We also have a basis for bringing normative considerations centrally into the theoretical enterprise: assessing the extent to which and how the present and alternative configurations of the world's political system are conducive to, or inhibit, the realization of certain morally consequential conditions and outcomes; and, in light of such assessments, indicating

---

[1]Kenneth E. Boulding, *The World as a Total System* (Beverly Hills: Sage Publications, 1985), p. 9.

where in the world's political system (at the general or particular subsystem levels) reform would be most desirable and feasible.

Essential Features of the Theory

The world polity first of all should be viewed as the global configuration of governance—meaning the enforceable rules, and the rule-making and rule-implementing processes and institutions, relied on around the world for regulating human behavior. It includes not only the prevailing configuration of governance but also efforts directed toward changing the prevailing configuration. As such the world polity is appropriately conceived of as a *sub*system of the world's social system. Other subsystems, at this level of analysis, would be the world economic system, the humanity-centered ecological system, the world's pattern of cultures, and so on.

The world polity, viewed as a system, itself comprises various political *sub*systems:

1. The "nation-state system" (often referred to as the "international system") of official government-to-government relations among countries, including the United Nations and other regional and functional intergovernmental agencies.
2. The rapidly proliferating "transnational" (really, trans-country nongovernmental) organizations and political movements operating largely beyond the direct control of national governments.
3. The internal or domestic systems of politics and government of each nation-state, comprising their own subsystems: provincial and local governments, party systems, interest-group organizations.
4. The individual as political actor.

The contemporary world polity, when viewed through this differentiated lens, exhibits a global configuration that, for lack of a better term, can be described as *polyarchic*. With neither a central system of order and justice nor a dominant hierarchy of power—and increasingly unable to rely on its anarchic state-sovereignty structure and interstate alliances to maintain global equilibrium and domestic well-being—today's polyarchic world is pervaded by a myriad of overlapping and crosscutting alignments and antagonisms.

Thus, the world polity and its various political subsystems are divided and conflicted among:

- champions of an open global market and defenders of localized protected markets;
- supporters of human-rights–based regimes and those who believe that long-established and deeply rooted cultural communities (such as nation-states) are the only legitimate sources of law and morality;

- devotees of the idea that a government is legitimate only to the extent that it is based on the uncoerced consent of the governed versus those who would repress and, if need be, incarcerate dissidents who are undermining the authority of the government;
- proponents of the self-determination of peoples and defenders of the sovereignty of states;
- religious fundamentalists who support theocracy and secularists who insist on a firm separation of church and state;
- altruists who believe that the affluent are morally obligated to help those who are without basic amenities and believers in Darwinistic or self-help philosophies who reject the idea that the poor have a moral claim on the rich;
- those who put economic growth ahead of environmental objectives under the premise that the value of anything in the natural world is solely a function of how it affects the well-being of humans versus those who hold that humans, as only one of the species in a vast natural universe, should refrain from disturbing natural ecosystems.

Even individuals are conflicted in their views on many of these issues.

To be useful analytically and prescriptively, a theory of the world polity must be intellectually congruent with these polyarchic realities. Rather than striving for parsimony, it should strive for inclusiveness. Instead of rigidly separating "levels of analysis" and thereby isolating the parts of the polities from the wholes they compose, the theory should be integrative—in both its explanatory and normative purposes.

Such a theory would treat the various systems of the world polity as open to one another, typically moving laterally from subsystem to subsystem, but also vertically from one level to the next, even leaping over levels. Yet each system or subsystem has its own partially unique configuration; and some of them, as a matter of policy, may try to restrict the extent to which they are open to influence from other systems. It may be theoretically valid, therefore, and often analytically useful, to heuristically treat them as closed systems. But particularly with the increasing mobility of persons, substances, and information, the *interpenetrability* (let alone simple interdependence) of the various systems that make up the world's political system would seem to be a more useful premise of a general theory of the world polity—certainly of any theory that attempts to understand (and normatively guide) systemic change.

The premise of open systems is consistent with the analytic strategy advanced by James Rosenau for understanding the turbulence of the contemporary era. We need, he advises, to "analyze world politics in such a way as to use labels that do not automatically accord superior status to nation-states." We should operate from the assumption that "subnational and supranational sovereignty-free actors may be as relevant as sovereignty-bound actors, . . . conceiving of whole systems and subsystems as the cast of characters at the macro level that, along with individuals at the micro level, act out global dramas."[2] This conceptual frame, says Rosenau, "facilitates inquiry into the conflicts that divide collectivities and the efforts they make to bridge the issues that separate them." It establishes a basis "for assessing parameter change and tracing turbulence."

> To distinguish between systems and subsystems is to provide a methodology for unraveling complexity. By their very nature, complex systems encompass both wholes and parts. We can begin to understand them only if we employ a method that allows us to move our analytic eyes back and forth between systems and subsystems and thus between collectivities, their subgroups, and the individuals who comprise them.[3]

The multilevel theory I am calling for, and which has been prefigured in the body of this book, can be constructed and elaborated through a wide variety of methodologies, ranging from impressionistic conjecture to highly formalistic models and rigorous empirical tests of propositions deduced from such models. It also provides many conceptual handles for relating scholarly work on international relations and world politics to many of the most important issues being fought over today in the world's political arenas—correcting what has been an increasingly uncommunicative discourse between the academic discipline of international relations and the world of applied statecraft.

Its most important potential contribution, and what has primarily driven my effort, is its usefulness for those who view the world polity as not merely something out there to be analyzed, but also as a normative project: that is, a set of phenomena whose structure and behavior can be significantly shaped by those among us who know what we want (or don't want) it to become. While according due weight to materially defined power and market relationships, it gives considerable influence to concepts of justice, particularly those targeted on the legitimacy of alternative power and market relationships.

The World Polity as a Normative Project

I have written out of a conviction that worldwide there is demand for polity models that are both practical *and* just. Despite cultural differences, most people seek ways of reconciling their immediate interests with what will also make life livable and better for their progeny. Most people seek ways of satisfying the self while contributing to the commonweal. Most people want to be treated fairly and also to treat others fairly.

---

[2]James N. Rosenau, *Turbulence in World Politics: A Theory of Change and Continuity* (Princeton: Princeton University Press, 1990), p. 41.

[3]*Ibid.*, pp. 123–124.

Models of practical and just political relationships that appeal to this human constituency can be debated and propagated across subsystems, both horizontally and vertically, to compete in the global marketplace for worldwide acceptance; alternatively, proponents can give priority to the acceptance and institutionalization of their normative commitments at any of the various subsystem levels of the world polity, from which base they will be in a better position to influence the behavior and ideas of other constituent units of the larger system.

Particularly at a time of increasing incongruence between inherited institutions of governance (and the norms that support them) and the dominant patterns of human interaction, scholars, other intellectuals, and artists can play an important role in the process of effecting change. They formulate and help others to visualize alternative patterns of human existence. In so doing, these ideational leaders play a crucial role in redefining or reinforcing prevailing standards of *political legitimacy* (not simply what is legal and enforceable, but what is in accord with accepted basic principles of right and wrong) that underlie all durable government authority.

Although disparaged by material determinists (Marxists and other "realists") as an instrument of more tangible wealth and power interests, by stimulus-response behaviorists (B. F. Skinner) as a nonobservable fiction, and by various political professionals (e.g., George Bush's political advisers) as "the vision thing"—that, like kissing babies, candidates for office are obligated to include in their repertoire of techniques—such vision, according to my reading of history, is one of the basic motive forces for change or stability in the world polity.

In this book, indeed in virtually all of my professional work, I have been operating under the assumption that I am not merely an observer/analyst of the world polity but also an active participant in the design of its structure and in the determination of its behavior. If this be arrogance, I willingly admit to it. Moreover, I invite readers to arrogate unto themselves a similar role: If they buy into or disagree with my argument, or parts of it, they can contribute to the discourse on the just world polity at whatever system or subsystem level they are in a position to provide inputs—as voters, role-holders in governmental or nongovernmental institutions, scholars, creative writers, artists, or simply as individuals in everyday dialogue. The alternative passive course simply leaves it by default to other more assertive individuals and groups (past, present, and future) to impose their world polity preferences on the rest of us.

References

Books and Articles

Almond, Gabriel A., and Stephen J. Genco. "Clouds, Clocks, and the Study of Politics." *World Politics.* Vol. 29, No. 4, 1977, pp. 489–522.

Art, Robert J., and Kenneth N. Waltz, eds. *The Use of Force: Military Power and International Politics.* Lanham: University Press of America, 1988.

Axelrod, Robert M. *The Evolution of Cooperation.* New York: Basic Books, 1984.

Baldwin, David A., ed. *Neorealism and Neoliberalism: The Contemporary Debate.* New York: Columbia University Press, 1993.

Ball, Desmond. "Can Nuclear War Be Controlled?" *Adelphi Papers,* No. 169. London: International Institute of Strategic Studies, 1981.

Beitz, Charles R. *Political Theory and International Relations.* Princeton: Princeton University Press, 1979.

Benedick, Richard Elliot. *Ozone Diplomacy: New Directions in Safeguarding the Planet.* Cambridge: Harvard University Press, 1991.

Berkowitz, Leonard. *Aggression: A Social Psychological Analysis.* New York: McGraw-Hill, 1962.

Bernstein, Victor H. *Final Judgment: The Story of Nuremberg.* New York: Boni & Gaer, 1947.

Blainey, Geoffrey. *The Causes of War.* New York: Free Press, 1973.

Blumenthal, W. Michael. "The World Economy and Technological Change." *Foreign Affairs.* Vol. 66, No. 3, 1987/88, pp. 537–538.

Bok, Sissela. *A Strategy for Peace: Human Values and the Threat of War.* New York: Pantheon Books, 1989.

Boulding, Kenneth E. *The World as a Total System.* Beverly Hills: Sage Publications, 1985.

Brandt Commission 1983. *Common Crisis North-South: Co-operation for World Recovery.* Cambridge: MIT Press, 1983.

Broad, Robin, John Cavanagh, and Walden Bello. "Development: The Market Is Not Enough." *Foreign Policy.* No. 81, Winter, 1990–91, pp. 144–162.

Brodie, Bernard. *Escalation and the Nuclear Option.* Princeton: Princeton University Press, 1966.

Brown, Chris. *International Relations Theory: New Normative Approaches.* New York: Columbia University Press, 1993.

Brown, Janet Welsh, ed. *In the U.S. Interest: Resources, Growth, and Security in the Developing World.* Boulder: Westview Press for the World Resources Institute, 1990.

Brown, Lester. *World Without Borders.* New York: Praeger, 1974.

Brown, Seyom. *The Causes and Prevention of War.* New York: St. Martin's Press, 1994.

———. *The Faces of Power: Constancy and Change in United States Foreign Policy from Truman to Clinton.* New York: Columbia University Press, 1994.

———. *New Forces, Old Forces, and the Future of World Politics.* Post–Cold War Edition. New York: HarperCollins, 1995.

Brown, Seyom, Nina W. Cornell, Larry L. Fabian, and Edith Brown Weiss. *Regimes for the Ocean, Outer Space and Weather.* Washington, D.C.: Brookings Institution, 1977.

Brubaker, Sterling. *To Live on Earth: Man and His Environment in Perspective.* Baltimore: Johns Hopkins University Press for Resources for the Future, 1972.

Bull, Hedley. *The Anarchical Society: A Study of Order in World Politics.* New York: Columbia University Press, 1977.

Bull, Hedley, and Adam Watson. *The Expansion of International Society.* New York: Oxford University Press, 1984.

Buzan, Barry, Charles Jones, and Richard Little. *The Logic of Anarchy: Neorealism to Structural Realism.* New York: Columbia University Press, 1993.

Caldwell, Lynton K. "International Response to Environmental Issues: Retrospect and Prospect." *International Studies Notes.* Vol. 16, No. 1, Winter 1991, pp. 1f.

Carson, Rachel. *Silent Spring.* Boston: Houghton Mifflin, 1962.

Chamberlain, M. E. *Decolonization: The Fall of the European Empires.* Oxford, UK: Blackwell, 1985.

Chambers, Frank P., Christina Phelps Harris, and Charles C. Bayley. *This Age of Conflict: Contemporary World History, 1914 to the Present.* New York: Harcourt, Brace, 1950.

Chayes, Abram. "Managing the Transition to a Global Warming Regime or What to Do til the Treaty Comes." In *Greenhouse Warming: Negotiating a Global Regime.* Washington, D.C.: World Resources Institute, 1991.

Christopher, Paul. *The Ethics of War and Peace: An Introduction to Legal and Moral Issues.* Englewood Cliffs: Prentice-Hall, 1994.

Clark, Grenville, and Louis B. Sohn. *World Peace Through World Law.* Cambridge: Harvard University Press, 1960.

Claude, Inis L., Jr. *Swords into Plowshares: The Problems and Progress of International Organization.* New York: Random House, 1984.

Claude, Richard Pierre, and Burns H. Weston, eds. *Human Rights in the World Community: Issues and Action.* Philadelphia: University of Pennsylvania Press, 1989.

Clausewitz, Karl von. *On War.* Translation by Michael Howard and Peter Paret. Princeton: Princeton University Press, 1976.

Cooper, Richard N. "A New International Economic Order for Economic Gain." *Foreign Policy.* No. 26, Spring 1977, pp. 65–120.

Crosette, Barbara. "U.N. Chief Ponders Future of Peacekeepers." *New York Times,* March 3, 1995.

———. "Talks in Denmark Redefine 'Foreign Aid' in Post–Cold-War Era." *New York Times,* March 10, 1995.

Deutsch, Karl W., et al. *Political Community in the North Atlantic Area: International Organization in the Light of Historical Experience.* Princeton: Princeton University Press, 1957.

Dollard, John, Leonard W. Doob, Neil E. Miller, et al. *Frustration and Aggression.* New Haven: Yale University Press, 1939.

Domke, William K. *War and the Changing Global System.* New Haven: Yale University Press, 1988.

Donnelly, Jack. *Universal Human Rights in Theory and Practice.* Ithaca: Cornell University Press, 1989.

———. *International Human Rights.* Boulder: Westview Press, 1993.

Draper, G.I.A.D. "Grotius' Place in the Development of Legal Ideas About War." In Hedley Bull, Benedict Kingsbury, and Adam Roberts, eds. *Hugo Grotius and International Relations.* Oxford: Clarendon Press, 1990, pp. 178–207.

Durant, Will, and Ariel Durant. *The Age of Reason Begins.* Vol. 7 of *The Story of Civilization.* New York: Simon and Schuster, 1961.

Easton, David. *The Political System: An Inquiry into the State of Political Science.* New York: Knopf, 1971, 2nd edition.

Eibl-Eibesfeldt, Irenaus. *The Biology of Peace and War: Men, Animals, and Aggression.* New York: Viking Press, 1979.

Etzioni, Amitai. *Political Unification.* New York: Holt, Rinehart & Winston, 1965.

Fabbro, David. "Peaceful Societies." In Richard A. Falk and Samuel S. Kim, eds. *The War System: An Interdisciplinary Approach.* Boulder: Westview Press, 1980, pp. 180–203.

Fabian, Larry L. *Soldiers Without Enemies: Preparing the United Nations for Peacekeeping.* Washington, D.C.: Brookings Institution, 1971.

Falk, Richard A. *A Study of Future Worlds.* New York: Free Press, 1975.

Fisher, Roger, and William Langer Ury. *Getting to Yes: Negotiating Agreement Without Giving In.* Boston: Houghton Mifflin, 1981.

Freud, Sigmund. Letter to Albert Einstein on war, September 1931. In William Ebenstein, *Great Political Thinkers: Plato to the Present.* New York: Rinehart, 1951, pp. 804–810.

Friedman, Milton. *Essays in Positive Economics.* Chicago: University of Chicago Press, 1953.

Gaddis, John Lewis. *The Long Peace: Inquiries into the History of the Cold War.* New York: Oxford University Press, 1987.

Galtung, Johan. *The True Worlds: A Transnational Perspective.* New York: Free Press, 1980.

Gilpin, Robert. *War and Change in World Politics.* Cambridge: Cambridge University Press, 1981.

———. *The Political Economy of International Relations.* Princeton: Princeton University Press, 1987.

———. "The Theory of Hegemonic War." In Robert Rotberg and Theodore Rabb, eds. *The Origin and Prevention of Major Wars.* Cambridge: Cambridge University Press, 1989, pp. 15–37.

Goldstein, Joshua S. *Long Cycles: Prosperity and War in the Modern Age.* New Haven: Yale University Press, 1988.

Goodin, Robert E. *Green Political Theory.* Cambridge: Polity Press, 1992.

Gottlieb, Gidon. *Nation Against State: A New Approach to Ethnic Conflicts and the Decline of Sovereignty.* New York: Council on Foreign Relations Press, 1993.

Gottmann, Jean. *The Significance of Territory.* Charlottesville: University Press of Virginia, 1973.

Gulick, Edward V. *Europe's Balance of Power.* Ithaca: Cornell University Press, 1955.

Gurr, Ted Robert. *Why Men Rebel.* Princeton: Princeton University Press, 1970.

———. *Minorities at Risk: A Global View of Ethnopolitical Conflicts.* Washington, D.C.: United States Institute of Peace Press, 1993.

Gurr, Ted Robert, and Barbara Harff. *Ethnic Conflict in World Politics.* Boulder: Westview Press, 1994.

Haas, Ernst B. *The Uniting of Europe: Political, Social, and Economic Forces, 1950–1957.* Stanford: Stanford University Press, 1958.

———. *Beyond the Nation State: Functionalism and International Organization.* Stanford: Stanford University Press, 1964.

Haas, Michael. *International Conflict.* Indianapolis: Bobbs-Merrill, 1974.

Haas, Peter M. *Saving the Mediterranean: The Politics of International Environmental Cooperation.* New York: Columbia University Press, 1990.

Halperin, Morton H. "Guaranteeing Democracy." *Foreign Policy.* No. 91, Summer 1993, pp. 105–123.

Hardin, Garrett. "The Tragedy of the Commons." *Science.* December 3, 1968.

Head, Ivan L. *On a Hinge of History: The Mutual Vulnerability of South and North.* Toronto: University of Toronto Press, 1991.

Hehir, J. Bryan. "The Politics and Ethics of Intervention." *Centerpiece.* Vol. 8, No. 2, Autumn 1994, pp. 4–5.

Henkin, Louis. "Law and Politics in International Relations: State and Human Values." In Robert L. Rothstein, ed. *The Evolution of Theory in International Relations: Essays in Honor of William T. R. Fox.* Columbia: University of South Carolina Press, 1991.

Hinsley, F. H. *Power and the Pursuit of Peace.* London: Cambridge University Press, 1963.

Hobbes, Thomas. *Leviathan* [1651]. London: Penguin Classics, 1985. Edited by C. B. Macpherson.

Hoffmann, Stanley. *The State of War: Essays on the Theory and Practice of International Politics.* New York: Praeger, 1965.

———. *Duties Beyond Borders: On the Limits and Possibilities of Ethical International Politics.* Syracuse: Syracuse University Press, 1981.

Hollifield, James L. *Immigrants, Markets and States: The Political Economy of Immigration in Postwar Europe and the United States.* Cambridge: Harvard University Press, 1993.

Huntington, Samuel P. "Civil Violence and the Process of Development." *Adelphi Papers,* No. 83. London: International Institute for Strategic Studies, December 1981.

Independent Commission on International Development Issues. *North-South: A Program for Survival.* Cambridge: MIT Press, 1980.

Jacobson, Harold. *Networks of Interdependence: International Organizations and the Global Political System.* New York: Knopf, 1984.

Jervis, Robert. "From Balance to Concert: A Study of International Security Cooperation." In Kenneth A. Oye, ed. *Cooperation Under Anarchy.* Princeton: Princeton University Press, 1985.

Johansen, Robert C. *The National Interest and the Human Interest: An Analysis of U.S. Foreign Policy.* Princeton: Princeton University Press, 1980.

———. "Building World Security: The Need for Strengthened International Institutions." In Michael Klare and Daniel Thomas *World Security: Challenges for a New Century.* New York: St. Martin's Press, 1994.

Johnson, Lawrence E. *A Morally Deep World: An Essay on Moral Significance and Environmental Ethics.* Cambridge: Cambridge University Press, 1991.

Jones, E. L. *The European Miracle: Environments, Economics, and Geopolitics in the History of Europe and Asia.* Cambridge: Cambridge University Press, 1981.

Kant, Immanuel. *Perpetual Peace: A Philosophical Essay* [1795]. Indianapolis: Bobbs-Merrill, 1957.

Kaplan, Morton A. *System and Process in International Politics.* New York: Wiley, 1962.

Kegley, Charles, ed. *The Long Postwar Peace: Contending Explanations and Projections.* New York: HarperCollins, 1991.

Kennedy, Paul M. *The Rise and Fall of the Great Powers: Economic Change and Military Conflict from 1500 to 2000.* New York: Random House, 1987.

Keohane, Robert O. *After Hegemony: Cooperation and Discord in the World Political Economy.* Princeton: Princeton University Press, 1984.

Kindleberger, Charles P. *Foreign Trade and the National Economy.* New Haven: Yale University Press, 1962.

———. "Dominance and Leadership in the International Economy: Exploitation, Public Goods, and Free Rides." *International Studies Quarterly.* Vol. 25, 1981, pp. 242–254.

Kissinger, Henry. *A World Restored: Metternich, Castlereagh, and the Problems of Peace.* Boston: Houghton Mifflin, 1973.

———. *White House Years.* Boston: Little, Brown, 1979.

Klare, Michael T., and Daniel C. Thomas, eds. *World Security: Challenges for a New Century.* New York: St. Martin's Press, 1994.

Kothari, Rajni. *Toward a Just World Order.* New York: Institute for World Order, 1980.

Krasner, Stephen D. *A Structural Conflict: The Third World Against Global Liberalism.* Berkeley: University of California Press, 1985.

———, ed. *International Regimes.* Ithaca: Cornell University Press, 1983.

Lasswell, Harold D. *The Political Writings of Harold D. Lasswell.* Glencoe: Free Press, 1951.

Lauterpacht, H. "The Grotian Tradition in International Law." In Richard Falk, Friedrich Kratochwil, and Saul H. Mendlovitz, eds. *International Law: A Contemporary Perspective.* Boulder: Westview Press, 1985, pp. 10–36.

Lebow, Richard Ned. *Nuclear Crisis Management: A Dangerous Illusion.* Ithaca: Cornell University Press, 1987.

Levy, Jack S. "Domestic Politics and War." In Robert Rotberg and Theodore Rabb, eds. *The Origin and Prevention of Major Wars,* pp. 79–99.

Lewis, W. Arthur. *Theory of Economic Growth.* New York: Harper & Row, 1970.

Lorenz, Konrad. *On Aggression.* New York: Harcourt Brace & World, 1966.

Luard, Evan. *Types of International Society.* New York: Free Press, 1976.

———. *War in International Society: A Study in International Society.* New Haven: Yale University Press, 1987.

MacNeil, Jim, Pieter Winsemius, and Taizo Yakishiji. *Beyond Interdependence: The Meshing of the World's Economy and the Earth's Ecology.* New York: Oxford University Press, 1991.

Masters, Roger. *The Political Philosophy of Rousseau.* Princeton: Princeton University Press, 1968.

Mathews, Jessica Tuchman. "Redefining Security." *Foreign Affairs.* Vol. 68, No. 2, Spring 1989, pp. 162–177.

———, ed. *Preserving the Global Environment: The Challenge of Shared Leadership.* New York: W. W. Norton, 1991.

Mayhew, Leon H. "Society." In the *International Encyclopedia of the Social Sciences.* Vol. 14. New York: Macmillan and the Free Press, 1968, pp. 577–586.

McDougal, Myers S., Harold D. Lasswell, and Lung-chu Chen. *Human Rights and World Public Order: The Basic Policies of an International Law of Human Dignity.* New Haven: Yale University Press, 1980.

McMichael, A. J. *Planetary Overload: Global Environmental Change and the Health of the Human Species*. Cambridge: Cambridge University Press, 1993.

Meadows, Donella H., Dennis L. Meadows, and Jorgen Randers. *Beyond the Limits: Confronting Global Collapse, Envisioning a Sustainable Future*. Post Mills, VT: Chelsea Green, 1992.

Mitrany, David. *A Working Peace System*. Chicago: Quadrangle Books, 1966 [1943].

Morgenthau, Hans J. *Politics Among Nations: The Struggle for Power and Peace*. New York: Knopf, 1954 [5th edition revised, 1978].

Mueller, John E. *Retreat from Doomsday: The Obsolescence of Major War*. New York: Basic Books, 1989.

Nardin, Terry. *Law, Morality, and the Relations of States*. Princeton: Princeton University Press, 1983.

Nardin, Terry, and David R. Mapel, eds. *Traditions of International Ethics*. New York: Columbia University Press, 1992.

National Conference of Catholic Bishops on War and Peace. *The Challenge of Peace: God's Promise and Our Response*. Washington, D.C.: United States Catholic Conference, 1983.

Nebel, Bernard J. *Environmental Science: The Way the World Works*. Englewood Cliffs, N.J.: Prentice-Hall, 1990.

Neff, Stephen C. *Friends But No Allies: Economic Liberalism and the Law of Nations*. New York: Columbia University Press, 1990.

North, Douglass C. *Structure and Change in Economic History*. New York: W. W. Norton, 1981.

Onuf, Nicholas Greenwood. *World of Our Making: Rules and Rule in Social Theory and International Relations*. Columbia: University of South Carolina Press, 1989.

Oye, Kenneth A., ed. *Cooperation Under Anarchy*. Princeton: Princeton University Press, 1986.

Parson, Edward A., Peter M. Haas, and Mark A. Levy. "A Summary of the Major Documents Signed at the Earth Summit and Global Forum." *Environment*, Vol. 34, No. 8 (October 1992), pp. 12–13.

Porter, Gareth, and Janet Welsh Brown. *Global Environmental Politics*. Boulder: Westview Press, 1991.

Porter, Gareth, with Inji Islam. *The Road from Rio: An Agenda for U.S. Follow-up to the Earth Summit*. Washington, D.C.: Environment and Energy Study Institute, 1992.

Raghavan, Chakravarthu. *Recolonization: GATT, the Uruguay Round & the Third World*. Penang, Malaysia: Third World Network, 1990.

Rawls, John. "The Law of Peoples." *Critical Inquiry*. Vol. 20, August 1993.

Reed, Laura W., and Carl Kaysen, eds. *Emerging Norms of Justified Intervention*. Cambridge: American Academy of Arts and Sciences, 1993.

Reich, Robert B. "Beyond Free Trade." *Foreign Affairs*. Vol. 61, No. 4, Spring 1983, pp. 773–804.

Richardson, Elliot L. "Elements of a Framework Treaty on Climate Change." *Greenhouse Warming: Negotiating a Global Regime*. Washington, D.C.: World Resources Institute, 1991.

Roosevelt, Grace G. *Reading Rousseau in the Nuclear Age*. Philadelphia: Temple University Press, 1990.

Rosecrance, Richard. *Action and Reaction in World Politics*. Boston: Little, Brown, 1963.

———. *International Relations: Peace and War*. New York: McGraw-Hill, 1973.

————. *The Rise of the Trading State: Commerce and Conquest in the Modern World.* New York: Basic Books, 1986.

Rosenau, James N. *Turbulence in World Politics: A Theory of Change and Continuity.* Princeton: Princeton University Press, 1990.

Rosenau, Pauline Marie. *Post-Modernism and the Social Sciences: Insights, Inroads, and Intrusions.* Princeton: Princeton University Press, 1992.

Rotberg, Robert I., and Theodore K. Rabb, eds. *The Origins and Prevention of Major Wars.* Cambridge: Cambridge University Press, 1989.

Schmookler, Andrew Bard. *Out of Weakness: Healing the Wounds That Drive Us to War.* New York: Bantam Books, 1988.

Sewell, John W. "The Metamorphosis of the Third World: U.S. Interests in the 1990s." In William E. Brock and Robert D. Hormats, eds. *The Global Economy: America's Role in the Decade Ahead.* New York: W. W. Norton for the American Assembly, 1990.

Shenon, Philip, and Alan Riding. "4 Parties in Cambodian War Sign U.N. Peace Pact." *New York Times,* October 24, 1991.

Shue, Henry. *Basic Rights: Subsistence, Affluence, and U.S. Foreign Policy.* Princeton: Princeton University Press, 1980.

Singer, J. David. "Accounting for International War: The State of the Discipline." *Journal of Peace Research.* Vol. 18, No. 1, 1981, pp. 1–18.

Sivard, Ruth Leger. *World Military and Social Expenditures 1993.* Washington, D.C.: World Priorities, 1993.

Steinberg, E. B., and J. A. Yager. *New Means of Financing International Needs.* Washington, D.C.: Brookings Institution, 1978.

Strong, Maurice. "Introduction." In Jim MacNeill, Pieter Winsemius, and Taizo Yakushiji. *Beyond Interdependence: The Meshing of the World's Economy and the Earth's Ecology.* New York: Oxford University Press, 1991.

Thomas, Elizabeth M. *The Harmless People.* New York: Knopf, 1959.

United Nations. *World Economic Survey, 1992.* New York: United Nations, 1993.

Vincent, R. J. *Nonintervention and International Order.* Princeton: Princeton University Press, 1974.

————. *Human Rights and International Relations.* Cambridge: Cambridge University Press, 1986.

Waltz, Kenneth N. *Theory of International Politics.* Menlo Park: Addison-Wesley, 1979.

Walzer, Michael. *Just and Unjust Wars: A Moral Argument with Historical Illustrations.* New York: Basic Books, 1977.

————. *Thick and Thin: Moral Argument at Home and Abroad.* Notre Dame: University of Notre Dame Press, 1994.

Ward, Barbara. *The Lopsided World.* New York: W. W. Norton, 1968.

Watson, Adam. *The Evolution of International Society: A Comparative Historical Analysis.* London: Routledge, 1992.

Weber, Max. *From Max Weber: Essays in Sociology.* Translated and edited by H. H. Gerth and C. Wright Mills. New York: Oxford University Press, 1946.

Weiner, Myron, ed. *International Migration and Security.* Boulder: Westview Press, 1993.

Wells, Donald A. *War Crimes and Laws of War.* Lanham: University Press of America, 1991.

Winston, Morton. *The Philosophy of Human Rights.* Belmont: Wadsworth, 1989.

Wiseman, Henry, ed. *Peacekeeping: Appraisals and Proposals.* New York: Pergamon Press, 1983.

World Commission on Environment and Development. *Our Common Future*. New York: Oxford University Press, 1987.

World Resources Institute. *World Resources 1988–89*. New York: Basic Books for the World Resources Institute, 1988.

————. *Greenhouse Warming: Negotiating a Global Regime*. Washington, D.C.: World Resources Institute, 1991.

Wynner, Edith, and Georgia Lloyd. *Searchlight on Peace Plans*. New York: Dutton, 1949.

Young, Oran R. *International Cooperation: Building Regimes for National Resources and the Environment*. Ithaca: Cornell University Press, 1989.

Official Documents

A Declaration by the Representative of the United States of America. In Congress Assembled. July 4, 1776.

"Basic Principles of Relations Between the United States of America and the Union of Soviet Socialist Republics." *Department of State Bulletin*, Vol. 66, No. 1722, June 29, 1972, pp. 898–899.

Boutros-Ghali, Boutros. *An Agenda for Peace: Preventive Diplomacy, Peacemaking, and Peacekeeping*. New York: United Nations, 1992.

Charter of the United Nations. 1945.

Clinton, William Jefferson. Address to the United Nations General Assembly, September 27, 1993. *Department of State Dispatch*, Vol. 4, No. 39.

Conference on Security and Cooperation in Europe, Final Act. Department of State Publication 8826. General Foreign Policy Series 298, 1975.

Convention on Biological Diversity. International Legal Materials, Vol. 31, No. 818. Adopted at Rio de Janeiro 1992.

Convention on the Prevention and Punishment of the Crime of Genocide. 78 United Nations Treaty Series 277. Adopted 1948. Entered into force 1951.

Covenant of the League of Nations. Signed at Versailles, June 28, 1919.

European Convention for the Protection of Human Rights and Fundamental Freedoms. 231 United Nations Treaty Series 221. Signed 1950. Entered into force 1953.

International Bank for Reconstruction and Development/The World Bank. *World Development Report 1990: World Development Indicators*. New York: Oxford University Press for the World Bank, 1990.

————. *World Development Report 1991: The Challenge of Development*. New York: Oxford University Press for the World Bank, 1991.

International Convention on the Elimination of All Forms of Racial Discrimination. 660 United Nations Treaty Series 195. Adopted 1966. Entered into force 1969.

International Covenant on Civil and Political Rights. 9 United Nations Treaty Series 171. Adopted 1966. Entered into force 1976.

International Covenant on Economic, Social, and Cultural Rights. 993 United Nations Treaty Series 3. Adopted 1966. Entered into force 1976.

International Institute for Sustainable Development. "Summary Report on the World Summit for Social Development." *Earth Negotiations Bulletin*, Vol. 10, No. 44, March 15, 1995.

Joint Communique of the United States of America and the People's Republic of China. Issued at Shanghai, February 27, 1972. *Department of State Bulletin.* Vol. 66, No. 1708, March 20, 1972, pp. 435–438.

Montreal Protocol on Substances That Deplete the Ozone Layer. International Legal Materials, Vol. 26, No. 1550. Done at Montreal, 1987. Entered in force 1989.

Non-Legally Binding Authoritative Statement of Principles for a Global Consensus on the Management, Conservation and Sustainable Development of All Types of Forests. United Nations Document A/Conf. 151/6/Rev. 1. 1992. Adopted at Rio de Janeiro 1992.

Optional Protocol to the International Covenant on Civil and Political Rights. 9 United Nations Treaty Series 171. Adopted 1966. Entered into force 1976.

Reagan, Ronald. "Address to the Board of Governors of the World Bank and International Monetary Fund, September 28, 1981." In *Weekly Compilation of Presidential Documents.* Vol. 17, No. 40, pp. 1052–1055.

Treaty on the Non-Proliferation of Nuclear Weapons. U.S. Arms Control and Disarmament Agency. *Arms Control and Disarmament Agreements.* Washington, D.C.: U.S. Government Printing Office, 1984, pp. 91–95.

United Nations Framework Convention on Climate Change. International Legal Materials, Vol. 31, No. 849. Adopted at Rio de Janeiro 1992.

United Nations General Assembly. "Uniting for Peace Resolution." United Nations Document A/1481, 1950.

United Nations Security Council Resolutions (concerning Iraq's invasion of Kuwait): 660, August 2, 1990; 661, August 6, 1990; 662, August 9, 1990; 664, August 18, 1990; 665, August 25, 1990; 666, September 13, 1990; 667, September 16, 1990; 669, September 24, 1990; 670, September 25, 1990; 674, October 29, 1990; 677, November 28, 1990; and 678, November 29, 1990. *United Nations Security Council Resolutions Relating to the Crisis in the Gulf.* United Nations: Department of Public Information, November 1990, DPI/1104–41090.

United States Senate, Subcommittee on Substances and Environmental Oversight, *Global Warming: Hearing, December 10, 1985.* Washington, D.C.: Government Printing Office, 1985.

About the Book and Author

The first edition of this successful text helped to define a new approach to the study of international relations, one suited to the realities of the post–cold war world. It broke the confines of the dominant "realist" paradigm to offer an intelligible theoretical discourse on how the world works.

In this thoroughly revised and updated edition, Professor Brown again presents a text exemplary both in its intellectual accessibility and its relevance to the real-world concerns of policymakers and the attentive public.

This new edition's approach, vindicated by world events since its original publication, expands and deepens the analysis that made the first edition such a unique text. Readers will especially appreciate the expanded treatment of the issues of ethnic and national self-determination, the controversial role played by the UN in humanitarian and peacekeeping missions, the growing importance of international trade and its impact on sovereignty, and the burgeoning of ethical inquiry in the analysis of international relations.

International Relations in a Changing Global System is still the ideal text to present the complexities of real-world analysis in a sophisticated but accessible manner.

Seyom Brown is the Lawrence A. Wien Professor of International Cooperation at Brandeis University. He is the author of *New Forces, Old Forces, and the Future of World Politics; The Causes and Prevention of War;* and many other books and articles in international relations and foreign policy.

Index